T0360874

EMOTIONAL INTELLIGENCE AND MARKETING

EMOTIONAL INTELLIGENCE AND MARKETING

Dr. Catherine Prentice
Griffith University, Australia

World Scientific

:W JERSEY · LONDON · SINGAPORE · BEIJING · SHANGHAI · HONG KONG · TAIPEI · CHENNAI · TOKYO

Published by

World Scientific Publishing Co. Pte. Ltd.

5 Toh Tuck Link, Singapore 596224

USA office: 27 Warren Street, Suite 401-402, Hackensack, NJ 07601

UK office: 57 Shelton Street, Covent Garden, London WC2H 9HE

British Library Cataloguing-in-Publication Data
A catalogue record for this book is available from the British Library.

EMOTIONAL INTELLIGENCE AND MARKETING

ISBN 978-981-120-354-1

For any available supplementary material, please visit
https://www.worldscientific.com/worldscibooks/10.1142/11363#t=suppl

Desk Editor: Sandhya Venkatesh

Typeset by Stallion Press
Email: enquiries@stallionpress.com

Printed in Singapore

CONTENTS

CHAPTER 1

EMOTIONAL INTELLIGENCE AND MARKETING

1.1 What is Marketing?

Marketing, as a business discipline, is the study and management of exchange relationships between parties involved to benefit stakeholders. Marketing is defined as "the activity, set of institutions, and processes for creating, communicating, delivering, and exchanging offerings that have value for customers, clients, partners, and society at large" (AMA, 2013). Marketing as an activity strikes consumers as advertising, sales promotion and other promotional related campaigns. As a set of institutions, marketing involves the functions that link the consumer, customer, and public to the marketer through marketing intelligence. As processes, marketing is to identify and define marketing opportunities and problems; generate, refine, and evaluate marketing actions; monitor marketing performance; and improve understanding of marketing by designing the method for collecting information, managing and implementing the data collection process, analysing the results, and communicating the findings and their implications (AMA, 2014).

1.2 Marketing Evolution

Marketing has evolved from a single production orientation focus on a holistic approach including, inter alia, integrated marketing,

1

internal marketing, corporate social responsibility, and relationship marketing. In this service and digital dominant era, marketing has been transformed into various unique forms to accommodate this dynamic business world. The parties that are involved in economic exchange relationships are no longer limited to Business-to-Business (B-to-B) and Business-to-Customer/Consumer (B-to-C) dyads but include Customer-to-Customer (C-to-C) or Peer-to-Peer (P-to-P) interactions and exchanges. The rapid development and increase use of internet and social media facilitate marketing evolution and business transactions. The rising popularity and evolution of artificial intelligence in this century has also transformed business operations and transactions. Although there is a growing concern of artificial intelligence's power of replacing manpower in various industries, researchers and practitioners affirm that it rather creates jobs and enhances productivity at the same time, dependent upon the industry. From marketing perspective, artificial intelligence has made marketing practice viable and efficient more than ever.

1.3 Offensive and Defensive Marketing

Despite emerging phenomenal technology advancements and transformations in marketing, the fundamental principles and ultimate goals of marketing remain unchanged: benefiting the exchange parties and maximising business profitability through acquiring and retaining customers. The marketing mix and its 4Ps or 7Ps are still the key strategies to attract target markets either for a discrete transaction or relational transactions. There are two key marketing mechanisms: offensive and defensive marketing. The former is focused on attracting new markets and customers extensively and expansively; whereas the latter is on engendering customer retention and loyalty. In the early stage of product life cycle, offensive marketing techniques with aggressive sales promotions and targeting competitors' weakness can be effective to attract new customers. However, this practice with a single-transaction focus entices match-up retaliation or exceeding offerings from competitors. On the customer end, the market saturation is inevitable.

From business growth and sustainability perspective, it is imperative for marketers to transfer marketing endeavours from a single transaction focus into ongoing exchanges with the selected target markets. Relationship marketing with a focus on attracting customers' positive attitudes and on optimising customer loyalty and retention has become and is still the central focus of various marketing practices in the long run.

1.4 Relationship Marketing

Relationship marketing is defined as a process of identifying and establishing, maintaining and enhancing and, when necessary, terminating relationships with customers and other stakeholders, at a profit (Gronroos, 1994). Depending on the context, relationship marketing also bears a few other names, for example, one-to-one marketing, continuity marketing or customer relationship management (CRM). Relationship marketing and CRM are often used interchangeably. Despite the different terms that are used to describe the relationship marketing practice, the central idea of this marketing practice is to retain customers by establishing individual relationships with clients, treating each customer differently, based on the information collected about them, and building trust between the exchange parties. The focal point of this marketing practice is to generate customers' positive attitudes and behaviours that are reflective of customer satisfaction and loyalty, which has long widely acknowledged to be related to business profitability (Anderson, Fornell and Lehmann, 1994; Hallowell, 1996).

1.5 Benefits of Relationship Marketing

Relationship marketing benefits both the company and the customer. For the company, the underlying assumption of relationship marketing is that customer loyalty and retention leads to business profitability. Customer loyalty expressed in the form of revisit intention, positive word of mouth, lower propensity to complain, and exercise more desirable consumption behaviours such as visiting the company or service provider more often as well as spending more time and money than one intended. Researchers identify that better financially performed firms are able to retain a higher level of brand image, brand awareness, and brand loyalty than less financially sound ones. In mid 1990s, researchers (e.g. Reichheld, 1996) identified that a 5 percent increase in customer retention can lead to a 25 to 85 percent increase in profitability. This can be construed by customer lifetime value (LTV). LTV is the revenue that one customer can spend with the company directly or indirectly through referral and recommendation over a nominal period of time. Directly, the more frequently a customer comes back to the business, the more his or her loyalty builds. A loyal customer tends to buy additional offerings and is less sensitive to tactical discounting. Furthermore, the initial costs of attracting and establishing relationships with these customers have already been absorbed due to experience-curve effects; on the other hand, as customers get to know the supplier through repeated purchases, they become less dependent on the employees for information and advice, and the effects of such learning are likely to translate into lower costs. Indirectly, loyal customers tend to be self-perpetuating advocates and spread favourable word-of-mouth communication, which, in turn, enhances company profitability.

For customers, having a relationship with the company has a range of commercial and social benefits (Berry, 1995). For complex products that requires high involvement in the purchase process, a relational and loyalty customer often receives customised product and service delivery and other individualised services as information technology enables the company to analyse customer profiles and become more knowledgeable about each individual customers' needs and wants. This relational approach enhances trust between buyers and sellers and reduces product related risks. Trust building is a prerequisite of establishment of long-term relationship. On the other hand, maintaining an ongoing relationship with the company also engenders various benefits for customers. Companies often reward loyal customers with financial (complimentary services) and non-financial rewards (tiered membership and associative benefits).

1.6 Marketing Strategies for Relationship Marketing

The focal outcomes that relationship marketing aims to achieve are customers' positive attitudes and behaviours towards the company including customer satisfaction, purchase and repurchase, and long-term loyalty. These relationship marketing-related outcomes can be achieved through different tools, methods and strategies, including marketing intelligence, customer relationship management software, and loyalty programs. These are organisational resources that are most commonly used by marketing practitioners and discussed by academics in the relationship marketing domain.

Admittedly these organisational resources are necessary, and to a certain degree, effective. However, the tools and programs embedded in relationship marketing practice can be excessively expensive, in particular the CRM software (Ang and Buttle, 2006; Colombo and Francalanci, 2004; Dubey and Wagle, 2007; Langerak and Verhoef, 2003). The effectiveness of loyalty programs is not guaranteed (Liu, 2007; meyer-Waarden, 2007; Sharp and Sharp, 1997; Uncles, Dowling and Hammond, 2003). Knowingly relationship marketing is essentially practised by employees, particularly customer-contact employees (either remote or personal contact), employees may be trained to use these organisational resources to achieve the relationship marketing goals. However, relationship marketing is not about employees' capabilities of using these resources, but a process of managing customer relationships. From customers' perspective, they are not in contact with these tools and methods, but drawn into interactions with employees. The abilities and competence manifested in employees and their interactions with customers play a critical role in attracting customer attention and loyalty. On this basis, this book proposes emotional intelligence as a non-organisational personal resource possessed by a cost-effective marketing tool practised by individual employees to implement relationship marketing.

1.7 Emotional Intelligence and Marketing

Emotional intelligence is a psychological concept that explains individuals' emotional abilities and competence. These individuals' abilities are manifested in recognising, using, understanding and managing one's emotions and those of others (Mayer and Salovey, 1993). Emotional intelligence is useful in predicting an individual's life and career success reflected in health, life satisfaction, personal and work relationships, and job efficiency and performance. How emotional intelligence as an individual's emotional competence can be integrated into marketing as an academic business discipline to facilitate business exchange?

Although emotional intelligence refers to individual emotional abilities, this book elevates these personal abilities to be a marketing tool that function like any other marketing strategies to achieve optimal business outcomes. Marketing and psychology disciplines are often intertwined to explain the attitudes and behaviours of employees and consumers/customers. Marketing, as a business discipline, contains multiple subcategories including services marketing, relationship marketing, digital marketing, strategic marketing, international marketing, and so on. Each sub-discipline has a specific focus. This book is not intended to position emotional intelligence as a panacea for all marketing activities and processes. Drawing on its conceptualisations and implications, the book proposes that emotional intelligence can be integrated into relationship marketing as a tool or a strategy utilised by relationship marketers or employees to establish and manage relationships with customers, which is the central focus of relationship marketing. The buyer-seller or customer-provider relationship is often established through interactions over the interpersonal encounter between employees and customers. This book reveals how employees' emotional intelligence can be used to manage the interpersonal interactions to achieve optimal relationship marketing outcomes manifested in customers' positive attitudes and behaviours such as satisfaction, product purchase, referral, and loyalty.

Given that businesses today are operating in a service dominant logic era, the service profit chain model proposed by Hesket and colleagues in 1997 is drawn upon to understand the link between employee emotional intelligence and marketing outcomes. This model depicts a few key marketing concepts, namely internal marketing, encounter marketing, and external marketing. Internal marketing refers to the marketing practice that views employees as internal customers and that aims to general positive attitudes and behaviours of these internal customers. This aim is achieved through managing internal personal encounter between co-workers, employees and supervisors. Encounter marketing refers to the marketing practice that is focused on managing the interpersonal interactions over the service encounter between employees (aka internal customers) and external customers. External marketing moves beyond the interpersonal encounter and is concentrated on how the attitudes and behaviours of employees or marketers affect those of customers.

To understand how emotional intelligence can be integrated into internal, encounter and external marketing as an effective relationship marketing tool, this book first provides the rationale for incorporating emotional intelligence into relationship marketing by discussing the importance of implementing this marketing practice for businesses and the role of employees in achieving relationship marketing goals. The importance of employees in marketing is elaborated. This discussion is focused on attributing frontline employees in the chain relationship between service quality, customer satisfaction, customer loyalty and business profitability described in the service profit chain model. Understanding the role of employees in marketing, the book subsequently introduces the concept of emotional intelligence and explains the logic behind the aim of this book. Consistent with this logic, the remaining chapters of this book integrate emotional intelligence into different marketing practices following the relationship sequence of the service profit chain model, namely internal marketing, encounter marketing, and internal marketing. Drawing upon the nature of different service encounters and the relationship marketing outcomes, this book coins a few marketing concepts to reflect the essence of these marketing practices. The new concepts are: dramaturgical marketing, relational encounter marketing and impersonal encounter marketing.

1.8 Brief Contents of Each Chapter

This book presents a series of conceptual and empirical discussions in a logic flow on how employee emotional intelligence affects customer attitudes and behaviours which subsequently lead to business profitability in service industries. The discussion provides the rationale for incorporating emotional intelligence into customer loyalty and company profitability analysis. The book begins with discussing the role of service employees in the service industries and reviewing the relevant theoretical models. The theoretical implications and potential applications of emotional intelligence are provided to reinforce the rationale. Subsequently, the book analyses all relevant factors that may contribute to customer loyalty and company profitability and delineates the impact of emotional intelligence on those factors. Following the chain relationships described in the service profit chain model, the book presents several chapters with each relating to a relationship on the chain. Specifically, the brief contents of the remaining chapters are as follows.

Chapter 2 discusses the power of employee influence in marketing. The discussion begins with contention for relationship marketing as an optimal marketing approach to maximising an organisation's financial performance, followed by identifying employees as a key factor of relationship marketing practice. The importance of employees is manifested in their key role in determining customers' assessment of service quality and rendering customer satisfaction and retention. These outcomes are derived from the transactions over the service encounter.

Chapter 3 presents the concept and characteristics of the service encounter. The book categorises the encounter to be personal and impersonal encounters. The personal encounter is characterised as being emotionally charged. This chapter elaborates the attributes of the service encounter and delineates affective contents relating to the personal encounter. The affective or emotional contents are specifically attributed to employees, customers and the nature of the service. Despite the causes and sources of emotions, from marketing perspective, employees are the incumbents to manage the emotions for marketing efficiency and financial performance. This view prompts the subsequent chapter to induce emotional intelligence into managing emotionally loaded service encounter.

Chapter 4 is dedicated to introducing and understanding emotional intelligence. This chapter elaborates everything about emotional intelligence. The elaboration includes discussion of the origins, conceptualisations, measurements of emotional intelligence, as well as debates and confirmation on its validities and applications in various fields. The elaborated discussion is necessary for readers to understand the concept of emotional intelligence and how it can be incorporated into marketing as a marketing strategy.

Consistent with the service profit chain model, **Chapter 5** discusses *internal marketing* and how it relates to emotional intelligence. Specifically, this chapter draws upon the internal marketing concept and explains how emotional intelligence affects employees' attitudes and behaviours which are related to the external marketing outcomes: customer attitudes and behaviours.

Adding to the internal marketing practice, **Chapter 6** introduces the concept of emotional labour and coins a new marketing concept *dramaturgical marketing* on the basis of acting strategies required of emotional labour performance. This chapter reviews the relevant literature to understand the positive and negative consequences of performing emotional labour. On this basis, the underlying motive of promoting emotional intelligence into emotional labour management is presented. The findings from empirical studies are provided to reinforce the influence of emotional intelligence on dramaturgical marketing.

Moving from discussion around emotional intelligence and internal marketing, the book focuses on the encounter marketing and the "Moment of Truth" between employees and customers. **Chapter 7** creates a new marketing concept *relational encounter marketing* to reflect employees' relationship-oriented behaviours over the service encounter with customers. The relationship between these behaviours and relationship marketing is revealed. Customer orientation and adaptability are opted as relational encounter behaviours in relational encounter marketing practice. The relationship between emotional intelligence and these relational encounter behaviours is discussed and confirmed with examples of empirical studies. The concepts of basic trait, surface trait and performance outcomes are reviewed to understand the hierarchical effect of emotional intelligence in optimising organisational efficiency.

Subsequent to the encounter marketing and management of moment of truth, the book proceeds to discuss how emotional intelligence is related to external marketing through linking employee behaviours and customer responses. **Chapter 8** sheds lights on integrating employee emotional intelligence and external marketing practice. Specifically, this chapter discusses how the level of employee emotional intelligence enhances rapport with customers, how it directly affects customer attitudes (e.g. satisfaction) and behaviours (e.g. purchase and loyalty).

Last but not the least, the book introduces a new marketing concept — *impersonal encounter marketing*. Impersonal encounter refers to customers' reaction and response toward the servicescape of a service organisation. **Chapter 9** discusses how emotional intelligence can be elevated as a personified concept to be incorporated into design of servicescapes, and how emotional intelligence can be practised as an impersonal encounter marketing tool to be infused in the design of servicescape to influence customers' attitudes and behaviours. This marketing concept is innovative and unprecedented. Nevertheless, it draws upon the evident impact of servicescape on customers' attitudes and behaviours.

1.9 Uniqueness of this Book

This book is intended to bridge three disciplines, namely psychology, marketing and human resource management in the service-dominant logic era, and discusses how employee emotional intelligence can be deployed to improve business profitability by analysing its impact on dyadic relationships between co-workers, between management and employees, between customer-contact employees and customers, and between tangible service environment and customers. The discussion draws upon the service profit chain model. The model depicts how business profitability can be achieved by the attitudes and behaviours of both customers and employees, and how these attitudes and behaviours are driven by the firm's internal service quality. Emotional intelligence is positioned as a marketing tool to influence implementation of marketing strategies for different dyads and to enhance each dyadic relationships through apprehending, managing and regulating emotions of the dyads.

The book provides empirical testing and results to support the discussion. Each section includes a thorough review of the relevant literature and selected empirical studies, and concludes with presenting results from empirical studies. This book sheds light on broadening the theoretical scope and practical applications of emotional intelligence, and promotes it as a marketing tool or strategy for improving and sustaining business growth.

Overall, this book provides a fresh perspective of the application of emotional intelligence in marketing. Emotional intelligence has been popularising in various communities, and primarily attracts attention from industry practitioners and consultants since its incept in 1990s. The majority of the existing books are focused on its impact on individuals personally and/or professionally. This book incorporates this concept into marketing discipline and analyses its contribution to business profitability through diagnosing its impact on different business stakeholders as well as on their interrelationships. For emotional intelligence researchers and practitioners, this book broadens their traditional mapping of its implications. For marketing researchers and practitioners, this book provides them with a fresh look into a new cost-effective marketing strategy to improve relationships among key stakeholders for profit maximisation.

References

Anderson, E.W., Fornell, C., & Lehmann, D.R. (1994). Customer satisfaction, market share, and profitability: Findings from Sweden. *The Journal of Marketing*, 53–66.

Ang, L. & Buttle, F. (2006). CRM software applications and business performance. *Journal of Database Marketing & Customer Strategy Management*, 14(1), 4–16.

Ang, L. & Buttle, F. (2006). Customer retention management processes: A quantitative study. *European Journal of Marketing*, 40(1/2), 83–99.

Berry, L.L. (1995). Relationship marketing of services — growing interest, emerging perspectives. *Journal of the Academy of Marketing Science*, 23(4), 236–245.

Colombo, E. & Francalanci, C. (2004). Selecting CRM packages based on architectural, functional, and cost requirements: Empirical validation of a hierarchical ranking model. *Requirements Engineering*, 9(3), 186–203.

Dubey, A. & Wagle, D. (2007). Delivering software as a service. *The McKinsey Quarterly*, 6.

Grönroos, C. (1994). From scientific management to service management: A management perspective for the age of service competition. *International Journal of Service Industry Management*, 5(1), 5–20.

Hallowell, R. (1996). The relationships of customer satisfaction, customer loyalty, and profitability: An empirical study. *International Journal of Service Industry Management*, 7(4), 27–42.

Langerak, F. & Verhoef, P.C. (2003). Strategically embedding CRM. *Business Strategy Review*, 14(4), 73–80.

Liu, Y. (2007). The long-term impact of loyalty programs on consumer purchase behavior and loyalty. *Journal of Marketing*, 71(4), 19–35.

Meyer-Waarden, L. (2007). The effects of loyalty programs on customer lifetime duration and share of wallet. *Journal of Retailing*, 83(2), 223–236.

Reichheld, F.F., Teal, T., & Smith, D.K. (1996). *The Loyalty Effect* (Vol. 1, No. 3, pp. 78–84). Boston, MA: Harvard Business School Press.

Sharp, B. & Sharp, A. (1997). Loyalty programs and their impact on repeat-purchase loyalty patterns. *International Journal of Research in Marketing*, 14(5), 473–486.

Uncles, M.D., Dowling, G.R., & Hammond, K. (2003). Customer loyalty and customer loyalty programs. *Journal of Consumer Marketing*, 20(4), 294–316.

CHAPTER 2

THE POWER OF EMPLOYEE INFLUENCE

Your employees have the power to influence your customers, your business, and your bottom line. For one to overlook their influence is to make a mistake. — GaggleAMP Employees are the brand ambassadors, brand maniacs, brand champions, brand evangelists, who transform brand vision into brand reality.

— VanAuken and Berry

2.1 Introduction

This chapter discusses the role of customer-contact employees in marketing. The rationale for promoting employees is provided by demonstrating its influence on the chain relationship between service quality, customer satisfaction, customer loyalty and business profitability. To understand this relationship, the chapter begins with explaining dominance of service industries in the economy and the characteristics of services, followed by explaining the marketing strategies that are commonly used to market services and how relationship marketing is practiced in service industries. On the basis of relationship marketing conceptualisation, the link between service quality and business profitability is elaborated with a focus on emphasising the role of frontline employees in this chain relationship.

2.2 Rise of the Service Sector

With the rapid rise of service industries, the service sector dominates the global economy (see Figure 2.1). In most developed countries, services account for over 80 percent of the national GDP (The World Factbook, 2018). Traditional manufacturing firms are also making every endeavour to move into service-oriented business. The services associated with producing, selling and serving the tangible products become a key component of competitive advantage. Microsoft, a product-oriented company, has moved into service-centric business and adopted a relationship marketing practice by focusing on relationship building with customers:

"We're ready to meet our customers at the right point in their journey, with the right touch at the right time to drive business success. With this

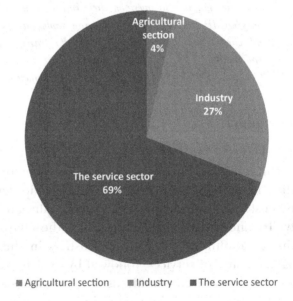

■ Agricultural section   ■ Industry   ■ The service sector

Figure 2.1   Contribution of services industries to GDP globally in 2016.

Source: *The Statistics Portal.*
https://www.statista.com/statistics/758809/distribution-of-gross-domestic-product-gdp-across-economic-sectors-global/

approach to customer engagement, we're creating an industry standard in digital selling." (Debbie Dunnam, Corporate Vice President)

"We're ready to meet our customers at the right point in their journey, with the right touch at the right time to drive business success. With this approach to customer engagement, we're creating an industry standard in digital selling." (Seth Young, Sales development specialist)

2.3 What is Service?

Services are defined as acts, deeds, performances and efforts that are offered as value-added activities for exchange to serve, help, and benefit the stakeholders (see Wirtz and Lovelock, 2018). There are many different types of service businesses including service product as the core offering, customer service and after-sale service. Wirtz and Lovelock (2018) classify these services into four broad categories on the basis of how the service is processed, namely, people processing, possession processing, mental stimulus processing and information processing.

People processing services refer to those that directly serve customers through appropriate locations, places and tools, such as airlines that transport passengers, beauty salons that "beautify" customers' physical appearance, medical centres that provide medical services to patients. This type of service is characterised as simultaneity i.e. offering of service by the service provider and consumption of service by customers take place over the service encounter simultaneously. Customer participation and cooperation is required in the service process. *Possession processing services* refer to offerings by service firms that are directed at customers' tangible possessions, such as car service and repairs, house cleaning, house moving, and freight transportation. *Mental stimulus processing services* refer to offerings that are aimed at serving mental capacity, such as education, news, religious and spiritual activities, professional counselling and services. This type of services can be provided through personal and impersonal encounters. The former includes face-to-face service delivery; whereas the latter indicates remote offering through electronic channels. *Information processing services* refer to those that the core component of the service offering is information based, such as banking, accounting and legal services.

2.4 Relationship Marketing in the Service Sector

Services are characterised as being intangible, perishable, inseparable, and heterogeneous (Zeithaml, Bitner, and Gremler, 2012). These characteristics are also referred to as challenges (Wirtz and Lovelock; 2018). Each type of services encompasses different degrees of intangibility, perishability, inseparability, and heterogeneity. People and possession processing services are highly perishable, inseparable from service providers and heterogeneous across different service representatives. Mental stimulus and information processing services are highly intangible and involve a high level of credence attributes. Customers are often unable to evaluate quality of the services, after experiencing and consuming them.

The characteristics or challenges of services become underlying motives for customers to establish and maintain relationships with the company and its service representatives. Although the service provider is compelled to take various marketing initiatives, such as providing attractive offerings, establishing online brand communities, offering a variety of loyalty programs, to stay competitive and attract customers' attention and engagement, customers often willingly engage with the provider and build a relationship with them to enjoy the relational benefits (e.g. complimentary services, reward programs, support from the brand communities). Having a relationship with the service provider enhances trust between the two parties. The trust instilled in customers facilitates their decision making and purchase from the favoured service provider, given the intangible and perishable nature of services. Relationship building requires trust in parties involved (Morgan and Hunt, 1994). Trust is even more important for the heterogeneous service delivered by the same or different service provider from different times since customers rely on their previous positive experiences with the service provider, as long as the discrepancy resulted from heterogeneity falls in the range of the tolerance zone. The simultaneous characteristic of service delivery and consumption entails interactions between the service provider and customers, and requires the latter's participation and cooperation to a great extent. These interactions enhance relationship building and become the "moment of truth" for customers to assess the company's service quality.

Admittedly, to efficiently and accurately deliver the service, the service provider and the employees need sufficient and reliable information to understand customers and their special needs or idiosyncrasies. Such information can be acquired through advanced technologies such as data warehousing, data mining and campaign management software. These technologies enable efficient customer relationship management and deliver more individualised and customised services based on each customer's respective needs and wants.

2.5 Services Marketing Mix

Since the ultimate goal of relationship marketing is to render customer loyalty and retention in order to reap long-term sustainable profitability, the question arises about what factors lead to these relationship marketing outcomes from service providers. Although the different categories of service businesses have different foci of offerings, the benefits of marketing are largely generated through the moment of truth: service encounter. Most services are produced and delivered through the service encounter. Customers receive and consume/experience the service over the service encounter.

The service encounter can be interpersonal involving employees and customers in a physical, impersonal with only employees and customers' possessions or with only customers and non-employee service settings, or remote encounter (e.g. call centre, e-encounter). To ensure a successful service transaction and establish a long-term relationship with customers, service delivery over each personal and impersonal encounter must meet or exceed customer expectation and steer a positive perception so that customer satisfaction can be rendered. Satisfying customers tend to repurchase from the service provider and engage in other loyal behaviours. Consistently, the marketing mix strategies have been extended from the 4Ps (product, price, promotion and place) for marketing tangible goods to the 7Ps for service products. The three additional Ps specifically refer to people, physical evidence and process respectively.

People, generally in the marketing literature, refer to service personnel who produce or perform services over personal and/or impersonal service encounter. However, since service production generally concurs with customers' consumption of the service, in some cases, customers to a great extent are required to participate in producing and creating the service. Co-production and co-creation have been widely discussed in the literature and applied in a broad range of businesses and industries (e.g. Chathoth *et al.*, 2013; Humphreys and Grason, 2008; Payne, Storbacka and Frow, 2008; Prahalad and Ramaswamy, 2004). The impetus of engaging customers in the co-production/creation process is value adding for both service providers and customers. Therefore, people strategy should include initiatives for both employees and customers. Employee service performance over the service encounter affects how customers assess the firm's service quality and customer satisfaction (Prentice, 2013). Customers' participation enhances efficiency and effectiveness of service delivery and service experience (Chandler and Lusch, 2015). The marketing strategy for people must instigate employee service encounter performance and customer participation and engagement to ensure generation of positive attitudes and behaviours from both employees and customers.

Physical evidence refers to the tangible elements that facilitate the service exchange, the physical settings and servicescape that customers experience and are in direct contact with, the ambience that is aimed to create an appropriate atmosphere to ensure a positive service experience for different market segments. Bitner (1992) initiated this domain of research. A plethora of research in recent years has examined the impact of physical evidence on customers' attitudes (e.g. satisfaction, experience) and behaviours (e.g. purchase, patronage, loyalty behaviours) from the environmental and psychological perspectives.

Process refers to service delivery logistics. The level of consistency and punctuality of service delivery is reflective of the process strategy. Service process from the organisations' perspective describe the means and sequences in the production and delivery process to ensure that the service in demand is delivered efficiently and effectively. Customers may be present in this process as a participant in people-process services (e.g. buffet restaurant; hairdressing) or simply receive the outcome of the service production (e.g. car services). In each case, the process can be utilised as a marketing strategy to defeat competitors and gaining customers' positive attitudes and behaviours. The commonly recommended process strategies are developing an appropriate blueprint to ensure optimal service process; and incorporating technologies and artificial intelligence to enhance self-service and service process. These strategies are aimed for customer satisfaction and subsequent behaviours.

Since most services are characterised as being intangible, inseparable, heterogeneous and perishable, these three marketing mix elements are crucial to ensure successful service delivery and customers' service experience which affects the service quality assessment. Service quality is widely acknowledged as a driver of organisations' profitability and a form of achieving a competitive advantage. At its core, it captures the meaning of excellence, coincides to specifications and meets or exceeds expectations. In service-marketing literature, service quality often reflects customers' perceptions and value-judgment of a product or service. Generally, two prominent views debate the operationalisation of Service Quality (Cronin Jr and Taylor, 1992; Grönroos, 1984; Zeithaml, 2000); as either a fit between customers perceptions and expectations, or a simple assessment at a perception-level (Gronroos, 1988; Parasuraman, Zeithaml and Berry, 1988).

2.6 Service Quality and Company Profitability

From a service viewpoint, service quality is widely recognised as an antecedent of satisfaction or a direct predictor of behavioural intentions (Eusébio and Vieira, 2013; Zeithaml, Berry and Parasuraman,

1996). The sequential process of the aforementioned relationships leads to the firm's long-term profitability. This relationship is widely supported in service settings (Cronin, Brady and Hult, 2000; Lee, Lee and Yoo, 2000; Prentice, 2013; Saleem *et al.*, 2017) including airports (Bogicevic *et al.*, 2013; Ching, 2014; Subha and Archana, 2013).

Despite recent research development in addressing the importance of service quality, marketing researchers in a few decades ago have already addressed a chain relationship of service quality, customer satisfaction, and customer retention theoretically and empirically for decades. In late 1980s, Woodside, Frey and Daly (1989) linked service quality, customer satisfaction and customer behavioural retention. Employing patients from two hospitals, the authors found that customer perceptions of service quality affect his or her overall satisfaction with the services, and customer satisfaction impacts on behavioural intention. Rust and Zahorik (1993) provided a mathematical framework for assessing the value of customer satisfaction, and indicated that customer satisfaction is linked sequentially to individual loyalty, aggregate retention rate, market share and profits. Storbacka, Strandvik and Gronroos (1994) provided a more comprehensive framework linking service quality, customer satisfaction, customer retention, and company profitability. This chain of relationship is based on the assumption that customer satisfaction is improved by enhancing service quality. A satisfied customer tends to have a strong and long relationship with the service provider, and long-term relationships generate stable revenues that improve customer relationship profitability. Hallowell (1996) examined the link between customer satisfaction, customer loyalty and profitability in the banking industry. The results show that customer satisfaction is responsible for as much as 37 percent of the difference in customer loyalty levels.

These studies show that service quality and customer satisfaction are significant antecedents to customer retention and company profitability. In the relevant marketing literature, there has been some confusion and debate about the differences between service quality and customer satisfaction. Most marketing researchers agree that service quality precedes customer satisfaction which subsequently affects customer loyalty. However, some researchers (Bowen and Chen, 2001; Sivadas and Baker-Prewitt, 2000) argue that customer satisfaction does not lead to customer loyalty, and the relationship can be non-linear. Studies (e.g. Dube and Renaghan, 1994) found that satisfied customers do not return to the business.

Satisfaction generally refers to a customer's attitudes towards the product or service in relation to the level of pleasure and fulfilment felt (Oliver, 1980). Customer satisfaction can be conceptualised by transaction-specific and cumulative evaluations. While transaction-specific evaluation is used to assess particular events in service encounters, cumulative evaluation is used to assess the overall impressions on a provider. These transaction-specific satisfaction is not necessarily correlated with overall satisfaction and customers' propensity to revisit and recommend the service provider. Satisfaction as an attitudinal construct can be unstable. Customers may be satisfied with one encounter but not the others, or vice versa. To a certain degree, service quality is more closely related to customer behavioural intentions.

Numerous studies have found that service quality has a direct influence on customer retention and loyalty. Zeithaml, Berry, and Parasuraman (1996) examined the relationship between service quality and customer behaviour intentions. The results from a multicompany empirical study showed that improving service quality increased favourable behavioural intentions and decreased unfavourable ones. A similar finding was reported by Rust, Zahorik, and Keiningham (1995). In the hospitality sector, Prentice (2013, 2014, 2018) also reported that service quality provided by casinos has a direct impact on player loyalty. Superior services result in favourable responses with a higher level of arousal and dominance emotion (Lio and Roy, 2009). Consequently, service operators have reaped value in the form of delivering exceptional service throughout the service encounter. Therefore, service quality is evidently a more stable predictor of customers' behavioural intentions. However, the importance of customer satisfaction must be acknowledged. Satisfied customers may not return, but unsatisfied customers are not conducive to business development. Hence, to better understand loyalty and retention, both service quality and customer satisfaction must be taken into account, despite of the sequence.

Research on this area is ongoing but targets different angles such as extending into different study contexts, identifying and incorporating a variety of factors (e.g. Bedi, 2010; Kassim and Abdullah, 2010; Maroco and Maroco, 2013; Prentice, 2013; Shi, Prentice and He, 2013). Recent research mostly delves into operationalisation and composition of service quality and debate on the relevant influences of service quality and customer satisfaction on the attitudinal and behavioural outcomes. Instead of discussing service quality as an overall assessment of the company's service offerings, researchers tend to operationalise service quality into tangible and intangible components. The former refers to any physical settings and technical quality such as amenities, facilities, and the atmosphere (servicescapes) relating to the service (McCain, Jang and Hu, 2005). The latter focus on employees and employee services. A large body of recent literature has emphasised the role of employees in customers' attitudes and behaviours (Keh *et al.*, 2013; Prentice, 2018; Subramony and Holtom, 2012; Yee *et al.*, 2010). Research shows that employee service has a direct impact on customer satisfaction and their subsequent behaviours.

2.7 Service Employees and Service Quality

Service quality is defined as a consumer's judgement or perception of an entity's overall excellence or superiority, often as a result of comparing expectations with perceived performance (Parasuraman, Zeithaml and Berry, 1988). It is also regarded as a form of attitude, a global attitude of a firm, related but not equivalent to satisfaction. Service quality can be measured at the encounter level to predict encounter satisfaction, or measured as a function of multiple experiences to predict overall service satisfaction. Furthermore, the evaluation of the one encounter may be correlated with the measures of overall satisfaction, which is then correlated with overall perceptions of service quality (Bitner and Hubbert, 1994). Although the overall service quality predicts customer satisfaction, and customer retention, which ultimately leads to a firm's profitability, it is every service encounter that adds up to the cumulative perception and judgement.

Research (e.g. Prentice, 2014) shows that service quality, in high intensity service contexts, is primarily formed by frontline employees' service behaviour during service encounters. Typically, these encounters involve personal interactions between employees and customers. Employee behaviours over service encounters are concerned with the employee's performance evaluation, particularly in relation to service. An employee's service performance is affected by his or her behaviour when interacting with customers over service encounters. Service quality assessments are related to employee service performances. From this perspective, employee service performance over personal encounters with customers has implications for customer retention and company profitability. This relationship chain is documented in the service profit chain model, which was originally developed by Heskett *et al.* (1994). The model indicates that business profit and growth are stimulated primarily by customer loyalty; loyalty is a direct result of customer satisfaction; satisfaction is largely influenced by the value of services provided to customers; value is created by satisfied, loyal, and productive employees; and employee satisfaction, loyalty, and productivity, in turn, result primarily from internal service. Employee service performance and productivity derived from internal service quality can be transferred to customer perception of service quality. Firms with efficient operating strategy and service delivery endeavour to improve service productivity through satisfied and loyal employees, which enhance customer value in the service delivery process.

To capture customer value and improve customer experience, service operators have designed offerings that go beyond traditional means in order to build long-term profitable relationship with their patrons. Firms have evolved in seeking new ways to differentiate their brands and properties through better service quality in respect to the intangible attributes. The intangible aspect of services is often referred to as functional quality germane to the employee service delivery process promptness, service reliability and accuracy, and employee empathy and professionalism. Parasuraman *et al.*'s (1991) service quality measure, the SERVQUAL model with five core dimensions: reliability, assurance, empathy, responsiveness, and tangible, the first four dimensions correspond to the service delivery performed by the employees with emphasis on service promptness, accuracy, consistency, and employee friendliness and caring. The last dimension corresponds to the physical setting of the service premises that includes employees' appearance.

2.8 Service Employees

Admittedly, tangible elements of a service are important for successful service business transactions. Fostering good interactions between customers and employees is imperative in high contact services. The importance of dyadic encounters between buyer and seller–client and service provider in service marketing lies in the interpersonal contact during service encounter being a factor in customers' perception of service quality and determining ultimate satisfaction. Interpersonal contact between frontline employees and customers is vital to customers' perception of a company's service quality because personal interactions involve dynamic bargaining and communication processes that can dramatically change the attitudes, intentions, and behaviours of the parties involved. Communication between employee and customer is interactive, a reciprocal process rather than a linear one. The service experience that distinguishes one service organisation from another is a result of the unique interaction between the experiencer and the contact person. Facilities offered may be spotless and the service may be delivered on time as ordered — however, the customer may have a negative impression of the attitude of an employee and may overlook other facilities.

Customer service representatives or frontline employees, normally in the marketing-oriented boundary spanning positions, are the first and primary contact point for the customer before, during and after the service process. They play an important role in influencing customers' perceptions of any service encounter (Prentice, 2013).

Customers often base their impression of the firm largely on the service received from customer contact employees. Frontline service employees are pivotal in forming a customer's idea of perceived service quality. These employees' behaviours and performance over the service encounter form customers' perceptions of service quality, which further leads to customer satisfaction and retention (Delcourt *et al.*, 2013).

Other researchers empirically uncovered the importance of customer contact employee's behaviour in affecting customer satisfaction and subsequent purchase behaviours. A few survey-based studies, from customer satisfaction point of view, indicated the significant role of the frontline employees during the service delivery process, and the association of their service performance and customer satisfaction or dissatisfaction. For example, Crosby and Stephen (1987) found the service performance of the customer contact person is a significant predictor of overall satisfaction of the service. In another study, Crosby *et al.* (1990) revealed that the employees' relationship selling behaviours are the major determinants of relationship quality composed of two dimensions: trust and customer satisfaction. A similar finding was also reported by Boles, Barksdale and Johnson (1996). As indicated in previous context, customer satisfaction, preceded by service quality, is an important antecedent of customer loyalty. Therefore, frontline employees in people-based service contexts become a key factor in customer loyalty.

However, not all loyal customers bring financial benefits to the business. Researchers have operationalised customer loyalty into different levels: true loyalty, latent loyalty, spurious loyalty and low loyalty (Dick and Basu, 1994). Truly loyal customers have a strong emotional commitment and trust in a firm or brand. They often spend more and patronise the business more regularly. Latent-loyal customers express a high level of emotional commitment and trust in a brand or firm, but spend on the brand and patronise the business less. Spurious-loyal customers express a lower level of trust and commitment to a brand, although they appear to regularly return to the business. These customers are prone to switch to competitors when they are offered with something better. Low-loyal customers do return to the business but they spend less and are less likely to become referrals or to spread word of mouth communication. The first three types of customers generally have a more favourable attitude toward reward programs, have a longer tenure of the loyalty membership.

To capture customer purchase and loyalty behaviours, it is imperative for the business to have a clear understanding of customers' purchasing and consumption behaviours exhibited by different level of loyalty before offering incentives and designing the loyalty programs. A customer tier system is, thus, suggested for service organizations in an attempt to provide better and more reliable products or services to the higher tier segment (Zeithaml *et al.*, 2001). The firms often dedicate the most important resources and special treatment to the core portfolio. This strategy mainly relies on service representatives, especially those focusing on the profitable and genuine loyal customers (Prentice, 2013). Service employees play an essential role in identifying profitable customers, building and maintaining relationships with them, improving communication and helping increase both the quality service and the coordination between the firm and these customers (Prentice, 2016).

On the basis of the above discussion, frontline employees play a significant role in determining a firm's service quality in "people" concentrated services, and overall service quality assessment is based on individual performance over each service encounter. Singh (2000) indicated that the service employee's performance is concerned with how the service is delivered over the encounter, and the service delivery process is represented by a series of employee's encounter behaviours (Gronroos, 1984). In other words, the evaluation of the employee's performance is affected by service employees' behaviours in every encounter with customers. Consequently, employees' skills and capability of dealing with customers over each encounter has direct impact on quality evaluation.

2.9 Summary

This chapter provides the rationale for understanding the powerful role of service employees in marketing. Service employees from a marketing perspective refer to those who occupy customer-contact or frontline positions. The power of these employees on marketing is approached from their influence on marketing outcomes: service quality assessment, customer satisfaction, customer loyalty and business profitability. To understand the chain effects of employees on business outcomes, the importance of service industries is discussed. Subsequently, the conceptualisation, categorisations and characteristics of services are explained. Consistent with the service characteristics, the service marketing mix strategies with a focus on the three additional Ps (people, physical evidence and process) are discussed to understand the link between service quality and business profitability. On this basis, the role of frontline employees in service quality assessment is elaborated to understand its influence on marketing outcomes. The influence of employees on service quality assessment and its subsequent outcomes is manifested in employees' performance over the service encounter. Therefore, the service encounter becomes a key element in relationship and service marketing practice. Managing the service encounter has strategical implications for marketing success. The next chapter helps understand the service encounter.

References

Bedi, M. (2010). An integrated framework for service quality, customer satisfaction and behavioural responses in Indian banking industry: A comparison of public and private sector banks. *Journal of Services Research*, 10(1), 157–172.

Bitner, M. & Hubbert, A. (1994). Encounter satisfaction versus overall satisfaction versus quality: The customer's voice. In Rust, R., & Oliver, R. (eds), *Service Quality: New Directions in Theory and Practice*, Sage, Newbury Park, CA.

Bogicevic, V., Yang, W., Bilgihan, A., & Bujisic, M. (2013). Airport service quality drivers of passenger satisfaction. *Tourism Review*, 68(4), 3–18.

Boles, J.S., Brashear, T., Bellenger, D., & Barksdale, H. Jr (2000). Relationship selling behaviours: Antecedents and relationship with performance. *Journal of Business and Industrial Marketing*, 15(2/3), 141–153.

Bowen, D.E. & Schneider, B. (1988). Services marketing and management: Implications for organizational behaviour. In Staw, B.M. & Cummings, L.L. (eds), *Research in Organizational Behaviour,* JAI Press, Greenwich, CT.

Chandler, J.D. & Lusch, R. F. (2015). Service systems: A broadened framework and research agenda on value propositions, engagement, and service experience. *Journal of Service Research,* 18(1), 6–22.

Chathoth, P., Altinay, L., Harrington, R.J., Okumus, F., & Chan, E.S. (2013). Co-production versus co-creation: A process based continuum in the hotel service context. *International Journal of Hospitality Management,* 32, 11–20.

Ching, F.D. (2014). *Architecture: Form, Space, and Order,* 4th Ed. Hoboken, New Jersey, USA: John Wiley & Sons Inc.

Cronin Jr, J.J. & Taylor, S. A. (1992). Measuring service quality: A reexamination and extension. *The Journal of Marketing,* 56(3), 55–68.

Cronin Jr, J.J., Brady, M.K., & Hult, G.T.M. (2000). Assessing the effects of quality, value, and customer satisfaction on consumer behavioral intentions in service environments. *Journal of Retailing,* 76(2), 193–218.

Crosby, L.A. & Stephens, N. (1987). Effects of relationship marketing on satisfaction, retention, and prices in the life insurance industry. *Journal of Marketing Research,* 24 (November), 404–411.

Crosby, L.A., Evans, K.A., & Cowles, D. (1990). Relationship quality in services selling: An interpersonal influence perspective. *Journal of Marketing,* American Marketing Association. 54(3), 68–81.

Delcourt, C., Gremler, D.D., Van Riel, A.C., & Van Birgelen, M. (2013). Effects of perceived employee emotional competence on customer satisfaction and loyalty: The mediating role of rapport. *Journal of Service Management,* 24(1), 5–24.

Dick, A.S. & Basu, K. (1994). Customer loyalty: Toward an integrated conceptual framework. *Journal of the Academy of Marketing Science,* 22(2), 99–113.

Dube, L. & Renaghan, L.M. (1994). Measuring Customer Satisfaction for Strategic Management: For financial success, a restaurant's management must make the connection between service attributes and return patronage. Here's a way to establish that connection. *Cornell Hotel and Restaurant Administration Quarterly,* 35(1), 39–47.

Eusébio, C. & Vieira, A.L. (2013). Destination attributes' evaluation, satisfaction and behavioural intentions: A structural modelling approach. *International Journal of Tourism Research,* 15(1), 66–80.

Gronroos, C. (1984). A service quality model and its marketing implications. *European Journal of Marketing,* 18(4), 36–44.

Gronroos, C. (1988). Service quality: The six criteria of good perceived service. *Review of business*, 9(3), 10.

Gronroos, C. (1994). From marketing mix to relationship marketing: Towards a paradigm shift in marketing. *Management Decision*, 32(2), 4–20.

Grönroos, C. (1995). Relationship Marketing: The Strategy Continuum. *Journal of the Academy of Marketing Science*, 23(4), 252–254.

Grove, S.J. & Fisk, R.P. (1992). The impact of other customers on service experiences: A critical incident examination of "getting along". *Journal of Retailing*, 73(1) (Spring), 63–85.

Hallowell, R. (1996). The relationships of customer satisfaction, customer loyalty, and profitability: An empirical study. *International Journal of Service Industry Management*, 7(4), 27–42.

Hallowell, R., Schlesinger, L.A., & Zornitsky, J. (1996). Internal service quality, customer and job satisfaction: Linkages and implications for management. *Human Resource Planning*, 19(2), 20–31.

Heskett, J.L., Jones, T.O., Loveman, G.W., Sasser, W. E., & Schlesinger, L.A. (1994). Putting the service-profit chain to work. *Harvard Business Review*, 72(2), 164–174.

Humphreys, A. & Grayson, K. (2008). The intersecting roles of consumer and producer: A critical perspective on co-production, co-creation and prosumption. *Sociology Compass*, 2(3), 963–980.

Kassim, N. & Asiah Abdullah, N. (2010). The effect of perceived service quality dimensions on customer satisfaction, trust, and loyalty in e-commerce settings: A cross cultural analysis. *Asia Pacific Journal of Marketing and Logistics*, 22(3), 351–371.

Keh, H.T., Ren, R., Hill, S. R., & Li, X. (2013). The beautiful, the cheerful, and the helpful: The effects of service employee attributes on customer satisfaction. *Psychology & Marketing*, 30(3), 211–226.

Lee, C.K, Lee, Y.K., Bernard, B.J., & Yoon, Y.S. (2005). Segmenting casino gamblers by motivation: A cluster analysis of Korean gamblers. *Tourism Management*, 27(5), 856–866.

Lio, H.L.M. & Rody, R. (2009). The emotional impact of casino servicescape. *UNLV Gaming Research & Review Journal*, 13(2), 17–26.

Maroco, A.L. & Maroco, J. (2013). Service quality, customer satisfaction and loyalty. *European Journal of Tourism, Hospitality and Recreation*, 4(3), 119–145.

McCain, S.L.C., Jang, S.S., & Hu, C. (2005). Service quality gap analysis toward customer loyalty: Practical guidelines for casino hotels. *International Journal of Hospitality Management*, 24(3), 465–472.

Morgan, R.M. & Hunt, S.D. (1994). The commitment-trust theory of relationship marketing. *Journal of Marketing*, 58(3), 20–38.

Oliver, R.L. (1980). A cognitive model of the antecedents and consequences of satisfaction decisions. *Journal of Marketing Research*, 17(4), 460–469.

Oliver, R.L. (1993). Cognitive, affective, and attribute bases of the satisfaction. *Journal of Consumer Research*, Inc. 20(3) 418–430.

Parasuraman, A., Zeithaml, V.A., & Berry, L.L. (1985). A conceptual model of service quality and its implications for future research. *Journal of Marketing*, 49, 41–50.

Parasuraman, A., Zeithaml, V.A., & Berry, L.L. (1988). SERVQUAL: A multiple-item scale for measuring consumer perceptions of service quality. *Journal of Retailing*, 64(1) 12–40.

Parasuraman, A., Zeithaml, V.A., & Berry, L.L. (1994). Reassessment of expectations as a comparison standard in measuring service quality: Implications. *Journal of Marketing*, American Marketing Association. 58(1), 111–124.

Payne, A.F., Storbacka, K., & Frow, P. (2008). Managing the co-creation of value. *Journal of the Academy of Marketing Science*, 36(1), 83–96.

Prahalad, C.K. & Ramaswamy, V. (2004). Co-creation experiences: The next practice in value creation. *Journal of Interactive Marketing*, 18(3), 5–14.

Prentice, C. (2013). Service quality perceptions and customer loyalty in casinos. *International Journal of Contemporary Hospitality Management*, 25(1), 49–64.

Prentice, C. (2014). Who stays, who walks, and why in high-intensity service contexts. *Journal of Business Research*, 67(4), 608–614.

Prentice, C. (2016). Service Quality Perception and Casino Player Loyalty *Let's Get Engaged! Crossing the Threshold of Marketing's Engagement Era* (pp. 405–410): Springer, Cham.

Prentice, C. (2018). Linking internal service quality and casino dealer performance. *Journal of Hospitality Marketing & Management*, 27(6), 733–753.

Rust, R.T. & Zaborik, A.J. (1993). Customer satisfaction, customer retention, and market share. *Journal of Retailing*, Elsevier Science Publishing Company, Inc. 69, 193.

Rust, R.T., Zahorik, A.J., & Keiningham, T.L. (1995). *Return of quality: Measuring the impact of your company's quest for quality*, Irwin Professional Publishing, Chicago, IL.

Shi, Y., Prentice, C., & He, W. (2014). Linking service quality, customer satisfaction and loyalty in casinos, does membership matter? *International Journal of Hospitality Management*, 40, 81–91.

Sivadas, E. & Baker-Prewitt, J.L. (2000). An examination of the relationship between service quality, customer satisfaction, and store loyalty. *International Journal of Retail & Distribution Management*, 28(2), 73–82.

Storbacka, K., Strandvik, T., & Grönroos, C. (1994). Managing customer relationships for profit: The dynamics of relationship quality. *International Journal of Service Industry Management*, Emerald. 5(5).

Subha, M.V. & Archana, R. (2013). Identifying the Dimensions of Service Quality as Antecedents to Passenger Satisfaction of Rajiv Gandhi International Airport. *Journal of Contemporary Research in Management*, 8(2), 50–63.

Subramony, M. & Holtom, B.C. (2012). The long-term influence of service employee attrition on customer outcomes and profits. *Journal of Service Research*, 15(4), 460–473.

The World Factbook (2018). Available at https://www.cia.gov/library/publications/the-world-factbook/fields/2012.html

Wirtz, J. & Lovelock, C. (2018). *Essentials of Services Marketing*, Global Edition. Pearson Education Limited, Great Britain.

Woodside, A.G., Frey, L.L., & Daly, R.T. (1989). Linking service quality, customer satisfaction, and behavioral intention. *Journal of Health Care Marketing*, 9(4), 5–17.

Yee, R.W., Yeung, A.C., & Cheng, T.E. (2010). An empirical study of employee loyalty, service quality and firm performance in the service industry. *International Journal of Production Economics*, 124(1), 109–120.

Zeithaml, V.A. (2000). Service quality, profitability, and the economic worth of customers: What we know and what we need to learn. *Journal of the Academy of Marketing Science*, 28(1), 67–85.

Zeithaml, V.A., Berry, L.L., & Parasuraman, A. (1996). The behavioral consequences of service quality. *Journal of Marketing*, 60, 31–46.

Zeithaml, V.A., Rust, R.T., & Lemon, K.N. (2001). The customer pyramid: Creating and serving profitable customers. *California Management Review*, 43(4), 118–142.

CHAPTER 3

SERVICE ENCOUNTER

Most services are characterized by an encounter between a service provider and a customer. This interaction, which defines the quality of the service in the mind of the customer, is called a 'moment of truth'. The often brief encounter is a moment in time when the customer is evaluating the service and forming an opinion of its quality.

— *Fitzsimmons & Bordoloi*

3.1 Introduction

Chapter 1 discussed the role of frontline employees in marketing and its related outcomes: customer perception of service quality, customer satisfaction and loyalty. The importance of employees is manifested in their attitudes and behaviours over the service encounter with the customer. This chapter introduces the concept and characteristics of service encounter with a focus on interpersonal encounter. Given the nature of interpersonal interactions, the affective element of the service encounter is elaborated by diagnosing the sources and attributes of the emotions associated with the encounter. This discussion pays the way for introducing emotional intelligence into management of the service encounter.

3.2 Understanding Service Encounter

Service encounter has a significant role in service marketing, and is described as having limited or narrow relational contact and communication, and characterised as a one-off or independent purchase (Grönroos, 1994). The service performed over each encounter impacts service differentiation, quality assessment, delivery systems, customer attitudes and behaviours (Lin and Mattila, 2010). Service encounters are dyadic with a beginning and end point, and some form of exchange takes place. The dyadic encounter can be divided into an encounter that requires presence of employees, and another one that requires presence of customers. The former includes personal interactions between one employee and the other (internal service encounter), a service employee and a customer, and an employee and customers' possessions. The latter refers to contact between customers and physical or online settings by the service providers but not necessarily with employees' presence. The physical settings include any tangible offerings, servicescape, ambience, or atmosphere. The online services include website design and other associated services that facilitate online delivery. Table 3.1 shows the categorisation of the service encounter.

The encounter that involves personal interactions between employees and customers is referred to as interpersonal encounter. This type of encounter can have only the presence of service employees with customers' possessions (e.g. car repairs), or have only the presence of customers with non-employee elements of the service provider (e.g. servicescape, website), which is hereafter referred to as impersonal encounter. Most processing and information

Table 3.1 Categorisations of the service encounter

Service encounter	Internal service encounter	Between employees within the same company
	Interpersonal encounter	Employees and customers (face to face, online)
	Impersonal encounter	Employees and customers' possessions
		Customers and tangible service environment
		Customers and online service environment

processing services involve personal interactions. These services largely rely on attitudes, behaviours and performance of service employees that have direct and/or indirect contact with customers. Customers' physical possessions refer to the services performed by service employees with or without the presence of customers. Most possessions processing and mental stimulus processing services involve impersonal encounters.

3.3 The Nature of Service Encounter

In most cases, a service encounter refers to a process that relies on the interaction between service employees and customers, and is considered interpersonally relational in nature, especially in services characterised by a high degree of person-to-person interaction and by the absence of an exchange of tangible goods. The idea originated from people-based "pure" services and focused primarily on the dyadic encounter between customers and frontline employees (including remote call centre employees) in the service sector. This view can be generalised to any marketing situation in which personal interaction is an important element of the total offering (Solomon *et al.*, 1985).

At the superficial level, the interpersonal encounter is a setting where a service employee produces, performs or deliver a service and a customer purchase, consume or experience a service concurrently. The impersonal encounter entails service employees performing the service and working on customers' possessions. Either type of service encounter involves a human element. Each individual has unique economic, social and personal characteristics. From the social psychological perspective, any encounter that involves the human factor can be characterised as an emotional event, and hence an emotionally charged encounter (Hartel *et al.*, 1999; Prentice and King, 2013). Both customers and employees enter and exit service encounters with associated cognitions and emotions. In some cases, the service itself contains high affective content and is intended to deliver emotional benefits to customers. Therefore, the emotions associated with a service encounter can be attributed by the "human" (customers or employees) or the nature of the service.

3.4 Attributions of Emotionally Charged Service Encounter

3.4.1 *Employee attributions*

An emotional service encounter can be attributed by employees. Employees can be emotional. Their emotions can be traced from, inter alia, internal service encounter with co-workers, inappropriate job assignments and tasks, emotional contagion, or emotional labour requirement. Internal service encounter refers to interactions between co-workers or between employees and supervisors within the same organisation, with one employee as an internal customer, the other as an internal service provider (Gremler, Bitner and Evans, 1994). This concept is derived from internal marketing that depicts employees as internal customers whose needs and wants should be satisfied to achieve optimal organisational performance, as opposed to external marketing that is focused on external customers' needs and wants. A smooth "transaction" over an internal service encounter is critical to engender customer satisfaction and positive assessment of the company's service quality as internal operations at the backstage influence implementation of marketing strategies and efficiency of external transactions (Gremler *et al.*, 1994; Gunawardane, 2011). Any internal conflict between co-workers or employees and supervisors could cause an employee to be emotional. Such emotions may be transferred to encounters with external customers.

On the basis of role theory, the role conflict, role ambiguity, and role overload contribute to employee emotions (Bateman and Strasser, 1984; Hrebiniak, 1974; Hartline and Ferrell, 1996). Emotions elicited from the job role may affect employee attitudes and behaviours over the service encounter. Some may vent their emotions out to the customer they are dealing with. Even in a low affect service encounter such as a bank transaction or hotel check in, service behaviour performed by an employee with negative emotions may trigger customer emotional reaction.

According to emotional contagion theory (Hatfield, Cacioppo and Rapson, 1994), emotions are contagious, despite who the transmitter is. Emotional contagion is the interactions that people automatically and continuously tend to mimic and synchronise their movements with the facial expressions, voices, postures movements, and the instrumental behaviours of others. Many scholars have suggested that emotions affect the dynamics of a conversation between a customer-contact employee and customer (e.g., Liljander *et al.*, 1995; Prentice, 2016; Prentice, Chen and King, 2013). Verbal cues, and especially nonverbal cues from the part of sender, which set the emotional tone in a conversation, make up for this process of impression (Weitz *et al.*, 1993). Once a person contacts another, this person arouses the other person. This process of arousal also takes place in the opposite direction. Seeing someone expresses an emotion can evoke that mood. Regardless of the facial expression mimicking, people become influenced in an unconscious manner (Goleman, 1995). In the case of employee-customer interactions, an emotional customer may cause an emotional employee or vice versa.

The job of service representatives involves high social components, and hence contains high emotional labour demand (Daus and Ashkanansy, 2005). Prior research into emotional labour has been concerned with service employees, and the concept of emotional labour has particular relevance to service encounters. The main reason, according to Ashforth and Humphrey, lies in the uncertainty created by "human" (employees or customers) participation in the service encounter, which often has a dynamic and emergent quality. Emotional labour is the process of managing (including suppressing and faking) feelings and expressions to fulfil the organisational requirements of a job (Hochschild, 1983). Employees are compelled to follow organisational scripts to engineer their emotions. Service employees are situated at the organisation-customer interface as the first contact point for customers. Service transactions often involve face-to-face interactions between these employees and customers. The process of performing emotional labour per se is an emotional experience.

3.4.2 *Customer attributions*

Customers are emotional. The emotion may be attributed to their good or bad moods, or unreasonable expectation before entering the service encounter, or irrational demands during the encounter. When customers are in good mood, they may tolerate some imperfection of the service. Their zone of tolerance may be expanded. When the service is delivered to their standards or better than they expected, they may be elated and express delightful attitudes and behaviours towards the service providers.

On the other hand, customers may be dissatisfied with the best service when they are in bad mood. Their dis/satisfaction is caused by their own behaviours (Bitner, Booms and Tetreault, 1990; Hartel *et al.*, 1999). Bitner *et al.* (1994) found that unsatisfactory service encounters may be due to inappropriate customer behaviours. Their study provides empirical evidence that these difficult customer types do exist and in fact can be the source of their own dissatisfaction. In some service industries, problem customers are the source of 22% of the dissatisfactory incidents. This group may be even larger in industries in which the customer has greater input into the service delivery process.

3.4.3 *The nature of a service*

Some services contain high affect contents, such as psychological reactance (bill collectors); invasive procedures on the self (e.g., tattooing); and risk associated with credence goods (e.g., financial advising). Customers are motivated by the expected functional benefits of service encounters, emotional content is nonetheless an important part of interaction and service satisfaction. Some services offer affective benefits, such as martial arts training, and adventure recreations (Arnould and Price, 1993; Siehl, Bowen and Pearson, 1992). Customers seek emotional benefits of these services. Emotions associated with these service encounters largely result from the cognitive and affective information processing initiated by the service event. Service employees convey the affective content of events through their own engagement, emotions, sense of drama and skills (Deighton, 1992; Grove and Fisk, 1992).

3.5 Managing the Service Encounter with Emotional Intelligence

Despite the emotional encounter caused by customers, employees, or the nature of the service, it is critical for employees to manage emotions associated with the service encounter. During an emotional counter, customers want the employee to interact with them on the basis of their emotional state, rather than according to a standardised script by the management (Price *et al.*, 1995). Emotional labour through engineering of emotion is not sufficient to render a satisfactory encounter. As emotional intelligence constitutes abilities of displaying strong self-awareness and high levels of interpersonal skills, and emotional intelligent individuals are empathetic, and adaptable (e.g., Bar-On, 2002; Boytzis, Goleman and Rhee, 2000; Goleman, 1995; 1998; Sjoberg and Littorin, 2003), hence highly emotionally intelligent people are more likely to harness the emotional level of the encounter (Fineman, 1996).

Emotional intelligence refers to individuals' abilities to understand and regulate their own emotions and those of others (Mayer and Salovey, 1997). People with higher than average emotional intelligence scores display strong self-awareness and better interpersonal skills. These emotional abilities can be utilised by service employees to manage their own attitudes and behaviours as well as those of others (internal and external customers) over the internal or external service encounter. The level of emotional intelligence demonstrated by employees is imperative to deliver quality service, ensure a successful service encounter and customers' positive service experience with the service provider that would affect customer assessment of the firm's service quality and customers' attitudes and subsequent behaviours manifested in their patronage and loyalty.

3.6 Emotional Intelligence for Employees

In the case of the emotions resulted from employees who perform emotional labour, emotional intelligence can manage the negative consequences of emotional labour (Daus and Ashkanasy, 2005). Studies have been undertaken to demonstrate and confirm the important relationships between emotional intelligence and emotional labour in both laboratory and field studies. With simulated customer service representatives, Daus (2002) found that people who could read emotions in faces felt less of an emotional load from the job, and people who could better manage emotions in themselves felt more of such load. Among actual customer service representatives and sales personnel, Cage *et al.* (2004) found that with respect to the dimensions of emotional intelligence, understanding emotions was positively related with the faking positive aspect of emotional labour, whereas expressing negative emotions was negatively associated with actual sales performance. Employing police officers as a sample, Daus, Rubin and Cage (2004) and Daus, Rubin, Smith and Cage (2004) quantitatively demonstrated a definitive link between aspects of emotional labour and emotional intelligence. Based on these studies, Daus and Ashkanasy (2005) concluded that emotional intelligence and its four branches proposed by Mayer and Salovey (1997) were significantly associated with deep acting of emotional labour; while the branch understanding emotions was associated with surface acting, the other three branches were significantly related to suppressing negative emotions; finally, using emotions was related to faking positive emotions.

When employees' emotions result from emotional contagion, emotional intelligence accounts for individual differences in dealing with these emotions. Individuals differ in their abilities to influence another person or to become influenced by another person's emotions. For example, when people mimic and synchronise reactions with one another, some might be powerful transmitters of emotions (they are able to influence others with their emotions) and others might be powerful catchers of emotions (they assume the senders' emotions) (Hatfield *et al.*, 1994). Transmitters, those who by their innate bodily circuitry transmit their emotions to others, are charismatic, colourful and entertaining, score high on dominance, affiliation, and exhibition (Hatfield *et al.*, 1994). In many cases, being able to transmit positive emotions to another person might cause this other person to become more accessible to the intention of the conversation (Isen and Means, 1983). On the other side, those susceptible to the emotions of others, are people whose attention tends to be riveted to others. Therefore, they are more likely to be affected by other people's emotions. According to Goleman (1995), those who can influence others or be influenced by others' emotions without suffering burnout or emotional dissonance could be perceived as emotionally intelligent people. Burnout and emotional dissonance have been empirically evidenced to be negatively related to one's behaviour and performance (Abraham, 1998a).

3.7 Employee Emotional Intelligence for Customers

Frontline employee's emotional abilities are believed to play an important role in solving customers' problems (Bitner *et al.*, 1990), and achieving customer satisfaction (Bardzil and Slaski, 2003). In a few qualitative studies, Bitner (1990) and Bitner *et al.* (1990) show that customers have positive emotions towards service encounters when employees exhibit emotionally competent behaviours. Bitner *et al.* also found that an employee's ability to adapt to special needs and requests enhances customers' positive perceptions of the service encounter. Furthermore, several studies have shown that the friendliness, enthusiasm and attentiveness of contact employees positively affect customers' perceptions of service quality (e.g., Bowen and Schneider, 1988; Rafaeli and Sutton, 2001). These characteristics demonstrated by employees imply emotional intelligent performance (Bar-On, 1997; Goleman, 1998).

In the case of customers seeking emotional services, employee emotional intelligence can manage a customer's attitudes and behaviours resulting from the employees' encounter behaviours (Hartel *et al.*, 1999). The influence of service employee's emotional intelligence on customer's quality perception and service satisfaction can be interpreted from two aspects. First, through the aspect of perceiving, understanding and managing an employee's own emotions, emotional intelligence exerts effect on preventing the detrimental side of emotional labour mentioned above that may affect the labourer's performance over the encounter with customers, thus influencing the customer's perceptions towards the firm's service quality. On the other hand, according to Hartel, Barker and Barker (1999), emotional intelligence, through the aspect of perceiving, understanding and managing customer's emotions, can be served as a vehicle by which service providers can affect a customer's emotion and appraisal process in service encounters.

3.8 Summary

The foregoing chapters discuss the rationale for incorporating emotional intelligence into marketing as a tool to manage the service encounter to generate positive quality assessment for the company, engender customer satisfaction and loyalty, and achieve company profitability. The service encounter is categorised as internal and external and as being emotionally charged. Hence, emotional intelligence is known to manage emotions associated with the service encounter. The emotions can be attributed to employees, customers and the nature of the service. Despite the causes and sources of emotions, from the marketing perspective, employees are the incumbents to manage the emotions for marketing efficiency and financial performance. In this sense, emotional intelligence becomes a marketing strategy to facilitate business transactions.

Consistent with the rationale elaborated in this chapter, the next chapter will first discuss what exactly emotional intelligence is. It elaborates everything relating to emotional intelligence. Since its inception in 1990s, this concept has been heavily debated and extensively discussed. The discussion is necessary for readers to understand the concept of emotional intelligence and how it can be incorporated into marketing as a strategy.

References

Abraham, R. (1998). Emotional dissonance in organizations: Antecedents, consequences, and moderators. *Genetic, Social and General Psychology Monographs,* 124(2), 229–246.

Arnould, E.J. & Price, L.L. (1993). "River magic": Hedonic consumption and the extended service encounter. *Journal of Consumer Research,* 20, 24–45.

Bardzil, P. & Slaski, M. (2003). Emotional intelligence: Fundamental competencies for enhanced service provision. *Managing Service Quality,* 13(2), 97–104.

Bar-On, R. (1997). *Bar-On Emotional Quotient Inventory: Technical Manual.* Toronto: Multi-Health Systems. *Business Networks.* Toronto, ON: MHS.

Bar-On, R. (2002). *Bar-On Emotional Quotient Short Form (EQ-i: Short):* *Technical Manual.* Toronto: Multi-Health Systems.

Bateman, T.S. & Strasser, S. (1984). A longitudinal analysis of the antecedents of organizational commitment. *Academy of Management Journal,* 27(1), 95–112.

Bitner, M.J. (1990). Evaluating service encounters: The effects of physical surroundings and employee responses. *Journal of Marketing,* American Marketing Association. 54(2), 69–82.

Bitner, M.J., Booms, B.H., & Tetreault, M.S. (1990). The service encounter: Diagnosing favorable and unfavorable incidents. *Journal of Marketing,* 54, 71–84.

Bitner, M.J., Booms, B.H., & Mohr, L.A. (1994). Critical service encounters: The employee's viewpoint. *Journal of Marketing,* American Marketing Association. 58(4), 95–106.

Bowen, D.E. & Schneider, B. (1988). Services marketing and management: Implications for organizational behaviour. In Staw, B.M., & Cummings, L.L. (eds), *Research in Organizational Behaviour,* JAI Press, Greenwich, CT.

Boyatzis, R., Goleman, D., & Rhee, K. (2000). Clustering competence in emotional intelligence: Insights from the emotional competence inventory (ECI). In Bar-On, R. and Parker, J.D.A. (eds.), *Handbook of Emotional Intelligence,* Jossey-Bass, San Francisco.

Cage, T., Daus, C.S., & Saul, K. (2004). An examination of emotional skill, job satisfaction, and retail performance. Paper submitted to the 19th Annual Society for *Industrial/Organizational Psychology,* as part of the symposium.

Daus, C.S., Rubin, R.S., Smith, R.K., & Cage, T. (2004). Police performance: Do emotional skills matter? Paper submitted to the 19th Annual Meeting of the Society for Industrial and Organizational Psychologists, as part of the symposium, Book 'em Danno!: New developments in law enforcement performance prediction.

Daus, C.S. & Ashkanasy, N.M. (2005). The case for the ability-based model of emotional intelligence in organizational behaviour. *Journal of Organizational Behaviour,* 26(4), 453–466.

Daus, C.S. & Jones, R.G. (2002). Emotional intelligence in everyday life. *Personnel Psychology,* Inc. 55.

Deighton, J. (1992). The consumption of performance. *Journal of Consumer Research,* 19(3), 362–372.

Fineman, S. (2000). *Commodifying the Emotionally Intelligence.* London: Sage.

Fitzsimmons, J.A., Fitzsimmons, M.J., & Bordoloi, S. (2006). *Service Management: Operations, Strategy, and Information Technology.* New York: McGraw-Hill.

Goleman, D. (1995). *Emotional Intelligence: Why It Can Matter More Than IQ.* USA: Bantam Books.

Goleman, D. (1998). *Working with Emotional Intelligence.* New York: Bantam Books.

Goleman, D. (1998b). What Makes a Leader? *Harvard Business Review,* November–December.

Gremler, D.D., Jo Bitner, M., & Evans, K.R. (1994). The internal service encounter. *International Journal of Service Industry Management,* 5(2), 34–56.

Gronroos, C. (1994). From marketing mix to relationship marketing: Towards a paradigm shift In marketing. *Management Decision,* 32(2), 4–20.

Grove, S. J. & Fisk, R. P. (1992). Observational data collection methods for services marketing: An overview. *Journal of the Academy of Marketing Science,* 20(3), 217–224.

Gunawardane, G. (2011). Reliability of the internal service encounter. *International Journal of Quality & Reliability Management,* 28(9), 1003–1018.

Hartel, C.E.J., Barker, S., & Barker, N.J. (1999). The role of emotional intelligence in service encounters. *Australian Journal of Communication,* 26(2), 77–87.

Hartline M.D. & Ferrell, O.C. (1996). The management of customer-contact service employees: An empirical investigation. *Journal of Marketing,* 60, 52–70.

Hatfield, E., Cacioppo, J.T., & Rapson, R.L. (1994). *Emotional Contagion.* New York, Cambridge University Press.

Hochschild, A. (1983). *The Managed Heart: Commercialization of Human Feeling.* Berkeley: University of California Press.

Hrebiniak, L.G. (1974). Effects of job level and participation on employee attitudes and perceptions of influence. *Academy of Management Journal,* 17(4), 649–662.

Isen, A.M. & Means, B. (1983). The influence of positive affect on decision-making strategy. *Social Cognition,* 2, 18–31.

Liljander, V. & Strandvik, T. (1995). The nature of customer relationships in services. In Swartz, T., Bowen, D., & Brown, S. (Eds), *Advances in Services Marketing and Management,* JAI Press, London.

Lin, I.Y. & Mattila, A.S. (2010). Restaurant servicescape, service encounter, and perceived congruency on customers' emotions and satisfaction. *Journal of Hospitality Marketing & Management,* 19(8), 819–841.

Mayer, J.D. & Salovey, P. (1997). What is emotional intelligence? In Salovey, P. & Sluyter, D. J. (eds.), *Emotional Development and Emotional Intelligence: Educational Implications,* 3–31. New York: Basic Books.

Prentice, C. (2016). Leveraging employee emotional intelligence in casino profitability. *Journal of Retailing and Consumer Services,* 33, 127–134.

Prentice, C. & King, B.E. (2013). Impacts of personality, emotional intelligence and adaptiveness on service performance of casino hosts: A hierarchical approach. *Journal of Business Research,* 66(9), 1637–1643.

Prentice, C., Chen, P.J., & King, B. (2013). Employee performance outcomes and burnout following the presentation-of-self in customer-service contexts. *International Journal of Hospitality Management,* 35, 225–236.

Price, L.L., Arnould, E.J., & Tierney, P. (1995). Going to extremes: Managing service encounters and assessing provider performance. *Journal of Marketing,* 59(2), 83–97.

Rafaeli, A. & Sutton, R.I., (2001). Expression of emotion as part of the work role. *Academy of Management Review* 12(1), 23–37.

Siehl, C., Bowen, D., & Pearson, C. (1992). Service encounters: An information processing model. *Organization Science,* 3(4), 537–555.

Sjöberg, L. & Engelberg, E. (2005). Measuring and validating emotional intelligence as performance or self-report. *Emotional intelligence. Research insights,* 18, 97–125.

Solomon, M.R., Surprenant, C., Czepiel, J.A., & Gutman, E.G. (1985). A role theory perspective on dyadic interactions: The service encounter. *Journal of Marketing,* 49(1), 99–111.

Weitz, D.A., Zhu, J.X., Durian, D.J., Gang, H., & Pine, D.J.F. (1993). Diffusing wave spectroscopy: The technique and some applications. *Physica Scripta (T49B),* 610.

CHAPTER 4

EMOTIONAL INTELLIGENCE

4.1 Introduction

The foregoing chapters discuss the role of frontline employees in marketing and how these employees influence marketing practice and outcomes through service encounter. The emotional nature of service encounter is elaborated to present the rationale for inducing emotional intelligence in service encounter management and marketing practice. This book adopts marketing and business perspectives to understand the relationship between emotional intelligence and marketing, and discusses how these two are related. Emotional intelligence is a psychology construct describing individual emotional abilities, and marketing is a business discipline. These individual abilities are elevated as a marketing strategy by demonstrating how they are related to employees' job attitudes and behaviours as well as to customer attitudinal and behavioural responses towards the employees and the firm which are the central focus of marketing activities. The remainder of this book discusses these relationships.

Despite being a popular topic, there has been substantial controversy and debate on emotional intelligence among researchers and practitioners, mainly in the areas of conceptualisation and assessments, which further led to arguments on its applicability and predictability. This chapter presents a thorough literature review on fundamental and essential issues and discussions around emotional intelligence including conceptualisations, measurements, and applications. This chapter begins with describing its historical and scientific background, moves into the conceptualisation and measurements, is concluded with its predictive validity and applications, which paves the foundation for introducing it into the marketing discipline as a marketing strategy.

The first section discusses the prevalence of emotions in a business/organisational context and presents the relevance of emotional intelligence, followed by discussion of the origin of emotional intelligence. The subsequent section reviews the conceptualisations of emotional intelligence. The conceptualisations proposed by three protagonists in this area are discussed, namely, the models of Mayer-Salovey-Caruso, Goleman and Baron-On. The three models have generated the most interest and claimed to complement each other in explaining the concept of emotional intelligence in the academic world and wider communities. Following discussion of these models, the measurement and predictive validity of emotional intelligence will be reviewed to clarify confusion of the models used in research and its applicability in practice. The measurement issue is revealed from the method of assessing emotional intelligence, on which the concepts of trait emotional intelligence and ability emotional intelligence are presented. The distinction between trait emotional intelligence and ability emotional intelligence is elaborated to delineate the differences of the three models. Lastly, the predictability of emotional intelligence is discussed to help readers understand the importance of emotional intelligence. To reinforce the predictability, the incremental validity of emotional intelligence is presented with regard to its relationship with the respective correlates in the psychological domain: personality or cognitive intelligence depending on the model in question.

4.2 Prevalence of Emotional Intelligence

Emotions are prevalent, in both personal, professional and business arenas. In the organisational context, emotions have been recognised as a fundamental and integral part of work life, for both employees and customers. Emotional dissonance, burnout, role theory concepts such as role conflict, role ambiguity, role overload to psychological stress have been popular topics in boundary spanning research on employees (Prentice, 2008; Prentice, Chen and King, 2013). Customer satisfaction, loyalty, commitment and retention are emotionally loaded terms describing customer emotional attachment to a firm that brings potential business profitability (Prentice and King, 2011). Emotional intelligence is emerged as a psychological concept accounting for intelligent behaviours in dealing with emotional related issues. Employees engage in these behaviours not only to manage their own performance but also to regulate customers' mood in order to influence their attitudes and behaviours towards the employee and the firm.

Emotional intelligence has been widely disseminated in various communities since early 1990s. Traditional intelligence often provides one accurate answer to a well-defined problem in the academic world, but it fails to do so in the daily life of organisations where emotions are prevalent. Emotional intelligence has been empirically proved to tap into a greater portion of unexplained variance in job performance left by traditional intelligence. In the academic community, publications around emotional intelligence are primarily centred on conceptualisations, construct validity, and measurement issues. Empirical studies are mostly focused on the impact of emotional intelligence on individuals' health, success, performance and relationships (e.g. Joseph *et al.*, 2015; Prentice, 2011; Schutte *et al.*, 2007; Wong and Law, 2002).

In the organisational context, research has extensively discussed its relationship with leadership (see McCleskey, 2014) and employees' job attitudes and behaviours (see Miao, Humphrey and Qian, 2017). A recent meta-analyses research (i.e. Joseph *et al.*, 2015) shows that emotional intelligence, to a certain degree, demonstrates substantial predictive validity. The degree of the predictive validity is dependent on the study settings, selected criterion as well as the model used. In particular, emotional intelligence can be a positive predictor for jobs logically requiring a high level of emotional skills. Such jobs normally contain high emotional labour demands, for instance, the job of customer service representatives or frontline employees (Prentice, Chen and King, 2013). Emotional intelligence could also be an important factor in employee performance for jobs that have important social components (Caruso, Mayer and Salovey, 2002). Mulki *et al.*, (2015) resonate with this view and indicate that emotional intelligence can be expected to contribute at a reasonable level of prediction of individual behaviours involving social components.

Empirical studies on its influence on customers' attitudes and behaviours are emerging (Kernbach and Schutte, 2005) but rather limited. However customers' responses towards a brand or firm are largely dependent upon those of customer contact employees. For instance, employee performance during interactions with customers largely influences the latter's perception of the firm's service quality and subsequent behaviours (Zablah *et al.*, 2016); employee commitment and retention relates to customer loyalty and retention (see Hogreve *et al.*, 2017). Therefore, customer response towards the brand or firm can be derived from the influence of emotional intelligence on employees' job attitudes and behaviours. To understand the influence of emotional intelligence on these business and organisational outcomes, the following reveals all the relevant issues relating to this concept including its origin, conceptualisation, measurements and explaining power in practice.

4.3 Origins of Emotional Intelligence

Thorndike and Gardener paved the way for the current interest in emotional intelligence. About a century ago, Thorndike (1920) suggested that intelligence could be organised under three broad dimensions: mechanical, abstract, and social. Mechanical intelligence reflects a person's ability to manage things and mechanisms; abstract intelligence is an ability to manage and understand ideas and symbols; and social intelligence refers to "the ability to understand and manage men and women, boys and girls — to act wisely in human relations" (p. 228) (cf. Newsome, Day and Catano, 2000). The last categorisation proposed by Thorndike is very similar to the concept of emotional intelligence.

Following Thorndike's ideas, Gardner (1993) included interpersonal and intrapersonal intelligences in his theory of multiple intelligences. According to Gardner, social intelligence, which is one among seven intelligence domains, comprises an individual's interpersonal and intrapersonal intelligence. Intrapersonal intelligence relates to one's ability to deal with oneself and to "symbolize complex and highly differentiated sets of feelings" (Gardner, 1993) within the self. Interpersonal intelligence relates to one's ability to deal with others and to "notice and make distinctions among other individuals and, in particular, among their moods, temperaments, motivations and intentions" (Gardner, 1993). Emotional intelligence can be viewed as a combination of the intrapersonal and interpersonal intelligence of an individual.

The first use of the term *emotional intelligence* appeared in a German publication in 1966. The author named Leuner (1966) discusses women who reject their social roles due to being separated at an early age from their mothers. He suggested that they had a low "Emotional Intelligence" and prescribed Lysergic Acid Diethylamide (LSD) for their treatment. Emotional intelligence first appeared in English in a doctoral dissertation by Payne (1983, 1986) who advocated fostering emotional intelligence in schools by liberating emotional experience through therapy.

The term emotional intelligence was brought into mainstream psychology in the early 1990s (Mayer, DiPaolo and Salovey, 1990; Salovey and Mayer, 1990). Mayer and Salovey (1997) presented a conceptual framework of emotional abilities that they believed constituted emotional intelligence. Daniel Goleman, a psychologist and science writer who has previously written on brain and behavioural research for the *New York Times*, popularised the term in the middle 1990s and conceptualised emotional intelligence as a general quality possessed by every normal person, a quantitative spectrum of individual differences in which people can be ranked on a type of emotional scale. Thus, so far, emotional intelligence has come to mean a measurement of emotions.

4.4 Emotional Intelligence Definitions

The definitions and conceptualisations of emotional intelligence in the literature are vastly different, and each of them bears little resemblance on their own. Among all the theories about emotional intelligence, those proposed by Mayer and Salovey, Bar-on and Goleman have generated the most interest in terms of research and application. Each of their theoretical paradigms conceptualise emotional intelligence from one of two perspectives: as a form of pure intelligence consisting of cognitive ability only (Salovey and Mayer, 1990), or as a mixed intelligence consisting of both cognitive ability and personality aspects, the differences in which are attributed to the different beliefs of what constitutes emotional intelligence (Bar-On, 1997; Goleman, 1998). The two perspectives revealed in depth below, although different, are, according to Ciarrochi, Chan and Caputi (2000), more complementary than contradictory.

4.4.1 *The Mayer-Salovey-Caruso ability model*

Relating emotional intelligence to Thorndike's social intelligence dimension, Salovey and Mayer (1990) perceive emotional intelligence as a form of pure intelligence, representing our potential for achieving mastery of specific abilities in this domain. The authors presented a conceptual framework of emotional abilities that they believed constituted emotional intelligence. To the authors, emotional intelligence should be integrated into the domains of intelligence and emotion. It involves capacity to carry out abstract reasoning about emotional signals that convey regular and discernible meanings about relationships and a number of universal basic emotions (Mayer, Salovey and Caruso, 2002). This idea can be thought of as one member of an emerging group of potential hot intelligences that include social intelligence (Sternberg and Smith, 1985, Thorndike 1920), practical intelligence (Sternberg and Caruso, 1985; Wagner and Sternberg, 1985), personal intelligence (Gardner 1993), non-verbal perception skills (Buck, 1984; Rosenthal *et al.*, 1979), and emotional creativity (Averill and Nunley, 1992). Each of these forgoing concepts forms coherent domains that partly overlap with emotional intelligence, but divide human intelligence in distinctive ways.

To establish emotional intelligence as a pure intelligence, Mayer, Caruso, Salovey (1999) used three criteria: conceptual, correlational and developmental. Conceptually, any intelligence must reflect actual mental performance rather than preferred behaviour patterns, self-esteem, or non-intellectual attainments (Carroll, 1993; Mayer and Salovey, 1993; Scarr, 1989). To Mayer *et al.* emotional intelligence does describe actual abilities. Secondly, from a correlation perspective, a new "intelligence" should describe a set of closely related abilities that are similar to, but distinct from, mental abilities described by existing intelligences (Carroll, 1993). Mayer *et al.* regard emotional intelligence as a type of social intelligence but in a broader scope, because it does not only include reasoning about the emotions in social relationships, but also reasoning about internal emotions that are important for personal growth. Finally, from a development point of view, intelligence should develop with age and experience. The results gained by Mayer *et al.* showed that adults did perform at higher ability levels than do adolescents.

Subsuming emotional intelligence under the domain of intelligence, Salovey and Mayer (1990, 1997) define emotional intelligence as the ability to perceive, respond and manipulate emotional information without necessarily understanding it and the ability to understand and manage emotions without necessarily perceiving feelings well or fully experiencing them. Their model of emotional intelligence is divided into four branches. The first branch is emotional perception, which includes the ability to identify emotion in one's physical states, feelings and thoughts, and emotions in other people, designs, artwork, *et cetera* through language, sound, appearance, and behaviour; the ability to express emotions accurately, and the needs related to those feelings; the ability to discriminate between accurate and inaccurate, or honest versus dishonest expressions of feelings.

The second branch is emotional assimilation, which includes emotion-prioritised thinking by directing attention to important information. Emotions are so sufficiently vivid and available that they can be generated as aids to judgement and memory concerning feelings. Emotional mood swings change the individual's perspective from optimistic to pessimistic, encouraging consideration of multiple points of view. Emotional states differentially encourage specific problem-solving approaches such as when happiness facilitates inductive reasoning and creativity.

The third branch is emotional understanding, which includes the ability to label emotions and recognise relations among the words and the emotions themselves, such as the relation between liking and loving; the ability to interpret the meanings that emotions convey regarding relationships, and that sadness often accompanies a loss; the ability to understand complex feelings, simultaneous feelings of love and hate or blends as *awe* as a combination of fear and surprise; the ability to recognise likely transitions among emotions, from anger to satisfaction or from anger to shame.

The fourth branch is emotion management, which includes the ability to stay open to feelings, including pleasant and unpleasant ones; the ability to reflectively engage or detach from an emotion depending upon it being judged to be informative or utility; the ability to reflectively monitor emotions in relation to oneself and others, such as recognising how clear, typical, influential or reasonable they are; the ability to manage emotion in oneself and others by moderating negative emotions and enhancing pleasant ones without repressing or exaggerating information they may convey.

Mayer, Salovey, Caruso and Sitarenios (2001) further explain that the four branches function hierarchically with the perception of emotions acting as the most basic or bottom branch, and emotional management as the most complex or top branch. Specifically, perception of emotions is a precursor to the next three branches. If an individual lacks the ability to process the lowest level of emotional input, he or she would also lack the ability to manage emotions at a higher level described in this model. Once perception has gained, emotions can be utilised to facilitate thought consciously or unconsciously. This is supported by Levine's (1997) (cited in Webb, 2004) study which shows that different emotions are related to different problem-solving strategies. For example, sadness leads to a coping strategy where coping is the most appropriate strategy (Levine, 1997). The next step involves cognitive processing to recognise how multiple emotions can combine and to anticipate how one emotion leads to another, until they finally translate emotional knowledge into behaviour.

4.4.2 *Goleman's model*

Being credited for popularising the concept of emotional intelligence in 1995, Daniel Goleman wrote the landmark book *Emotional Intelligence*. The author describes emotional intelligence as "abilities such as being able to motivate oneself and persist in the face of frustrations; to control impulse and delay gratification; to regulate one's moods and keep distress from swamping the ability to think; to empathize and to hope." Therefore, emotional intelligence is defined as "the capacity for recognizing our own feelings and those of others, for motivating ourselves, and for managing emotions well in ourselves and in our relationships" (Goleman, 1998, p. 317).

The model of emotional intelligence proposed by Goleman involves cognitive ability and personality factors. It focuses on the domain of work performance that is evaluated on social and emotional competencies. These competencies represent the degree to which an individual has mastered specific skills and abilities that build on emotional intelligence and allow them greater effectiveness in the workplace (Goleman, 1998). The competency-based approach reflects a tradition emphasising the identification of competencies that can be used to predict work performance across a variety of organisational settings, often with an emphasis on those in leadership positions (Boyatzis, 1982; Bray, Campbell and Grant, 1974; Kotter, 1982; Luthans, Hodgetts and Rosenkrantz, 1998; McClelland, 1973; Thornton and Byham, 1982). In the book, *Working with Emotional Intelligence* (1998), Daniel Goleman set out a framework of emotional intelligence based on emotional competencies that have been identified in internal research at hundreds of corporations and organisations as distinguishing outstanding performers. The author distinguishes emotional intelligence from emotional competence by defining emotional competence as "a learned capability based on emotional intelligence that results in outstanding performance at work" (Goleman, 1998b).

According to Goleman, our emotional intelligence determines our potential for learning the practical skills that underlie the emotional competence clusters; our emotional competence shows how much of that potential we have realised by learning and mastering skills and translating intelligence into on-the-job capabilities. For example, to be adept in emotional competence like customer service or conflict management requires an underlying ability in emotional intelligence fundamentals, specifically, social awareness and relationship management. Goleman (1998) argued that emotional intelligence underlies emotional competence and that emotional competence is a required antecedent to performance. Emotional intelligence enhances employee potential for learning, and emotional competence translates that potential into task-mastering capabilities.

Dulewicz and Higgs (2000) also distinguished emotional competencies from emotional intelligence and alleged that a competence framework appears to hold more empirical promise. In relation to organisational application, Dulewicz and Herbert (1996, 1999) demonstrate a clear linkage between competencies and elements of advancement within an organisational context. The relationship between individual attributes and differentiation between "average" and "outstanding" performance is at the heart of the case for considering emotional intelligence by tracking the career progress of General Managers over a seven-year period. The competencies of emotional awareness, accurate self-assessment, and self-confidence may be perceived as providing a road map toward making necessary adjustments on the job, managing uncontrolled emotions, motivating oneself, and assessing others' feelings, thereby developing the social skills to lead and motivate. However, existing research mainly draws on physiological research developments, educational-based research and developments in the therapy field. According to Dulewicz and Higgs (2000), research about emotional intelligence in organisational contexts has mainly been based on derivative arguments and largely anecdotal case descriptions.

From the perspective of competence, Goleman (1998) identified four components of emotional intelligence: self-awareness, self-management, social awareness, and relationship management. According to Goleman, self-awareness is the ability to read one's emotions and recognise their impact on decision-making. He refers to self-awareness as "knowing what we are feeling in the moment, and using those preferences to guide our decision making; having a realistic assessment of our own abilities and a well-grounded sense of self-confidence" (p. 318). Self-management involves controlling one's emotions and impulses and adapting to changing environments and is defined as "handling our emotions so that they facilitate rather than interfere with the task at hand; being conscientious and delaying gratification to pursue goals; recovering well from emotional stress" (Goleman, 1998, p. 318). Social awareness is defined as "sensing what people are feeling, being able to take their perspective, and cultivating rapport and attunement with a broad diversity of people" (Goleman, 1998, p. 318). It includes the ability to sense, understand, and react to other's emotions while comprehending social networks. Finally, relationship management entails the ability to inspire, influence, and develop others while managing conflict (Goleman, 1998).

In an analysis of data on workplace effectiveness, Boyatzis, Jacobs and Goleman (2000) found that the four clusters are related hierarchically. According to these authors, emotional self-awareness is a prerequisite for effective self-management, which in turn predicts greater social skills. A secondary pathway runs from self-awareness to social awareness to social skill. Managing relationships well then depends on a foundation of self-management and empathy, each of which in turn requires self-awareness. Goleman believes this evidence that empathy and self-management are foundations for social effectiveness finds support at the neurological level.

From the perspective of competence, Goleman developed a measure called *Emotional Competence Inventory* (ECI) based on social and emotional competencies in organisational settings with an emphasis on those in leadership positions. The ECI is a 360-degree tool designed to assess emotional competencies of individuals and organisations. It is based on emotional competencies identified by Goleman (1998) in *Working with Emotional Intelligence* and on competencies from Hay/McBer's *Generic Competency Dictionary* (1996) as well as Richard Boyatzis's *Self-Assessment Questionnaire* (SAQ). Initial concurrent validity studies using assessments based on Goleman's model have been able to account for a larger amount of variance in work performance than emotional intelligence measures based on the Mayer and Salovey model of emotional intelligence (Bradberry and Greaves, 2003), as ECI demonstrates the utility of this approach for assessment, training, and the development of social and emotional competencies in the workplace.

The ECI is complete in that it can classify each respondent within the range of self and others' ratings. Evidence for content validity is reported in the technical manual through an accurate self-assessment study in which those individuals who were not aware of their strengths and weaknesses also had trouble evaluating themselves on emotional intelligence competencies (Sala, 2002). Measures of criterion validity found that the emotional intelligence of college principals was significantly associated with college student retention. Other researchers (e.g. Stys and Brown, 2004) reported emotional intelligence measured by ECI was significantly positively correlated with salary, job success and life success. Construct validity was established through convergent validity studies with a variety of measures of similar constructs. Goleman's model of emotional intelligence was found to correspond significantly with the sensing/intuiting and thinking/feeling dimensions of the Myers-Briggs Type indicator and with the extroversion, agreeableness, and conscientiousness factors of the NEO Personality Inventory. A study of divergent validity found no significant correlations between the ECI and a measure of analytical/critical thinking (Sala, 2002).

4.4.3 *Bar-On's model*

Bar-On (1997) coined the term Emotional Quotient (EQ) in his doctoral dissertation as an analogue to Intelligent Quotient (IQ). His model of emotional intelligence can be viewed as a mixed intelligence, also consisting of cognitive ability and personality aspects. It includes: the ability to be aware of, to understand, and to express oneself; the ability to be aware of, to understand and relate to others; the ability to deal with strong emotions and control one's impulses; and the ability to adapt to change and to solve problems of a personal or social nature. Emphasising its influence on general wellbeing and adaptation, Bar-On (1997) defines emotional intelligence as "an array of non-cognitive capabilities, competencies, and skills that influence one's ability to succeed in coping with environmental demands and pressures." (p. 14)

Bar-On's model of emotional intelligence relates to the potential for performance and success, rather than performance or success itself, and is considered process-oriented rather than outcome-oriented (Bar-On, 2002). It focuses on an array of emotional and social abilities, including the ability to be aware of, understand and express oneself and the ability to adapt to change and solve problems of a social or personal nature (Bar-on, 1997). This model hypothesises that individuals with higher than average EQ's are generally more successful in meeting environmental demands and pressures. A deficiency in emotional intelligence likely means a lack of success and the existence of emotional problems. According to Bar-On (2002), emotional intelligence and cognitive intelligence contribute equally to a person's general intelligence, which then indicates potential success in one's life.

4.4.4 *Evaluations of the three models*

The three models presented above have been widely discussed in in the literature (see Stys and Brown, 2004). Each model attempts to interpret and operationalise what emotional intelligence as an incepted psychological construct connotes and implies from a different angle. However, the different conceptualisations for the same construct also create confusion, as emotional intelligence is often classified as a state of cognitive intelligence or a trait. Subsuming emotional intelligence under the "intelligence" domain, Mayer, Salovey and Caruso (1999) indicate the models proposed by Goleman and Bar-On include not only emotion and intelligence, but also motivation, non-ability dispositions and traits, and global personal and social functioning. Therefore, these broadened emotional intelligence concepts are classified as mixed models (Mayer *et al.*, 1999). They are more closely related to personality traits (Mayer *et al.*, 1999). Thus the model proposed by Mayer *et al.* (1997) is regarded as an ability model, because it emphasises the cognitive components of emotional intelligence.

Mayer *et al.*'s view has been mostly received in consensus, although some researchers (e.g. Roberts, Zeidner and Matthews, 2001) reveal scepticism. In review of the different viewpoints, Van Rooy and Viswesvaran (2003) commented that it is difficult to provide an operational definition for emotional intelligence accepted by all, as researchers interested in this area are constantly amending their own definitions of the construct. Goleman and Emmerling (2003) indicate that it is an inherent part of the process of theory development and scientific discovery in any field as specific theories within a mature paradigm begin to emerge and differentiate. Goleman (2002) acknowledges that the existence of several theoretical viewpoints within the paradigm of emotional intelligence indicate the robustness of the field but not a weakness. As each theory represents the theoretical orientation and context in which each of these authors have decided to frame their theory, all researchers share a common desire to understand and measure the abilities and traits related to recognising and regulating emotions in ourselves and others (Goleman, 1998). All theories in this paradigm tend to understand how individuals perceive, understand, utilise and manage emotions in an effort to predict and foster personal effectiveness (Goleman and Emmerling, 2003).

4.5 Measurements of Emotional Intelligence

Given that emotional intelligence is a scientifically founded and empirically validated construct, the issue of assessing and measuring this construct has fundamental significance for research on organisational behaviours. Although emotions have been viewed as unpredictable, irrational and not worth measuring, the conceptualisations of emotional intelligence have helped counter this view and offer a promise of a useful concept for predicting workplace performance. However, the use of emotional intelligence measures in research and organisational settings is vastly varied and controversial. The reason lies in how the construct should be measured, and which theory it shall be based on. The following section presents a general review of emotional intelligence measures in the relevant literature. This book takes into account all relevant views and perspectives and opts for a bipartisan approach and a less biased stance to achieve its aim: to reinforce the importance of emotional intelligence, its predictive validity is discussed following the issues of measurement.

4.5.1 *Measures of emotional intelligence*

In the emotional intelligence literature, both self-report questionnaires and performance-based tests have been used to measure this construct, which adds confusion to the findings and its relationship with personality and cognitive ability. Following the confusion, emotional intelligence researchers have not reached consensus on which method is most suitable to assess it. Ability model protagonists mentioned before indicate that performance scales are standard for intelligence research because they are based on the capacity to solve mental tasks. Objective performance scales measure objective performance with items having correct or incorrect responses, and are normally used for assessing ability construct. On the other hand, self-report scales of intelligence can be an accurate measure only if people can accurately report their own abilities. They are normally used for assessing personality construct and for those types of responses concerning self-perceptions, personal reactions, preferences, interests, attitudes, and values (Schutte *et al.*, 1998).

To exacerbate the confusion on different models and measures for the same concept, a few studies show very low correlations between performance and self-report measures of emotional intelligence. In one study, Bar-On's self-report Emotional Quotient Inventory is only modestly correlated ($r = 0.46$) with the Mayer-Salovey MEIS ability test (Van Rooy and Viswesvaran, 2003). Brackett and Mayer (2003) suggested that the ability and self-report measures might likely yield different representations of the same person; that self-report measures of emotional intelligence seem more strongly related to personality than objective measures, while objective measures appear more strongly related to cognitive ability than personality. Nevertheless, Van Rooy and Viswesvaran's (2003) meta-analytical study reported an unsubstantial, albeit significant correlation ($r = 0.33$) between MEIS (an objective measure) and General Mental Ability (GMA) (a cognitive ability measure).

4.5.2 *Ability-based measures*

Classifying emotional intelligence as a set of mental abilities, a domain of human performance, Mayer and Salovey (1999) argued that emotional intelligence should be best studied with ability measures. The ability-based emotional intelligence measures, purporting to assess emotional intelligence involving a series of solving items for emotion-based problem, are considered objective-based assessments (MacCann *et al.*, 2004). Mayer *et al.* (1999) suggested that emotional intelligence should be assessed most directly by asking a person to solve emotional problems, such as identifying the emotion in a story or painting, and then evaluating the person's answer against criteria of accuracy. Therefore, the authors developed an objective, performance-based assessment for emotional intelligence called Multifactor Emotional Intelligence Scale (MEIS) and its successor MSCEIT (Mayer — Salovey — Caruso Emotional Intelligence Test) by Mayer, Salovey and Caruso (2002).

MEIS, which consists of 12 subscale measures of emotional intelligence, indicates that emotional intelligence is a distinct intelligence with 3 separate sub factors: emotional three perception, emotional understanding, and emotional management. It found evidence for discriminant validity in that emotional intelligence was independent of general intelligence and self-reported empathy. However, the authors failed to provide evidence for the integration branch of the Four Branch Model.

For this reason, Mayer *et al.* (2002) further developed a new ability measure of emotional intelligence — MSCEIT. The MSCEIT aims to measure the four abilities described in Salovey and Mayer's model of intelligence: the experiential area comprising of Perceiving Emotions Branch and Facilitating Thinking Branch, and the strategic area including Understanding Emotional Meaning Branch and Managing Emotions Branch. Perception of emotion is measured by rating the extent and type of emotion expressed on different types of pictures. Facilitation of thought is measured by asking people to draw parallels between emotions and physical sensations as well as emotions and thoughts. Understanding emotions is measured by asking the subject to explain how emotions can blend from other emotions. Management of emotions is measured by having people choose effective self and other management techniques (Brackett and Mayer, 2003).

The MECEIT produced a factor structure congruent with the four-part model of emotional intelligence. This measure presents excellent reliability and content validity. The authors assert that the MSCEIT meets several standard criteria for a new intelligence:

1) It is objective in that answers on the test are either right or wrong as determined by consensus or expert scoring.
2) Its scores correlate with existing intelligence measures.
3) It accounts for unique variance.
4) The scores increase with age (Mayer, Caruso and Salovey, 1999; Mayer *et al.*, 2002; Mayer and Geher, 1996).

The measures are claimed to correlate with existing intelligences but independent of personality measure. The meta-analysis conducted by Van Rooy and Viswesvaran (2003) shows that the ability measure of emotional intelligence is indeed significantly associated with general cognitive ability measured by General Mental Ability (GMA). On the other hand, using emotional intelligence measured by MEIS to examine its relationship with personality measured by 16PF, Caruso, Mayer and Salovey (2002) found that the ability test of emotional intelligence is generally not associated with the 16PF primary factor scores, although the results did show a few statistically significant correlations between emotional intelligence and some branch scores of personality measures. The authors, therefore, concluded that the ability measure was separate from several standard personality traits and the ability approach places emotional intelligence in an intelligence framework.

Although Mayer *et al.* (1999) strongly believe the performance-based assessments are the best approach to measuring emotional intelligence since it is classified as a form of intelligence; the method also has its downside. According to Pérez, Petrides and Furnham (2005), unlike standard cognitive ability tests, tests of ability emotional intelligence (referred to as ability EI) cannot be objectively scored because there are no clear-cut criteria for what constitutes a correct response. Ability emotional intelligence tests have attempted to bypass this problem by relying on alternative scoring procedures, which have also been used in the past for addressing similar difficulties in the operationalisation of social intelligence. According to Petrides, Furnham and Frederickson (2004), much of the intrapersonal component of ability emotional intelligence is not amenable to objective scoring, because the information required for such scoring is available only to the test taker. Psychological indices of emotion have to be validated with reference to people's own reports of their feelings.

4.5.3 *Self-report measures*

A few self-report measures for assessing emotional intelligence emerged in the literature. One of the most recognised measures is Bar-On's Emotional Quotient Inventory (EQ-i). The measure is designed for individuals of sixteen years of age and over. Developed as a measure of emotionally and socially competent behaviour that provides an estimate of one's emotional and social intelligence, the EQ-i is not meant to measure personality traits or cognitive capacity, but rather to measure one's ability to be successful in dealing with environmental demands and pressures (Bar-On, 2002). The use of a self-report measure to assess individuals on this model is consistent with established practice within personality psychology, where self-report measures represent the dominant, if not the only method of assessment.

The EQ-i is a complete test in that it can classify each respondent within the range of EQ scores and can be used in a multitude of settings and situations, including corporate, educational, clinical, medical, research, and preventative settings. The author reports that content validity is adequate in that items for each subcomponent were generated and selected in a systematic approach. Measures of criterion validity found that emotional intelligence measured by EQ-i could accurately differentiate between those who were successful and those who were unsuccessful in various settings. Those individuals who were suspected to intuitively have higher levels of emotional intelligence were found to have EQ-i scores significantly higher than the mean (Bar-On, 2002). Measures of construct validity found no significant correlations between EQ-i and several measures of standard intelligence (Bar-On, 2002), although the EQ-i has been found to be significantly correlated to measures of psychological and subjective wellbeing and to all of the Big Five personality factors as measured by the NEO-PI-R (Brackett and Mayer, 2003). Furthermore, research has found that total EQ scale was positively correlated with three of the best indicators of emotional functioning in a measure of personality, while being negatively correlated with other indicators of abnormal emotional functioning (Bar-On, 2002). Overall, the EQ-i seems to provide a valid and reliable estimate of an individual's ability to effectively cope with the pressures and demands of daily life, as conceptualised by Bar-On (2000).

Researchers (e.g., Mayer and Salovey, 1997; Zeidner *et al.*, 2004) have raised concerns about self-report measures of emotional intelligence. The issue about the self-report measures normally contains two aspects: one is the test-taker's social desirability response; the other is the overlap with personality measures. Social desirability can be defined as a response pattern where test-takers systematically represent themselves with an excessive positive bias (Paulhus, 2002). This bias has long been known to contaminate responses on personality inventories (Holtgraves, 2004; McFarland and Ryan, 2000; Peebles and Moore, 1998; Nichols and Greene, 1997; Zerbe and Paulhus, 1987), and act as a mediator of the relationships between self-report measures (Nichols and Greene, 1997; Ganster *et al.*, 1983). Some researchers (e.g. McFarland, 2003) suggest one way of off-setting "faking good" responses, that is to use the psychometric technique of consensus-based technique to create standards for assessing emotional intelligence that cannot be faked.

The main concern about self-report measures is that this method is normally considered a common way of measuring things such as personality traits. Generally, self-report emotional intelligence measures and personality measures have been said to converge because they both purport to measure traits, and because they are both measured in the self-report form (Zeidner, Roberts and Matthews, 2002). Specifically, there appear to be two dimensions of the Big Five that stand out as most related to self-report emotional intelligence measures — neuroticism and extraversion, particularly the former. Neuroticism has been said to relate to negative emotionality and anxiety (Costa and McCrae, 1992). Intuitively, individuals scoring high on neuroticism are likely to score low on self-report emotional intelligence measures (Zeidner, Roberts and Matthews, 2002).

More studies have shown that self-report measures are independent of intelligence tests, but highly correlated with existing personality questionnaires. The results of meta-analysis conducted by Van Rooy and Viswesvaran (2003) did show that self-report emotional intelligence measures are highly associated with personality. For example, three of the Big Five factors of personality had correlations with emotional intelligence with $r > 0.31$. A few recent published studies have shown that Bar-On's self-report Emotional Quotient Inventory correlates strongly with a number of personality measures. For example, Stys and Brown (2004) reviewed that highly significant correlations were between Emotional Quotient Inventory and four of the Big Five personality factors, namely: Neuroticism, Extraversion, Agreeableness and Conscientiousness ($r = 0.27$ to 0.57), and moderately significant correlations were found with Openness ($r = 0.16$). Brackett and Mayer (2003) reported that this measure correlated significantly with all five factors of personality, particularly Neuroticism ($r = -0.57$). Other self-report measures, such as Goleman's ECI and Schutte *et al.*'s (1998) self-report emotional intelligence test (SREIT), have been shown to have significant relationships with personality factors. For example, Sala (2002) reported ECI was significantly correlated with three of the Big Five personality factors:

Extraversion, Openness and Conscientiousness. Brackett and Mayer (2003) found SREIT was correlated with four of the Big Five factors. Austin, Saklofske and Egan (2005) reported similar findings. When the MSCEIT was used, only Openness to experience and Agreeableness were found to relate to emotional intelligence (Brackett and Mayer, 2003). Surprisingly there was no significant relationship found between the two constructs when the MEIS and MSCEIT were adopted (Caruso, Mayer and Salovey, 2002). Weak relationships with personality are construed as that the two measures are through performance-based tests, which is more related to cognitive-ability measures (Petrides, Furhnam and Frederickson, 2004; Van Der Zee and Wabeke, 2004).

However, it is worth noting that, the interpretations of moderate-to-high correlations between self-report emotional intelligence and personality have been varied and inconsistent. Some researchers (e.g. Davies, Stankov and Roberts, 1998) have asserted that correlations in the 0.40 range constitute outright construct redundancy, while others have suggested 0.70 (Cohen, 1960). Gignac (2005) indicated that it would be difficult for any self-report individual difference measure to demonstrate exceptional incremental validity above and beyond the Big Five, and recommended that factor analytic methodology be used to test for construct redundancy (as opposed to zero-order correlations), whereas others (e.g. Davies *et al.*, 1998) questioned the psychometric properties of self-report emotional intelligence inventories.

Despite the question regarding relevance to personality traits, in their meta-analysis, Van Rooy and Viswesvaran (2003) found that self-report measures of emotional intelligence were used in more settings than other reports and demonstrated most validity. The reasons may lie in that only the individuals who are being assessed better know some aspects of emotional intelligence; or because the questionnaires are more straightforward compared to task-based assessment, and the self-report method has possibilities for unsupervised use (e.g. in postal surveys) (Van Rooy and Viswesvaran, 2003; Austin, Saklofske and Egan, 2005).

4.5.4 *Ability and trait emotional intelligence (EI)*

The lack of a coherent operational framework of emotional intelligence has led to the haphazard development of the construct and numerous conflicting findings. In recognition of the problem, Petrides and Furnham (2001) suggested the terminology "ability EI" and "trait EI" to distinguish the two measurement approaches. The measurement of emotional intelligence through self-report questionnaires leads to the operationalisation of the construct as a personality trait, and is classified as trait EI, while the measurement through performance tests lead to the operationalisation of the construct as a cognitive ability, and therefore is classified as ability EI.

Based on this classification, trait EI was concerned with cross-situational consistencies in behaviour, and was embedded within the personality framework and assessed via validated self-report inventories that measure typical behaviour (e.g. Bar-on, 1997; Salovey, Mayer, Goldman, Turvey and Palfai, 1995). This approach to emotional intelligence research draws heavily on personality variables such as empathy, optimism and impulsivity. Considering the five-factor model of personality, trait emotional intelligence measures are generally found to have large significant correlations with Extraversion and Neuroticism, while smaller significant positive correlations with Openness, Agreeableness and Conscientiousness have also been found (Petrides and Furnham, 2001; Schutte *et al.*, 1998). By contrast, the ability emotional intelligence is much more focused, as explicit as traditional intelligence and can be measured through maximal performance. Therefore, trait emotional intelligence should not be expected to correlate strongly with measures of general cognitive ability or proxies, whereas ability emotional intelligence should not be strongly correlated with factors of personality measures.

Furthermore, Petrides and Furnham (2001) clarified that the distinction between trait and ability emotional intelligence is predicated on the method used to measure the construct and not on the elements that the various models are hypothesised to encompass. As such, it is unrelated to the distinction among the models of emotional intelligence conceptualised by Mayer and Salovey, Goleman and Bar-On. The emotional intelligence scale (EIS) developed by Schutte and her colleagues in 1998 is a good example for this clarification. EIS is a self-report measure but based on the ability model of emotional intelligence developed by Salovey and Mayer (1990). It is classified as trait emotional intelligence because it is measured through self-report questionnaires; however, it is founded on a cognitive-based conceptualisation. This distinction between ability emotional intelligence and trait emotional intelligence sheds light on the measure-related confusion and provides basis in selecting an appropriate measure for relevant studies.

Consistent with the foregoing discussion, this book is not intended to be situated on any particular model for the remaining chapters. The empirical studies drawn to discuss the relationship between emotional intelligence and marketing are focused on its impact not on a specific model. However, prior to setting about incorporating emotional intelligence into marketing, the following section presents discussion on the validity issues of emotional intelligence to reinforce its predictive abilities. This discussion is essential to understand its link to marketing.

4.6 Validity of Emotional Intelligence

4.6.1 *Predictive validity*

In addition to its measurability, the issue of emotional intelligence's predictive validity is crucial to establishing its scientific importance. As early as 1920, Thorndike, in reviewing the predictive power of IQ, found variations in outcome measures not accounted for by IQ (cited by Dulewicz and Higgs, 2000). In comparing the predicting utility of emotional intelligence with traditional intelligence, Goleman (1998, p. 19) argued that IQ is estimated to account for only 25 percent in explaining how well people perform in their careers. More accurately, it may be no higher than 10 percent, and in some cases, perhaps as low as 4 percent (Sternberg, 1997). The appeal of emotional intelligence lies in the possibility of accounting for some portion of the remaining variance in predicting work performance and career success which traditional intelligence has left unexplained. Indeed, the results from Van Rooy and Viswesvaran's (2003) meta-analysis showed that all emotional intelligence measures demonstrated predictive validity.

However, studies show that the predictive validity of emotional intelligence is widely varied. It largely depends on the study settings, selected criterion as well as the model of emotional intelligence used (Emmerling and Goleman, 2003). Dividing relevant studies to three categories in their meta-analysis, Van Rooy and Viswesvaran (2003) reported that all emotional intelligence measures have a respective operational validity of 0.10, 0.24 and 0.24 in academic settings, life outcomes and employment settings.

4.6.2 *Emotional intelligence and study settings*

In general, emotional intelligence is not so promising in predicting academic achievement. In fact emotional intelligence measured by Schutte *et al.*'s (1998) self-report scales was found in one study to be inversely related to academic achievement. Using Bar-On's Emotional Quotient Inventory, Newsome, Day and Catano (2000) found that neither the total score of emotional intelligence nor the sub-dimension scores were significantly related to academic achievement. This is plausible as academic results are more related to an individual's IQ (Goleman, 1998). Emotional intelligence appears to be more prominent in predicting criteria in life settings and work-related outcomes. For example, using both Bar-On's Emotional Quotient Inventory and Schutt *et al.*'s self-report emotional intelligence scale, Austin, Saklofske and Egan (2004) found that emotional intelligence was positively associated with life satisfaction, social network size and quality, but negatively associated with alexithymia and alcohol consumption.

In work settings, emotional intelligence has been claimed to affect a wide variety of job attitudes and behaviours. First, emotional intelligence has been extensively discussed to exert a positive influence on job satisfaction because it may influence one's ability to succeed in coping with environmental demands and pressures, thus managing stressful work conditions (Bar-On, 1997) (Meisler, 2014;

Shi *et al.*, 2014), and employee commitment because emotional intelligence facilitates communication, and emotionally intelligent people make others feel better suited to the occupational environment (Goleman, 1998; Nikolaou and Tsaousis, 2002; Rozell, Pettijohn and Parker, 2004). With regards to work behaviours, emotional intelligence significantly impacts team work, because emotionally intelligent people have better social skills which are needed for group work (Mayer and Salovey, 1997; Sjöberg, 2001); and leadership, because leaders with higher level of emotional intelligence may affect the relationship in the work setting. Researchers (e.g. Cooper, 1997) allege that people with high levels of emotional intelligence experience more career success, build stronger personal relationships, lead more effectively, and enjoy better health than those with low levels of emotional intelligence.

Consequently, emotional intelligence has been extensively discussed as a valid predictor of job performance (see Joseph *et al.*'s meta-analytical study on the relationship between emotional intelligence and job performance published in 2015). Furthermore, the efficiency of emotional intelligence in predicting job behaviours depends on the type of job. According to Ashkanasy and Daus (2005), it is the profession that often requires high emotional labour, such as the job of customer service representatives. Sjöberg and Littorin (2005) noted that emotional intelligence could be an important factor in job performance for jobs that have important social components. In one study, Caruso, Mayer and Salovey (2002) found that emotional intelligence was related to a self-report measure of social behaviour and social needs. The authors conclude that emotional intelligence can be expected to contribute at a reasonable level of prediction of some criterion outcomes, for example, behaviours involving social components.

4.7 The Incremental Validity of Emotional Intelligence

Either as an ability or a trait, emotional intelligence should not only demonstrate criterion and predictive validity, but also incremental validity over those well-established constructs to be induced as a valid psychological construct in the relevant domains (see Brackett and Mayer, 2003; Zeidner, Matthews and Roberts, 2004). Due to various measures of emotional intelligence in the literature, such as self-report questionnaires or performance-based tests, caution should be taken in evaluating its incremental validity to account for additional variance, as different methods of measuring this construct lead to the differences in its incremental validity.

With regards to its relationship with personality (the case of mix model), apart from their significant correlations (depending on the choice of measure), emotional intelligence and personality have been constantly used in the comparison of their individual variance within the criterion variables (e.g., Vakola, Tsaousis, and Nikolaou, 2004; Van Der Zee and Wabeke, 2003). Trait EI is expected to provide additional variance in the selected criteria outcomes over and above personality measures. A number of empirical studies have demonstrated incremental validity over the Big Five personality factors.

In discussing if trait emotional intelligence is simply or more than a trait, Van Dan Zee *et al.* (2004) found that trait emotional intelligence as measured by Bar-On's Emotional Intelligence Quotient was not only substantially related to most dimensions of personality measure, but also explained additional variance over and above the personality measure in the identified two dimensions of competencies: support and leadership. In a study to compare the predictive validity in attitudes towards organisational change, Vakola, Tsaousis and Nikolaou (2003) found that the overall emotional intelligence score explained additional variance over personality measure. However, when using the sub-scales of emotional intelligence, only one dimension of trait emotional intelligence — the use of emotions scale demonstrated more effect than personality measure in the criterion variable.

Day, Therrien and Carroll (2005) conducted a study to explore the relationships among emotional intelligence assessed by Bar-On's EQ-i, Big Five personality factors, Type A Behaviour Pattern (TABP), daily hassles, and psychological health/strain factors (in terms of perceived wellbeing, strain, and three components of burnout). The results showed that the EQ-i was highly correlated with most aspects of personality and TABP. After controlling for the impact of hassles, personality, and TABP, the five EQ-i subscales accounted for incremental variance in two of the five psychological health outcomes. Similar results were found in Chapman and Hayslip's (2005) study. The authors reported that emotional intelligence measured by Schutte *et al.*'s (1998) self-report emotional intelligence scale significantly and uniquely predicted variance beyond personality measured by NEO Five–Factor Inventory (NEO–FFI; Costa and McCrae, 1992) in loneliness and social stress.

Defining emotional intelligence as a constellation of emotion-related self-perceptions and dispositions located at the lower levels of personality hierarchies, Petrides, Pérez-González and Furnham (2007) attempted to investigate the criterion and incremental validity of trait emotional intelligence and found that trait emotional intelligence is more related to measures of rumination, life satisfaction, depression, dysfunctional attitudes, and coping. Most relationships remained statistically significant even after controlling for Big Five variance. The authors concluded that trait emotional intelligence has a role to play in personality, clinical, and social psychology, often with effects that are incremental over the basic dimensions of personality and mood.

With regards to its incremental variance in explaining job performance, a number of studies have provided empirical evidence. For example, Sy, Tram and O'Hara's (2006) study shows that employees' emotional intelligence positively predicts job performance after controlling for the Big Five personality factors. O'Boyle *et al.*'s (2011) meta-analytical study used the most current perspectives and accepted practices to prove that emotional intelligence has the predictive validity in terms of job performance, above and beyond the FFM and cognitive intelligence. The study found that all three streams of emotional intelligence (ability-based models, self-report or peer report measures, and mixed models) correlated with job performance. Streams 2 and 3 incrementally predicted job performance over and above cognitive intelligence and the FFM. In addition, dominance analyses showed that when predicting job performance, all three streams of EI exhibited substantial relative importance in the presence of the FFM and intelligence.

To examine whether emotional intelligence explains additional variance in employee service performance over the FFM of personality, Prentice and King (2011) examined the respective influences of personality and emotional intelligence on employee service performance. The Five Factor Model of personality factors (FFM) and a self-report emotional intelligence measure were used in that study. The results show that the whole model from the five personality factors explained 38 percent variance in the service performance: $R^2 = 0.38$, $F(5, 146) = 17.83$, $p < 0.0005$. However, among the five personality factors, only Extraversion and Conscientiousness made statistically significant unique contribution to employee service performance. The beta weight for Extraversion was 0.20, $t = 2.25$, $p < 0$ .05, and for Conscientiousness 0.29, $t = 2.92$, $p < 0.01$. Examination of the Coefficients table shows that Conscientiousness makes the strongest contribution to employee performance, followed by Extraversion, Openness to Experience ($\beta = 0.14$, $t = 1.73$), Neuroticism ($\beta = -0.09$, $t = -1.09$) and Agreeableness ($\beta = 0.05$, $t = 0.55$).

The hierarchical regression analysis was subsequently performed to demonstrate the additional variance explained by emotional intelligence. The results presented in Table 4.1 show that the whole model explained 42 percent variance in employee service performance, R-squared = 0.42, $F(6, 145) = 17.25$, $p < 0.0005$. After the personality factors were controlled for, it resulted in a change in R-squared of 0.04, F Change = 9.29, Sig. F Change < 0.005. Thus, emotional intelligence did explain an additional 4 percent of the variance in the criterion variable, over and above the effects of the FFM of personality. Further investigation shows that utilisation of emotions made a unique significant contribution to employee service performance. The beta weight obtained from this analysis for the utilisation of emotion was 0.30, $t = 3.31$, $p < 0.005$.

There are relatively few studies that show emotional intelligence as providing incremental validity in performance over other cognitive ability measures. Lam and Kirby (2002) examined the relationships between emotional intelligence, general intelligence, and individual

Table 4.1 Hierarchical regression analysis for incremental validity of trait EI in explaining variance of the service performance over the FFM of personality

	Coefficients		
Predictor	Beta	t	Sig.
Step 1			
Extraversion	0.20	2.25	0.02
Agreeableness	0.05	0.55	0.58
Conscientiousness	0.29	2.92	0.00
Neuroticism	−0.09	−1.09	0.27
Openness to Experience	0.14	1.73	0.08
Step 2			
Total trait EI	0.29	3.05	0.00
Mood Regulation	0.13	1.21	0.22
Social Skills	−0.07	−0.82	0.41
Utilisation of Emotions	−0.05	−0.57	0.57
Appraisal of Emotions	0.30	3.31	0.00
df (6, 145) F = 17.25	Sig. = 0.00	R-squared = 0.38	
R-squared Change = 0.04	F Change = 9.29	Sig. F Change= 0.00	

cognitive-based performance. The participants were 304 undergraduates (152 men and 152 women) at a university in Western United States. Among the emotional intelligence dimensions, perceiving emotions (R-squared change = 0.074, $F(2, 292)$ = 23.24, $p < 0.001$), regulating emotions (R-squared change = 0.024, $F(2, 291)$ = 7.59, $p < 0.01$) significantly and uniquely contributed to individual cognitive-based performance over and above the level attributable to general intelligence. Understanding emotions in this study did not contribute to individual cognitive-based performance over and above the level attributable to general intelligence, with R-squared change = 0.008, $F(2, 291)$ = 2.75, $p > 0.05$. Nevertheless, the results show that overall emotional intelligence contributed to individual cognitive-based performance over and above the level attributable to general intelligence, and the relationship was positive, R-squared change = 0.034, $F(2, 291)$ = 11.37, $p < 0.001$.

However, the results from Van Rooy and Viswesvaran's (2003) meta-analysis showed that ability emotional intelligence only demonstrated incremental validity over GMA by 0.02, while incremental validity of GMA over emotional intelligence is as large as 0.31. This finding may be attributed to the phenomenon that very limited studies used ability-based emotional intelligence measures to explain performance; or that cognitive ability measures may be more conductive to explaining cognitive-based performance.

Cote and Miners (2006) examined how emotional intelligence and cognitive intelligence are associated with job performance. The authors develop and test a compensatory model to examine the association between emotional intelligence and job performance. The study shows that performance becomes more positive as cognitive intelligence decreases. The finding indicates that individuals with high emotional intelligence and low cognitive intelligence may employ their abilities to manage emotions to develop good social relationships that may in turn enhance task performance via advice and social support (Pearce and Randel, 2004; Sparrowe *et al.*, 2001; Wong and Law, 2002). Good social relationships may also compel employees to engage in organisational citizenship behaviours frequently to benefit close colleagues.

4.8 Summary

This chapter presents a thorough and comprehensive review and discussion on all the relevant issues relating to emotional intelligence. This review includes the origins and incept of emotional intelligence, its conceptualisations and popular models in the literature, measurement to clarify confusion of different models, and validity to understand the practicality and importance of the concept of emotional intelligence. This review aims to pave the way for an application of the concept to marketing throughout the following chapters of this book. The marketing practices that are related to emotional intelligence and selected for inclusion in this book are internal marketing, relational encounter marketing, external marketing, and impersonal encounter marketing. The chapter on internal marketing is focused on discussing how emotional intelligence as a marketing tool affects employees' attitudes and behaviours. Given this book is focused on frontline employees who perform emotional labour, the relationship between emotional intelligence and emotional labour is presented as a separate chapter to understand the influence of emotional intelligence on internal marketing practice. The discussion relating to relational encounter centres on how emotional intelligence can be used to manage service encounter and employees' relational encounter behaviours. Subsequently, the book moves on to elaborate how emotional intelligence directly affects customers' responses toward the company and their employees from marketing perspective. Finally, this book coins a new concept named *emotional intelligent servicescape* to understand the influence of emotional intelligence on the impersonal encounter between customers and the physical evidence of the company. The discussion continues to explain how a company's service environment can be designed by incorporating the concept of emotional intelligence to influence customers' attitudes and behaviours.

References

Ashkanasy, N.M., & Daus, C.S. (2005). Rumors of the death of emotional intelligence in organizational behaviour are vastly exaggerated. *Journal of Organizational Behaviour*, 26, 441–452.

Austin, E.J., Saklofske, D.H., & Egan, V. (2005). Personality, well-being and health correlates of trait emotional intelligence. *Personality and Individual Differences*, 38(3), 547–558.

Averill, J.R., & Nunley, E.P. (1992). *Voyages of the Heart: Living an Emotionally Creative Life.* New York: Free Press.

Bar-On, R. (1997). Bar-On Emotional Quotient Inventory: Technical manual. Toronto: Multi-Health Systems.

Bar-On, R. (2002). Bar-On Emotional Quotient Short Form (EQ-i: Short): Technical manual. Toronto: Multi-Health Systems.

Boyatzis, R.E. (1982). *The Competent Manager: A Model for Effective Performance.* New York: John Wiley & Sons.

Boyatzis, R.E., Goleman, D., & Rhee, K. (2000). Clustering competence in emotional intelligence: Insights from the emotional competence inventory (ECI). In R. Bar-On and J.D.A. Parker (Eds.), *Handbook of Emotional Intelligence*. San Francisco: Jossey-Bass

Brackett, M.A., & Mayer, J.D. (2003). Convergent, discriminant, and incremental validity of competing measures of emotional intelligence. *Personality and Social Psychology Bulletin*, 29(9), 1147–1158.

Bradberry, T., & Greaves, J. (2003). *Emotional Intelligence Appraisal: Technical Manual*. TalentSmart, Inc.: San Diego.

Bray, D.W., Campbell, R.J., & Grant, D.L. (1974). *Formative Years in Business: A Tong Term AT&T Study of Managerial Lives*. New York: John Wiley & Sons.

Buck, R. (1984). *The Communication of Emotion*. Guilford Press.

Buck, R. (1984). Rapport, emotional education, and emotional competence. *Psychological Inquiry*. 1990, 1(4), 301–302. (doi:10.1207/s15327965pli 0104_4)

Carroll, J.B. (1993). *Human Cognitive Abilities: A Survey of Factor-analytic Studies*. Cambridge: Cambridge University Press.

Caruso, D.R., Mayer. J.D., & Salovey, P. (2002). Relation of an ability measure of emotional intelligence to personality. *Journal of Personality Assessment*, 79(2), 306–320.

Chapman, B.P., & Hayslip, J.B. (2005). Incremental validity of a measure of emotional intelligence. *Journal of Personality Assessment*, 85(2), 154–169.

Ciarrochi, J., Chan, A., & Caputi, P. (2000). A critical evaluation of the emotional intelligence construct. *Personality and Individual Differences*, 28(3), 539–561.

Cohen, J. (1960). A coefficient of agreement for nominal scales. *Educational and Psychological Measurement*, 20(1), 37–46.

Cooper, R. (1997). *Executive EQ*. New York: Grosset/Putnam.

Costa, P.T., & McCrae, R.R. (1992). Normal personality assessment in clinical practice: The NEO personality inventory. *Psychological Assessment*, 4(1), 5–13.

Cote, S. and Miners, S.T. (2006). Emotional intelligence, cognitive intelligence, and job performance. *Administrative Science Quarterly*, 51(1), 1–28.

Davies, M., Stankov, L., & Roberts, R.D. (1998). Emotional intelligence: In search of an elusive construct. *Journal of Personality & Social Psychology*, 75(4), 989–1015.

Day, A.L., Therrien, D.L., & Carroll, S.A. (2005). Predicting psychological health: Assessing the incremental validity of emotional intelligence beyond personality, type A behaviour, and daily hassles. *European Journal of Personality*, 19, 519–536.

Dulewicz, V. & Herbert, P.J.A. (1996). General management competencies and Personality: A 7-year fellow-up study. Henley Working Paper 9621, Henley Management College.

Dulewicz V. & Herbert, P.J.A. (1999). Predicting advancement to senior management from competencies and personality data: a 7-year follow-up study. *British Journal of Management*, 10(1), 13–22.

Dulewicz, V. & Higgs, M. (2000). Emotional intelligence: A review and evaluation study. *Journal of Managerial Psychology*, 15(4), 341–372.

Emmerling, R.J. & Goleman, G. (2003). Emotional intelligence: Issues and common misunderstandings. *Issues and Recent Developments in Emotional Intelligence*, 1(1). Consortium for Research on Emotional Intelligence in Organizations.

Ganster, D., Hennessey, H., & Luthans, F. (1983). Social desirability response effects: Three alternative models. *Academy of Management Journal*, 26(2), 321–331.

Gardner, H. (1993). *Multiple Intelligences: The Theory in Practice*. New York: Basic Books.

Gignac, G.E. (2005). Evaluating the MSCEIT V2.0 via CFA: Comment on Mayer *et al.* (2003). *Emotion*, 5(2): 233–235.

Goleman, D. (1998). *Working with Emotional Intelligence*. New York: Bantam Books.

Goleman, D. (1998b). What makes a leader? *Harvard Business Review*, November-December.

Goleman, D. (2002). *Primal Leadership*. Boston, MA: Harvard Business School Publishing.

Hogreve, J., Iseke, A., Derfuss, K., & Eller, T. (2017). The service–profit chain: A meta-analytic test of a comprehensive theoretical framework. *Journal of Marketing*, 81(3), 41–61.

Holtgraves, T. (2004). Social desirability and self-reports: Testing models of socially desirable responding. *Personality and Social Psychology Bulletin*, 30(2), 161–172.

Joseph, D. L., Jin, J., Newman, D. A., & O'Boyle, E. H. (2015). Why does self-reported emotional intelligence predict job performance? A meta-analytic investigation of mixed EI. *Journal of Applied Psychology*, 100(2), 298.

Kernbach, S. & Schutte, N. S. (2005). The impact of service provider emotional intelligence on customer satisfaction. *Journal of Services Marketing*, 19(7), 438–444.

Kotter, J.P. (1982). *The General Managers*. New York: Free Press.

Lam, L.T. & Kirby, S.L. (2002). Is emotional intelligence an advantage? An exploration of the impact of emotional and general intelligence on individual performance. *The Journal of Social Psychology,* 142(1), 133–143.

Leuner, B. (1966). Emotional intelligence and emancipation. *Praxis der Kinderpsychologie und Kinderpsychiatrie,* 15, 193–203.

Levine, P.A. (1997). *Waking the Tiger: Healing Trauma: The Innate Capacity to Transform Overwhelming Experiences.* Berkeley, CA: North Atlantic Books.

Luthans, F., Hodgetts, R.M., & Rosenkrantz, S.A. (1998): *Real Managers.* Cambridge, MA: Ballinger.

MacCann, C., Roberts, R.D., Matthews, G., & Zeidner, M. (2004). Consensus scoring and empirical option weighting of performance-based emotional intelligence (EI) tests. *Personality and Individual Differences,* 36(3), 645–662.

Mayer, J.D., DiPaolo, M., & Salovey, P. (1990). Perceiving affective content in ambiguous visual stimuli: A component of emotional intelligence. *Journal of Personality Assessment,* 54(3–4): 772–81.

Mayer, J.D. & Geher, G. (1996). Emotional intelligence and the identification of emotion. *Intelligence,* 22, 89–113.

Mayer, J.D. & Salovey, P. (1993). The intelligence of emotional intelligence. *Intelligence,* 17(4), 433–442.

Mayer, J.D. & Salovey, P. (1997). What is emotional intelligence? In P. Salovey and D. Sluyter (Eds.), *Emotional Development and EI: Educational Implications* (pp. 3–34). New York: Basic Books.

Mayer, J.D., Salovey, P., & Caruso, D.R. (2002). *Mayer-Salovey-Caruso Emotional Intelligence Test. (MSCEIT) User's Manual.* Toronto: MHS Publishers.

Mayer, J.D., Salovey, P., & Caruso, D.R. (1999). *MSCEIT Item Booklet (Research Version 1.1).* Toronto, ON: MHS Publishers.

Mayer, J.D., Salovey, P., & Caruso, D.R. (2002). *MSCEIT — User's Manual.* Toronto: Multi-Health Systems Inc.

Mayer, J.D., Salovey, P., Caruso, D.R., & Sitarenios, G. (2001). Emotional intelligence as a standard intelligence. *Emotion,* 1(3), 232–242.

McClelland, D.C. (1973). Testing for competence rather than intelligence. *American Psychologist,* 28(1), 1–14.

McCleskey, J.A. (2014). Situational, transformational, and transactional leadership and leadership development. *Journal of Business Studies Quarterly,* 5(4), 117.

McFarland, L.A. (2003). Warning against faking on a personality test: Effects on applicant reactions and personality test scores. *International Journal of Selection and Assessment,* 11(4), 265–276.

McFarland, L.A. & Ryan, A.M. (2000). Variance in faking across non-cognitive measures. *Journal of Applied Psychology*, 85, 812–821.

Meisler, G. (2014). Exploring emotional intelligence, political skill, and job satisfaction. *Employee Relations*, 36(3), 280–293.

Miao, C., Humphrey, R.H., & Qian, S. (2017). A meta — analysis of emotional intelligence and work attitudes. *Journal of Occupational and Organizational Psychology*, 90(2), 177–202.

Mulki, J.P., Jaramillo, F., Goad, E.A., & Pesquera, M.R. (2015). Regulation of emotions, interpersonal conflict, and job performance for salespeople. *Journal of Business Research*, 68(3), 623–630.

Newsome, S., Day, A. L., & Catano, V.M. (2000). Assessing the predictive validity of emotional intelligence. *Personality and Individual Differences*, 29(66), 1005–1016.

Nichols, D.S. & Greene, R.L. (1997). Dimensions of deception in personality assessment: The example of the MMPI-2. *Journal of Personality Assessment*, 68(2), 251–266.

Nikolaou, I. & Tsaousis, I. (2002). Emotional intelligence in the workplace: Exploring its effects on occupational stress and organizational commitment. *The International Journal of Organizational Analysis*, 10(4), 327–342.

O'Boyle, E.H., Forsyth, D.R., & O'Boyle, A.S. (2011). Bad apples or bad barrels: An examination of group-and organizational-level effects in the study of counterproductive work behavior. *Group & Organization Management*, 36(1), 39–69.

Paulhus, D.L. (2002). Socially desirable responding: The evolution of a construct. In H.I. Braun, D.N. Jackson and D.E. Wiley (Eds.). *The Role of Constructs in Psychological and Educational Measurement* (pp. 49–69). Mahwah, NJ: Erlbaum. Retrieved May 10, 2006 from the University of British Columbia, via the homepage of Del Paulhus' site: http://neuron4.psych.ubc.ca/~dpaulhus/research/SDR/downloads/ETS%20chapter.pdf

Payne, W.L. (1983/1986). A study of emotion: developing emotional intelligence; self integration; relating to fear, pain and desire. Dissertation Abstracts International, 47, p. 203A. (University microfilms No. AAC 8605928).

Pearce, J.L. & Randel, A.E. (2004). Expectations of organizational mobility, workplace social inclusion, and employee job performance. *Journal of Organizational Behavior: The International Journal of Industrial, Occupational and Organizational Psychology and Behavior*, 25(1), 81–98.

Peebles, J. & Moore, R.J. (1998). Detecting socially desirable responding with the Personality Assessment Inventory: The Positive Impression

Management scale and the Defensiveness index. *Journal of Clinical Psychology*, 54(5), 621–628.

Pérez, J.C., Petrides, K.V., & Furnham, A. (2005). Measuring trait emotional intelligence. *Emotional Intelligence: An International Handbook* (pp. 181–201). Ashland, OH: Hogrefe & Huber Publishers.

Petrides, K.V. & Furnham, A. (2001). Trait emotional intelligence: psychometric investigation with reference to established trait taxonomies. *European Journal of Personality*, 15(6), 425–448.

Petrides, K.V., Furnham, A., & Frederickson, N. (2004). Emotional intelligence. *The Psychologist*, 17, 574–577.

Petrides, K.V., Pérez-González, J.C., & Furnham, A. (2007). On the criterion and incremental validity of trait emotional intelligence. *Cognition and Emotion*, 21(1), 26–55.

Prentice, C., Chen, P.J., & King, B. (2013). Employee performance outcomes and burnout following the presentation-of-self in customer-service contexts. *International Journal of Hospitality Management*, 35, 225–236.

Prentice, C. & King, B. (2011). The influence of emotional intelligence on the service performance of casino frontline employees. *Tourism and Hospitality Research*, 11(1), 49–66.

Roberts, R.D., Zeidner, M., & Matthews, G. (2001). Does emotional intelligence meet traditional standards for an intelligence? Some new data and conclusions. *Emotion*, 1(3), 196–231.

Rosenthal, R. Archer, D. Hall, J. A., DiMatteo, M. R., & Rogers, P. L. (1979). Measuring Sensitivity to Nonverbal Communication: The PONs Test. In *Nonverbal Behavior*, 67–98. Academic Press.

Rozell, E.J., Pettijohn, C.E., & Parker, R.S. (2004). Customer-oriented selling: Exploring the roles of emotional intelligence and organizational commitment. *Psychology and Marketing*, 21(6), 405–424.

Sala, F. (2002). *Emotional Competence Inventory (ECI)*. McClelland Centre for Research & Innovation.

Salovey, P. & Mayer, J.D. (1990). Emotional intelligence. *Imagination, Cognition and Personality*, 9(3), 185–211.

Salovey, P., Mayer, J.D., Goldman, S.L., Turvey, C., & Palfai, T.P. (1995). Emotional attention, clarity, and repair: Exploring emotional intelligence using the trait meta-mood scale. In J. W. Pennebaker (Ed.). *Emotion, Disclosure, & Health* (pp. 125–154). Washington, DC: APA.

Scarr, S. (1989). Progress in Child Psychiatry & Child Development. *American Psychologist*, 43(1), 56–59.

Schutte, N.S., Malouff, J.M., Hall, L.E., Haggerty, D.J., Cooper, J.T., & Dornheim, L. (1998). Development and validation of a measure of emotional intelligence. *Personality and Individual Differences*, 25, 167–177.

Schutte, N.S., Malouff, J.M., Thorsteinsson, E.B., Bhullar, N., & Rooke, S.E. (2007). A meta-analytic investigation of the relationship between emotional intelligence and health. *Personality and Individual Differences*, 42(6), 921–933.

Shi, Y., Prentice, C., & He, W. (2014). Linking service quality, customer satisfaction and loyalty in casinos, does membership matter? *International Journal of Hospitality Management*, 40, 81–91.

Sjöberg, L. (2001). Emotional intelligence: A psychometric analysis. *European Psychologist*, 6(2), 79.

Sjöberg, L. & Littorin, P. (2003). *Emotional Intelligence, Personality and Sales Performance* (No. 2003: 8). Stockholm School of Economics.

Sjöberg, L. & Littorin, P. (2005). Emotional intelligence, personality and sales performance. In K. B. S. Kumar (Ed.), *Emotional Intelligence. Research Insights* (pp. 126–142). Hyderabad, India: ICFAI University Press.

Sparrowe, R.T., Liden, R.C., Wayne, S.J., & Kraimer, M.L. (2001). Social networks and the performance of individuals and groups. *Academy of Management Journal*, 44(2), 316–325.

Sternberg, R. & Caruso, D. (1985). Practical modes of knowing in learning and teaching the ways of knowing. Eisner, E. (Ed.). *84th Yearbook of NSEE Learning and Teaching the Ways of Knowing*. Chicago: Chicago University Press.

Sternberg, R.J. (1997). Managerial intelligence: Why IQ isn't enough. *Journal of Management*, 23(3), 475–493.

Sternberg, R.J. & Smith, C. (1985). Social intelligence and decoding skills in nonverbal communication. *Social Cognition*, 3(2), 168–192.

Stys, Y. & Brown, S.L. (2004). *A review of the Emotional Intelligence Literature and Implications For Corrections*. Research Branch, Correctional Service of Canada.

Sy, T., Tram, S., & O'Hara, L.A. (2006). Relation of employee and manager emotional intelligence to job satisfaction and performance. *Journal of vocational behavior*, 68(3), 461–473.

Thorndike, E.L. (1920). Intelligence and its uses. *Harper's*, 140, 227–235.

Thornton, G.C.III & Byham, W.C. (1982). *Assessment Centers and Managerial Performance*. New York: Academic Press.

Vakola, M., Tsaousis, I., & Nikolaou, I. (2004). The role of emotional intelligence and personality variables on attitudes toward organizational change. *Journal of Managerial Psychology*, 19(2), 88–110.

Van der Zee, K. & Wabeke, R. (2004). Is trait-emotional intelligence simply or more than just a trait? *European Journal of Personality*, 18(4), 243–263.

Van Rooy, D.L. & Viswesvaran, C. (2004). Emotional intelligence: A meta-analytic investigation of predictive validity and nomological net. *Journal of Vocational Behavior*, 65(1), 71–95.

Wagner, R.K. & Sternberg, R.J. (1985). Practical intelligence in real-world pursuits: the role of tacit knowledge. *Journal of Personality and Social Psychology*, 49(2), 436–458.

Webb, S. (2004). *Exploring the Relationship of Emotional Intelligence to Transformational Leadership within Mentoring Relationships*. Master thesis approved 3 Feb 2004. University of South Florida.

Wong, C.S. & Law, K.S. (2002). The effects of leader and follower emotional intelligence on performance and attitude: An exploratory study. *The leadership Quarterly*, 13(3), 243–274.

Zablah, A.R., Carlson, B.D., Donavan, D.T., Maxham III, J.G., & Brown, T.J. (2016). A cross-lagged test of the association between customer satisfaction and employee job satisfaction in a relational context. *Journal of Applied Psychology*, 101(5), 743.

Zeidner, M., Roberts, R.D., & Matthews, G. (2002). Can emotional intelligence be schooled? A critical review. *Educational Psychologist*, Lawrence Erlbaum Associates. 37(4), 215–231.

Zeidner, M. Matthews, G., & Roberts, R. (2004). Emotional intelligence in the workplace: A critical review. *Applied Psychology*, 33, 371–399.

Zerbe, W. & Paulhus, D. (1987). Socially desirable responding in organizational behavior: A reconception. *Academy of Management Review*, 12, 250–264.

CHAPTER 5

EMOTIONAL INTELLIGENCE AND INTERNAL MARKETING

5.1 Introduction

Chapter 4 provides a comprehensive review and discussion on emotional intelligence in relation to its history, conceptualisations, measurements, validities and applicability. The review serves as a foundation for the remainder of this book, which is focused on how to apply and incorporate emotional intelligence into marketing. The areas of marketing that the book covers are determined based on the relevance of employees to and the level of their involvement in the marketing practice. Employee involvement is manifested in the service encounter with customers. The service encounter in this book includes the internal service encounter between co-workers (i.e. employees, supervisors) within the same organisation from internal marketing perspective, interpersonal encounter between employees and customers from relationship marketing perspective, and impersonal encounter between customers and the physical evidence of the service organisation. The sequence of these discussions is in accordance with the service profit chain model proposed by Heskett *et al.* (1994). The model depicts the chain of internal → external marketing relationship and how business profitability is derived from employees through internal marketing. Hence, this chapter employs the internal marketing concept to explain the role of emotional intelligence in strategising internal marketing.

Emotional intelligence is proposed as a marketing tool and non-organisational resource to achieve internal marketing outcomes.

5.2 Internal Marketing

Building upon the concept that delivering superior service and satisfying customers are key premises to achieving customer loyalty and business profitability, internal marketing has been proposed as a solution to drive employees to deliver consistently high quality of service in order to achieve customer satisfaction. This solution views employees as internal customers and their jobs as internal products that can be managed through a marketing approach to satisfy their needs and wants, so that they can be motivated to satisfy external customers to optimise organisational goals. This logic is well documented in Heskett *et al.*'s (1994) service profit chain model (see Figure 5.1). The model depicts that business profit and growth as generated by obtaining a large share of genuinely loyal customers; customer loyalty is a direct result of customer satisfaction; satisfaction is influenced by the value of services provided to customers; value is created by satisfied, loyal, committed and productive

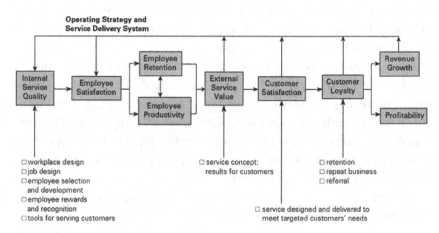

Figure 5.1   The links in the service profit chain from Heskett *et al.*, 2008

Source: https://hbr.org/2008/07/putting-the-service-profit-chain-to-work

employees; employee satisfaction, loyalty, and productivity, in turn, result primarily from internal service quality, which is a core component of internal marketing.

The model provides an ideology on how human resources can be translated into revenue growth for the organisation through employees-customers link. Employees' attitudes and behaviours can shape those of customers during their interactions. For example, Sears' top management examined about 800 stores and discovered that a 5% increase in employee attitude scores resulted in a 1.3% increase in customer satisfaction and a 0.5% increase in revenue (Lowenstein, 2008). While businesses enter an automated and digital-dominant era, and robots and artificial intelligence pay an important role in enhancing business operations and facilitating service delivery, employees still play a pivotal role in driving company profitability. Clearly, employees are not robots, they cannot be automated or engineered to deliver quality service and satisfy customers without meaningful incentives and appropriate motivational means. Internal marketing provides such mechanism to motivate employees and optimise use of their competency and capabilities to benefit key stakeholders.

Ultimately, internal marketing aims to satisfy and retain the right employees to achieve organisational objectives. The right employees must be loyal and productive. Loyal employees, like loyal customers, tend to stay with the company for a long time and bear financial implications for the business such as in allowing for less expenses on recruiting and training of new personnel. In the case of customer contact employees, studies have shown that regular customers prefer to engage in business transactions with long-term employees (Prentice, 2008). Loyal employees are generally committed to their organisation and jobs, and hence more productive. They view themselves as an integral part of the organisation and are proud of their organisational identity. The logical premises to loyal and productive employees are employee satisfaction and commitment. Employees must be happy with their jobs and the company, have a pleasant relationship with co-workers and supervisors, and receive their financial and non-financial rewards fairly, so that they can be "right" for the business. To stay loyal to the company, they must be able to commit to and identify themselves with the organisation and their jobs. In other words, employee commitment is prerequisite to their organisational loyalty. The foregoing discussion informs that the causes of employee satisfaction and commitment ultimately affect employee retention and performance.

Most researchers and practitioners tend to address employee satisfaction and commitment from organisational perspectives such as having appropriate leadership and supervisor support. From internal marketing perspective, researchers propose that internal service quality is key to achieving employee satisfaction. This proposition is consistent with the logic of treating employees as internal customers since service quality is widely acknowledged as an empirically verified antecedent to customer satisfaction. Internal service quality refers to employees' perception and assessment of service quality provided by other members of the organisation to carry out their jobs. Service provided by co-workers within the same organisation, and support from supervisors are considered vital components of internal service quality.

Admittedly these elements are important for employees to accomplish their job tasks. However, co-workers and supervisors are also part of internal customers and the receivers of internal service. Co-workers need to be cooperative with one or another to ensure efficiency of internal transactions. Supervisors need subordinates' support and cooperate to achieve organisation-set goals. These outcomes cannot be generated by only resorting to the supply of material resources. Personal resources from employees such as their personalities, competencies and capabilities have been proven to substantially contribute to employees' performance and work relationships (Barrick and Mount, 1991; Judge and Bono, 2001; O'Boyle *et al.*, 2011; Tett, Jackson and Rothstein, 1991). Personal characteristics and abilities play an important role given that delivering internal service quality entails interactions among co-workers including supervisors over the internal service encounter. Emotional intelligence is one of these personal characteristics that can facilitate

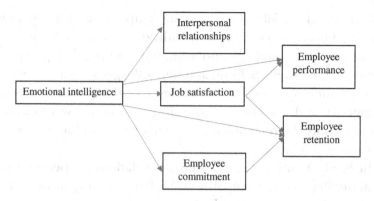

Figure 5.2 The relationships to be discussed in this chapter

internal marketing process. Since the central aim of internal marketing is to achieve employee satisfaction, commitment, employee loyalty and productivity, the rest of this chapter discusses how emotional intelligence can facilitate internal marketing mechanism and influence these employee outcomes.

Consistent with the service profit chain model, the employee outcomes opted for discussion here include employee job satisfaction, employee commitment and retention, which is reflective of employee loyalty, and employee performance. To ensure success of internal marketing and efficient delivery of internal service quality, employees must build sound relationship with co-workers and supervisors. Hence, the following section presents empirical studies from the relevant literature to illustrate how emotional intelligence impacts interpersonal relationships, followed by a demonstration of its influence on other employee outcomes including satisfaction, commitment, performance and retention. A few relationship links are discussed in this chapter as shown in Figure 5.2.

5.3 Emotional Intelligence and Interpersonal Relationships

According to Goleman (1995), emotional competence is a crucial component of social development and contributes to the quality of interpersonal relationships. Emotional intelligent individuals tend to have good social kills including empathy and cooperation. Building upon the concept that individuals with high emotional intelligence are capable of understanding and regulating emotions of oneself and others, Schutte and her colleagues in early 2000 conducted 7 studies in the United States (2 of them tested emotional intelligence and romantic relationships and hence were excluded here) to testify the relationship between emotional intelligence and interpersonal relations.

In **Study 1**, the authors tested the relationship between emotional intelligence and empathy and self-monitoring in view of that emotional intelligent individuals are able to perceive and understand others' emotions. Self-monitoring is referred to as the ability to (a) understand others' emotions and behaviours, (b) understand environmental contexts, and (c) modify self-presentation in response to such understanding (Lennox and Wolfe, 1984). 24 participants (17 women, 7 men) were recruited in this study. The participants who scored higher for emotional intelligence scored significantly higher for self-monitoring, $r(23) = 0.59$, $p < 0.001$, and for empathic perspective taking, $r(23) = 0.35$, $p < 0.045$. Empathic perspective taking is clearly emotionally adaptive. Taking another's perspective allows one to understand the other person better and to interact with that person more effectively. **Study 2** was to replicate the first. 37 teaching interns completed the emotional intelligence measure (Schutte *et al.*, 1998) and the Empathic Perspective Taking subscale (Davis, 1980). The participants who scored higher for emotional intelligence scored significantly higher for perspective taking, $r(36) = 0.59$, $p < 0.0005$.

Study 3 was to test the relationship between emotional intelligence and social skills. This testing draws on the logic that emotional intelligent individuals are able to understand others' emotions and to regulate and harness one's own emotions adaptively, one would expect persons with higher emotional intelligence to be more socially adept and to display better social skills. Social skills are the lubricants of social life that help individuals interact in mutually beneficial ways (Shutte *et al.* 1998). Furthermore, social skills tend to be reciprocal; persons who display good social skills tend to receive good treatment in return (Gouldner, 1960) and to be liked by others. 77 university employees and students participated in this study (44 women, 33 men). Higher scores for emotional intelligence were significantly associated with higher scores for social skills, r (76) = 0.41, $p < 0.0001$.

Study 4 tested emotional intelligence and cooperation. The authors argue that the central elements of emotional intelligence are the ability to understand and regulate the emotions oneself and others. This ability can be important foundations for cooperating with others. Cooperation, in turn, is an essential element in building and maintaining relationships. Persons who cooperate tend to have more positive relationships with each other (Austin and Worchel, 1979; Deutsch, 1980). 38 public school employees and college students (25 women, 13 men) participated in this study. The results show that those with higher scores for emotional intelligence were significantly more cooperative, r (37) = 0.72, $p < 0.0001$.

Study 5 tested emotional intelligence and relations with others. Emotionally intelligent individuals are more understanding others' emotions, are able to help others regulate their moods positively, and able to regulate and harness their emotions when interacting with others. These abilities are essential foundations for building good relationships and enable a highly emotionally intelligent person to be more socially connected with better relationships. Good relationships fulfil basic needs for belonging and nurturance; the social support provided by relationships buffers the negative impact of life stressors (House, Robbins and Metzner, 1982; Oxman *et al.*, 1992; Pilisuk and Parks, 1986). 43 college students and church attendees with over half being females participated in this study. The participants completed the measures of emotional intelligence described in Study 1 (Schutte *et al.*, 1998) and the Fundamental Interpersonal Relations Orientation-Behavior Inventory (FIRO-B; Schütz, 1978). The FIRO-B measures wanted and expressed (a) inclusion, (b) affection, and (c) control in interpersonal relationships. *Inclusion* refers to the degree to which a person associates with others; *affection* refers to how emotionally involved with others a person becomes; and *control* refers to the extent to which a person assumes responsibility, makes decisions, and dominates in relationships. Higher emotional-intelligence scores were also significantly related to higher scores on the Inclusion subscale, r (42) = 0.31, $p < 0.021$, and to higher scores on the Affection subscale, (42) = 0.29, $p < 0.029$. Overall, the results of the 5 studies supported the proposition that emotional intelligence is significantly associated with interpersonal relations in several important ways with interpersonal relationships.

This section employs existing empirical studies to demonstrate how emotional intelligence can affect interpersonal relationship, which is an important premise to achieve the outcomes of internal marketing practice, namely, employee performance and loyalty. The following sections discus how emotional intelligence is related to these outcomes.

5.4 Emotional Intelligence and Internal Marketing Outcomes

5.4.1 *Emotional intelligence and employee performance*

Emotional intelligence has been widely acknowledged to predict employee performance, in particular the performance of service employees. Employees with a high level of emotional intelligence are more likely to have personal and professional success, which is often from the result of superior performance. The emotional intelligence–job performance relationship has generated a great deal of interests among the general public, managers, academics, and business consultants alike. Proponents claim that emotional intelligence can do everything from improving the general quality of work life to enhancing career success. For example, employees would employ the ability to *use emotions,* one of the four dimensions of emotional intelligence, to improve performance by using both positive and negative emotions to their advantage. Positive emotions, such as excitement or enthusiasm, could stimulate employees to provide better customer service, complete their work assignments, or contribute to the organisation. Conversely, negative emotions, such as anxiety, could facilitate employees' ability to focus on their work tasks. Employees with high emotional intelligence should be more adept at regulating their own emotions and managing others' emotions to foster more positive interactions, which could lead to more organisational citizenship behaviours that contribute to job performance. The influence of emotional intelligence on job performance can be accounted for by multiple complementary mechanisms.

The first mechanism concerns expertise at identifying and understanding the emotions of other individuals. In most, if not all jobs, organisation members interact with supervisors, co-workers, support staff, and outsiders such as customers, clients, or patients. These individuals publicly display their emotions through facial, vocal, and bodily signals that provide important information about their goals, attitudes, and intentions (Rafaeli and Sutton, 1987; Sutton, 1991). This information may in turn, be converted into high task performance by individuals with high emotional intelligence and low cognitive intelligence. An employee who accurately detects colleagues' emotions may facilitate coordination and interpersonal functioning that may, in turn, enhance task performance (Law, Wong and Song, 2004). Information about other people's goals, attitudes, and intentions may also be converted into frequent organisational citizenship behaviours by individuals with high emotional intelligence and low cognitive intelligence. For example, these individuals can detect other individuals' sadness and anxiety, which often signal a need for assistance (Eisenberg, 2000), and therefore they may exhibit frequent organisational citizenship behaviours.

A second mechanism concerns how regulating emotion influences the quality of social relationships. Employees who generate and display genuine emotions elicit more favourable reactions than employees who choose to display fake emotions (Grandey, 2003; Grandey *et al.*, 2005). Employees who display genuine concern about their co-workers' problems should build stronger relationships than employees whose concern may appear to be less genuine.

A third mechanism concerns the effects of emotions on how people think and act (Loewenstein and Lerner, 2003). Emotionally intelligent individuals may achieve high levels of task performance and organisational citizenship behaviours in most, if not all jobs by managing their emotions in ways that enhance their motivation and the quality of their decisions (Law *et al.*, 2004). A manager who understands that anger tends to lead people to underestimate the degree of risk in situations (Lerner and Keltner, 2001) may suppress anger before making an important financial decision and, in turn, exhibit good task performance. In addition, an organisation member who understands that motivation is often enhanced by positive emotions (Erez and Isen, 2002) and successfully boosts positive emotions may exert more effort to engage in organisational citizenship behaviours.

Law *et al.* (2004) and Wong and Law (2002) show that highly emotionally intelligent employees seem to be more aware of how certain emotions can influence their behaviours and work outcomes, and be more adept at regulating their emotions in such a manner that they are aligned with the requirements of the task. For example, employees with high emotional intelligence could be better at regulating their emotions so they experience more confidence and control over the task requirements of their job, which in turn enables them to be more proactive and influence work outcomes positively. Alternatively, it is possible that employees with high emotional intelligence are better at dealing with superiors and management. For example, emotionally intelligent employees strive for optimal approach to managing their relationships with their managers who are more likely to evaluate their performance positively. Research has shown that the quality of relationship between manager and employee influences job performance evaluations (Sy, Tram and O'Hara, 2006).

An empirical study undertaken by Prentice and King (2011) on frontline employees working in the casino tested the relationship between emotional intelligence as the predictor and employee service performance as the dependent variable. Schutte *et al.*'s (1998) emotional intelligence measure was used in that study. Four dimensions were identified from the measure: mood regulation, appraisal of emotions, social skills and utilisation of emotions. The results from multiple regression analysis show that overall emotional intelligence explained 35 percent of variance in the service performance: R-squared = 0.35, $F(4, 147) = 19.76$, $p < 0.0005$, which indicates a

Table 5.1 Multiple regression analysis of emotional intelligence as predictor of service employees' performance

Predictor	Coefficients		
Emotional intelligence	Beta	T-value	P-value
Mood Regulation	0.34	3.48	0.00
Social Skills	−0.07	−0.80	0.42
Utilisation of Emotions	−0.09	−1.04	0.30
Appraisal of Emotions	0.41	4.47	0.00
df (4, 147)	$F = 19.76$	Sig. $F = 0.00$	R-squared = 0.35

statistically significant result, although only two sub-dimensions of emotional intelligence made statistically significant unique contributions to the performance outcome. They are mood regulation and appraisal of emotions, with $\beta = 0.34$, $t = 3.48$, $p < 0.001$ and $\beta = 0.41$, $t = 4.47$, $p < 0.0005$ respectively as shown in the following Table 5.1.

5.4.2 *Emotional intelligence and retention*

Emotional intelligent employees not only excel in performance at work, they also enable for lower turnover. A study on 350 nurses in a large medical centre in Hawaii shows that emotional intelligence measured by the Mayer-Salovey-Caruso EI test is strongly related to both performance and employee retention. Three emotional intelligence subscale scores (Experiencing Emotions, Perceiving Emotions, and Using Emotions to Facilitate Reasoning) emerged recurrently as significant correlates with both performance and retention indicators. Nurses with high emotional intelligence scores demonstrated greater job retention and longer careers.

In addition to a direct influence on employee performance and retention, emotional intelligence exerts indirect effects on these outcomes through mediators. The most commonly researched mediators are job satisfaction and employee commitment. Numerous empirical studies have shown that employees with high emotional intelligence demonstrate high level of job satisfaction and commitment (Aghdasi, Kiamanesh and Ebrahim, 2011; Brunetto *et al.*,

2012; Güleryüz *et al.*, 2008; Naderi Anari, 2012; Sy, Tram and O'Hara, 2006). Job satisfaction and employee commitment are key antecedents of employee performance and retention. Logically, emotional intelligence can predict these outcomes through job satisfaction and commitment.

5.5 The Hierarchical Effect of Emotional Intelligence in Internal Marketing Outcomes

Emotional intelligence not only has a direct relationship with internal marketing outcomes, but also influences them hierarchically through mediators. Among all the mediation relationships identified in the literature, from a service profit chain perspective, job satisfaction and employee commitment are the most common mediators in hierarchical relationships. The following discusses these relationships with illustration of empirical studies.

5.5.1 *The mediation of job satisfaction*

5.5.1.1 *Emotional intelligence and job satisfaction*

To ensure positive outcomes (high performance, low turnover or high retention), the key issue is to identify causes of job satisfaction. *Inter alia*, organisational variables (supervisory behaviours, job characteristics), role perceptions, and individual differences are the commonly studied antecedents or causes of job satisfaction. Organisational and role variables are beyond employees' control. Individual characteristics, such as emotional intelligence explain significant portion of job satisfaction. Employees with high emotional intelligence are more likely to have higher levels of job satisfaction because they are more adept at appraising and regulating their own emotions than are employees with low emotional intelligence. For example, highly emotionally intelligent employees may be better at identifying feelings of frustration and stress, and subsequently, regulating those emotions to reduce stress. Highly emotionally intelligent employees are more resilient because they are able to understand the causes of stress and develop strategies and perseverance to deal with the negative consequences of stress (Cooper and Sawaf, 1997). Conversely, employees with low emotional intelligence are likely to be less aware of their emotions and possess fewer abilities to cope with their emotions when faced with difficult situations, thereby, exacerbating their level of stress and decreasing their level of job satisfaction.

Furthermore, employees with high emotional intelligence can utilise their ability to appraise and manage emotions in others. This skill becomes significant in group settings where employees with high emotional intelligence can use their skills to foster positive interactions that help boost their own morale, as well as the morale of the group, and contribute positively to the experience of job satisfaction for all (Shimazu, Shimazu and Odahara, 2004).

Emotional intelligence is particularly important for the job satisfaction of employees who are positioned in the frontline as these employees have direct interactions with customers. These interactions often contain high-affect content. Employees' emotional intelligence is essential in managing emotional encounters in order to create positive service experience for both employees and customers (Kernback and Schutte, 2005; Varca, 2004). An emotionally intelligent employee often enjoys interpersonal interactions with customers (Goleman, 1998; Prentice *et al.*, 2013).

An empirical study conducted with 187 food service workers at 9 different locations of the same restaurant franchise found that employees' emotional intelligence is correlated positively with job satisfaction. The relationship between EI and job satisfaction was established using hierarchical regression after controlling for personality factors because of concerns with the limited evidence regarding the distinctiveness of emotional intelligence from personality. Hospital nurses with higher emotional intelligence tend to report higher satisfaction with their job (Güleryüz *et al.*, 2008). A study on 193 Australian police officers also found that the relationship between emotional intelligence and job satisfaction was positive and statistically significant (coefficient = 0.21, t-statistic = 3.19, $p < 0.001$).

Jobs that involve more intense affective contents, for example, the job of casino employees, require a high level of emotional labour. Casino employees, especially dealers are positioned in a very high-affect service context, dealing with intense customers (aka gamblers). Gambling, as a risk-taking activity and the primary service offered by casinos, has high affective content in both the gambling process (the functional aspect) and outcome (the technical component). The emotions displayed during gambling are attributed to uncertainty of the outcome (winning or losing). Studies (Mellers, Schwartz, and Ritov, 1999; O'Connor, 2000; Schellinck and Schrans, 1998) show that regular gamblers experience the range and strength of emotions during gambling on the basis of their cortical responses to the expectation of winning. They often appear to be anxious and hysterical, as reflected in their impatience towards the dealer's performance and yelling while expecting the outcome of turning the cards. Gambling outcomes also trigger gamblers' emotional responses. Win-seeking is one of the primary motives that people come to a casino to play and the feeling of fulfilment from winning can be very emotional (Lee *et al.*, 2005). Admittedly, the odds are generally not in their favour (Watson and Kale, 2003). Whilst some gamblers treat gambling as a recreational activity and accept the outcome (either win or loss) without making a fuss; others who have experienced a big loss can be wildly emotional and abusive, complaining about the dealer for their own mistakes and bad play (Prentice, 2008).

Gamblers' emotions during gambling or after each play are often transferred to the interactions with casino dealers who are in direct contact with the gambler. The dealers not only bear a noisy working environment and physical exhaustion from conducting croupier duties (Chan, Wan and Kuok, 2015), but they are also the victims of gamblers' emotional outbursts (Prentice, 2016). Following organisational job descriptions, the dealers are compelled to deal with these outbursts to ensure a smooth operation, acting in a friendly manner with smiling faces towards emotional customers. On the flipside of the coin, the dealer's job can be rather mechanical and mundane.

In that circumstance, emotional intelligence logically plays a significant role in adjusting dealers' job attitudes and behaviours. Highly emotional intelligent dealers may treat their monotonous dealing task as a means to enjoy connecting and interacting with customers and gamblers. Their skilful dealing and professionalism often attract gambling customers' compliments and generous tips. In turn, the dealers would feel rewarded, which would enhance their job satisfaction. This is confirmed in an empirical study on casino dealers (Prentice, 2018). The research finds that emotional intelligence has a significant influence on dealer's job satisfaction ($\beta = 0.616$, $p < 0.0005$).

5.5.1.2 *Job satisfaction and performance*

Job satisfaction generally refers to an emotional state resulting from one's job experiences or the level of content that an employee feels about his or her work (Locke, 1976; Spector, 1997). This is often reflected in financial (e.g. salary, promotion) and non-financial facets including perception of fairness of workload, relationships with co-workers and supervisors. Job satisfaction has been widely discussed as an antecedent of employee performance, turnover intention, and job retention.

Judge *et al.* (2001) provided a comprehensive literature review on job satisfaction–performance relationship and presented seven models describing their relationship. Among those proposed models, job satisfaction preceding performance relationship is most dominant in the literature. This model is based on attitudes literature in social psychology that "higher morale would lead to improved productivity", and "people who evaluate an attitude object favourably tend to engage in behaviours that foster or support it, and people who evaluate an attitude object unfavourably tend to engage in behaviours that hinder or oppose it" (Eagly and Chaiken, 1993, p. 12).

5.5.1.3 *Job satisfaction and employee retention*

Job satisfaction is a common factor of employee retention. This relationship has been extensively tested in certain professions: nurse, teachers and other service occupations. These occupations are highly stressful due to their boundary positions with demands from customers (patients, students and commercial customers) and from the management. Numerous empirical studies have examined and confirmed that job satisfaction is a key determinant of employee retention (e.g. Coomber and Barriball, 2007; Cowin *et al.*, 2008; Farrell and Rusbult, 1981).

5.6 The Mediation of Employee Commitment

5.6.1 *Emotional intelligence and employee commitment*

Commitment is considered as "a force that binds an individual to a target (social or non-social) and to a course of action of relevance to that target" (Meyer, Becker, and Van Dick, 2006, p. 666).) Commitment is a persistent, positive affective-motivational state of vigor, dedication, and absorption (Schaufeli *et al.*, 2002). Vigor is indicative of high levels of energy and resilience; dedication refers to voluntary involvement in one's work; and absorption indicates an individual's total immersion in work (Maslach, Schaufeli and Leiter, 2001). Employee commitment can be reflected in both attachment to the organisation (organisational commitment) and to the occupation (occupational commitment). Organisational commitment is viewed as a sophisticated construct involving an employee's identification and involvement with the organisation, willingness to exercise effort on behalf of the organisation, and desire to remain with the organisation (Porter, Crampon, and Smith, 1976; Wright, and Bonett, 2002). Occupational commitment represents the psychological link between an individual and his/her occupation on the basis of an affective attachment to the occupation and is defined as the extent to which an individual identifies with, and feels involved in a particular profession (Ciftcioglu, 2011; Lee *et al.*, 2000; Mathieu and Zajac, 1990). Occupational commitment is reflective of the degree of their engagement with the occupation. Both commitments are highly correlated. Employees who are committed to their occupations are more likely to be committed to their organisations where they find best fit. Committed employees tend to stay loyal to the organisation.

Employee commitment generates lots of organisational benefits: employee retention and performance. Hence the causes of such commitment are critical to achieve these benefits. Meyer *et al.*'s (2002) meta-analysis summarises the causes and outcomes of employee commitment. Their study clearly shows that employee personal characteristics are one of the key antecedents of employee commitment. Emotional intelligence is such a personal characteristic to maintain commitment. This relationship can be approached from understanding the impact of occupational stress.

Occupational stress is conceived mainly as an emotional reaction (usually negative) to various environmental stimuli (Selye, 1956). The most common definitions of stress may be categorised into three types (Beehr and Franz, 1987). The first type is stimulus-based, which views stress as a situational or environmental based stimulus, impinging upon the person. The second type is response-based, defining stress as an individual's psychological or physiological response to environmental/situational forces. The third definition applies an interactive approach, which has often been called the stressor-strain approach. This approach combines the first two types and defines stress as both the stimulus (source of stress or stressor) and the response (outcome or manifestation of stress or strain). Emotional intelligence could be used as a framework, within which the individual could learn how to cope with it and how to control strong emotions. Slaski and Cartwright (2002) have found that managers high in emotional intelligence suffered less subjective stress, had better physical and psychological wellbeing, and demonstrated higher-in-role job performance.

Bar-On, Brown, Kirkcaldy, and Thome (2000) investigated the differences in emotional intelligence between two distinct occupational groups, both of which suffered high levels of occupational stress: police officers and professional personnel in mental health and child care professions (Bar-On *et al.*, 2000). The results of their study indicated that police officers scored significantly higher than either of the care worker practitioner groups on most of the primary measures of emotional intelligence, suggesting that the ability of police officers to be more aware of themselves and of others makes them more adaptable to stressful events, and with better coping strategies (Bar-On *et al.*, 2000). A concept that the stress model used in the present study considers as a consequence of occupational stress is organisational commitment. Salancik (1977) defined organisational commitment as a state of being, in which an employee becomes bound by his actions and through these actions, to beliefs, which sustain them. He argued that commitment concerns the process by which individuals come to develop a sense of psychological ownership of their actions and hence a commitment to following those actions. This approach has roots in Festinger and Carlsmith (1959) theory of cognitive dissonance, which describes people's tendency to reconcile internal inconsistencies, for example between actions in one situation and actions in another. A recent approach in clarifying the concept of organisational commitment has taken two directions. The first claims that the relationship between an employee and an organisation can take various forms (i.e. multidimensional approach), whereas the second involves the distinction among specific entities within the organisation to which the employees become committed (Meyer, Allen and Allen 1997).

The study on professionals from mental health institutions revealed positive correlations between four of the five dimensions of emotional intelligence and both types of commitment. The findings suggest that employees with high scores in emotional intelligence tend to show increased levels of organisational commitment. This might be explained by the fact that emotionally competent employees who may be offered by top management have increased occupational opportunities and/or simultaneously they are better equipped to identify and effectively use them for their own benefit, resulting in increased organisational commitment.

5.6.2 *Commitment and performance*

From a conservation of resources theory perspective, employees need to have both willingness and ability to devote valuable resources in order to sustain a high level of emotional attachment to their occupations and organisations. Employees usually possess different needs and resources, which can be invested in an occupation and organisation. Individuals with higher occupational commitment strongly identify with and have positive feelings about their occupation and organisation. Employee commitment has positive influence on an individual's attitude toward their occupation and organisation. Committed individuals are more likely to invest resources in their occupation such as trying to improve their occupational knowledge and qualifications and work diligently to develop their career (Lee *et al.*, 2000, Meyer, Allen and Smith, 1993). According to the COR theory, lower commitment also results in inadequate resources invested in the profession, leading to lower energy and negative feelings, and ultimately poor performance (Ciftcioglu, 2011).

On the other hand, emotional labour is particularly relevant to customer service roles in fields such as hospitality services, health care, social service work, teaching, and other "caring" professions (see Ashkanasy and Humphrey, 1993; Brotheridge and Grandey, 2002). Such occupations have a higher than average incidence of employee burnout, poor performance and high turnover (Brotheridge and Grandey, 2002; Cherniss, 2017; Leiter and Maslach, 1998). However, in circumstances where employees within such professional areas identify themselves with their roles and with their organisations and regard them as a central, salient and valued component of their identity, they may ultimately acquire their identity with their occupations and organisations. Identity motivates the person to follow the stereotype when acting or behaving. Such motivations prevent the employee from feeling emotionally exhausted, thus enhancing the sense of personal achievement, which leads to enhanced performance.

Social identify theory indicates that employees who identify with their occupation and organisation may have a stronger sense of authenticity when conforming to role expectations including display rules and experience less alienation and emotional dissonance. Social identity theorists (Ashforth and Humphrey, 1993) suggest that individuals who identify strongly with their occupation and organisation feel more authentic in conforming with organisational display rules, and are most truly themselves when fulfilling their roles (Ashforth and Humphrey, 1993; Suh *et al.*, 2011). The type of "acting" that is described in the emotional labour process and expected by the organisation as a component of the rules of display may be enjoyable for occupants who are attached to their occupations and organisations. Alternatively, occupants may be capable of "acting" effectively, thereby reducing the likelihood of burnout and leading to better performance. Ashforth and Humphrey have proposed that such identity enhances psychological wellbeing and performance outcomes. A study conducted with 600 frontline employees shows that occupational commitment moderates the influence of emotional labour on consequences. In the case of emotional labour and performance, the moderating effect of occupational commitment is 0.18, ($p < 0.0005$) for surface acting — task performance is 0.18, ($p < 0.0005$), 0.16, ($p < 0.0005$) for surface acting — OCB. The incorporation of occupational commitment as a moderator of EL has enhanced both task performance and OCBs.

5.6.3 *Employee commitment and retention*

The relevant literature presents three major categories of antecedents of employee retention or turnover: (1) demographic factors, both personal and work-related; (2) employee attitudes reflected in organisational commitment and job satisfaction; and (3) organisational factors such as organisational culture and supervisor support. Researchers have not reached consensus on which condition or factor has a most significant influence on employee retention. However, most researchers agree that employee commitment is predictive of retention or turnover. The commitment–retention relationship has been discussed in the literature since 1970s. Although other organisational factors may affect this relationship, committed employees generally have low turnover. When an employee enjoys his/her assigned or signed-up job within an organisation, this employee is naturally committed to the job and the organisation, which provides the platform and support for execution of the job. Such commitment is reflective of individual identity, values and beliefs, which would enhance the employee's affinity with the organisation, and hence reduce the likeliness of the employee leaving the job.

5.7 Summary

This chapter draws upon the service profit chain model and discusses how emotional intelligence as a marketing tool and non-organisational resource influences common internal marketing outcomes: employee performance and retention which have implications for external marketing goals. Given that internal marketing is centred on managing interpersonal relationships over internal encounters among co-workers, the discussion begins with demonstrating the impact of emotional intelligence on interpersonal relationship and moves on to elaborate the link between emotional intelligence and internal marketing objectives. The relevant theories are identified to support the argument. The empirical findings are presented to confirm this link. The subsequent discussion moves on from internal encounter with employees to the external encounter with customers to identify how employees' emotional intelligence affects their encounter behaviours for external customers to achieve marketing goals. To understand the influence of emotional intelligence on external service encounter, it is imperative to explain the relationship between emotional intelligence and emotional labour as employees' encounter behaviours are related to emotional labour strategies. Therefore, Chapter 6 elaborates what emotional labour is and how emotional intelligence affects it.

References

Aghdasi, S., Kiamanesh, A.R., & Ebrahim, A.N. (2011). Emotional intelligence and organizational commitment: Testing the mediatory role of occupational stress and job satisfaction. *Procedia-Social and Behavioral Sciences*, 29, 1965–1976.

Ashforth, B.E. & Humphrey, R.H. (1993). Emotional labor in service roles: The influence of identity. *Academy of Management Review*, 18(1), 88–115.

Ashkanasy, N.M. & Humphrey, R.H. (2011). Current emotion research in organizational behavior. *Emotion Review*, 3(2), 214–224.

Austin, W.G. & Worchel, S. (Eds.). (1979). *The Social Psychology of Intergroup Relations*. Monterey, CA: Brooks/Cole Pub. Co.

Bar-On, R., Brown, J.M., Kirkcaldy, B.D., & Thome, E.P. (2000). Emotional expression and implications for occupational stress; an application of the Emotional Quotient Inventory (EQ-i). *Personality and Individual Differences*, 28(6), 1107–1118.

Barrick, M.R. & Mount, M.K. (1991). The big five personality dimensions and job performance: A meta-analysis. *Personnel Psychology*, 44(1), 1–26.

Beehr, T.A. & Franz, T.M. (1987). The current debate about the meaning of job stress. *Journal of Organizational Behavior Management*, 8(2), 5–18.

Brotheridge, C.M. & Grandey, A.A. (2002). Emotional labor and burnout: Comparing two perspectives of "people work". *Journal of Vocational Behavior*, 60(1), 17–39.

Brunetto, Y., Teo, S.T., Shacklock, K., & Farr Wharton, R. (2012). Emotional intelligence, job satisfaction, well-being and engagement: Explaining organisational commitment and turnover intentions in policing. *Human Resource Management Journal*, 22(4), 428–441.

Chan, S.H., Wan, Y.K.P., & Kuok, O.M. (2015). Relationships among burnout, job satisfaction, and turnover of casino employees in Macau. *Journal of Hospitality Marketing & Management*, 24(4), 345–374.

Cherniss, C. (2017). Role of professional self-efficacy in the etiology and amelioration of burnout. In W.B. Schaufeli, C. Maslach, & T. Marek (Eds.), *Professional Burnout: Recent Developments in Theory and Research* (pp. 135–149). London: Routledge.

Ciftcioglu, A. (2011). Investigating occupational commitment and turnover intention relationship with burnout syndrome. *Business and Economics Research Journal*, 2(3), 109–119.

Coomber, B. & Barriball, K.L. (2007). Impact of job satisfaction components on intent to leave and turnover for hospital-based nurses: A review of the research literature. *International journal of nursing studies*, 44(2), 297–314.

Cooper, R.K. & Sawaf, A. (1997). *Executive EQ: Emotional Intelligence in Leadership and Organization*. New York: Grosset/Putnam.

Cowin, L.S., Johnson, M., Craven, R.G., & Marsh, H.W. (2008). Causal modeling of self-concept, job satisfaction, and retention of nurses. *International Journal of Nursing Studies*, 45(10), 1449–1459.

Davis, M.H. (1980). A multidimensional approach to individual differences in empathy. *JSAS Catalog of Selected Documents in Psychology*, 10, 85.

Deutsch, D. (1980). The processing of structured and unstructured tonal sequences. *Perception & Psychophysics*, 28(5), 381–389.

Eagly, A.H. & Chaiken, S. (1993). *The Psychology of Attitudes*. Orlando, FL: Harcourt Brace Jovanovich College Publishers.

Eisenberg, N. (2000). Emotion, regulation, and moral development. *Annual Review of Psychology*, 51(1), 665–697.

Erez, A. & Isen, A. (2002). The influence of positive affect on components of expectancy motivation. *Journal of Applied Psychology*, 87(6), 1055–1067.

Farrell, D. & Rusbult, C.E. (1981). Exchange variables as predictors of job satisfaction, job commitment, and turnover: The impact of rewards, costs, alternatives, and investments. *Organizational Behavior and Human Performance*, 28(1), 78–95.

Festinger, L. & Carlsmith, J.M. (1959). Cognitive consequences of forced compliance. *The Journal of Abnormal and Social Psychology*, 58(2), 203.

Goleman, D. (1995). *Emotional Intelligence: Why It Can Matter More Than IQ.* New York: Bantam Books.

Goleman, D. (1998). *Working with Emotional Intelligence*. New York: Bantam Books.

Gouldner, A.W. (1960). The norm of reciprocity: A preliminary statement. *American Sociological Review*, 25, 161–178.

Grandey, A.A. (2003). When "the show must go on": Surface acting and deep acting as determinants of emotional exhaustion and peer-rated service delivery. *Academy of Management Journal*, 46(1), 86–96.

Grandey, A.A., Fisk, G.M., Mattila, A.S., Jansen, K.J., & Sideman, L.A. (2005). Is "service with a smile" enough? Authenticity of positive displays during service encounters. *Organizational Behavior and Human Decision Processes*, 96(1), 38–55.

Güleryüz, G., Güney, S., Aydın, E.M., & Aşan, Ö. (2008). The mediating effect of job satisfaction between emotional intelligence and organisational commitment of nurses: A questionnaire survey. *International journal of Nursing Studies*, 45(11), 1625–1635.

Heskett, J.L., Jones, T.O., Loveman, G.W., Sasser, W.E., & Schlesinger, L.A. (1994). Putting the service-profit chain to work. *Harvard Business Review*, 72(2), 164–174.

House, J.S., Robbins, C., & Metzner, H.L. (1982). The association of social relationships and activities with mortality: Prospective evidence from the Tecumseh Community Health Study. *American Journal of Epidemiology*, 116(1), 123–140.

Judge, T.A. & Bono, J.E. (2001). Relationship of core self-evaluations traits — self-esteem, generalized self-efficacy, locus of control, and emotional stability — with job satisfaction and job performance: A meta-analysis. *Journal of Applied Psychology*, 86(1), 80.

Kernbach, S. & Schutte, N.S. (2005). The impact of service provider emotional intelligence on customer satisfaction. *Journal of Services Marketing*, 19(7), 438–444.

Law, K.S., Wong, C.S., & Song, L.J. (2004). The construct and criterion validity of emotional intelligence and its potential utility for management studies. *Journal of Applied Psychology*, 89(3), 483.

Lee, H.S., Lemanski, J.L., & Jun, J.W. (2008). Role of gambling media exposure in influencing trajectories among college students. *Journal of Gambling Studies*, 24(1), 25–37.

Lee, J.Y., Cole, T.B., Palmiter, R.D., & Koh, J.Y. (2000). Accumulation of zinc in degenerating hippocampal neurons of ZnT3-null mice after seizures: evidence against synaptic vesicle origin. *Journal of Neuroscience*, 20(11), RC79–RC79.

Lee, C.K., Lee, Y.K., Bernhard, B.J., & Yoon, Y.S. (2006). Segmenting casino gamblers by motivation: A cluster analysis of Korean gamblers. *Tourism Management*, 27(5), 856–866.

Leiter, M.P. & Maslach, C. (2003). Areas of worklife: A structured approach to organizational predictors of job burnout. In *Emotional and Physiological Processes and Positive Intervention Strategies* (pp. 91–134). Bingley, Eng.: Emerald Group Publishing Limited.

Lennox, R.D. & Wolfe, R.N. (1984). Revision of the self-monitoring scale. *Journal of Personality and Social Psychology*, 46(6), 1349–1364.

Lerner, J.S. & Keltner, D. (2001). Fear, anger, and risk. *Journal of Personality and Social Psychology*, 81(1), 146.

Locke, E.A. (1976). The nature and causes of job satisfaction. In M.D. Dunnette (Ed.), *Handbook of Industrial and Organizational Psychology* (pp. 1297–1343). Chicago: Rand McNally College Pub. Co.

Loewenstein, G. & Lerner, J.S. (2003). The role of affect in decision making. In R. Davidson, H. Goldsmith, and K. Scherer (Eds.), *Handbook of Affective Science* (pp. 619–642). Oxford: Oxford University Press.

Lowenstein, A. (2008). Review of liquid desiccant technology for HVAC applications. *Hvac&R Research*, 14(6), 819–839.

Maslach, C., Schaufeli, W.B., & Leiter, M.P. (2001). Job burnout. *Annual Review of Psychology*, 52(1), 397–422.

Maslach, C. & Leiter, M.P. (2008). Early Predictors of job burnout and engagement. *Journal of Applied Psychology*, 93(3), 498–512.

Mathieu, J.E. & Zajac, D.M. (1990). A review and meta-analysis of the antecedents, correlates, and consequences of organizational commitment. *Psychological Bulletin*, 108(2), 171.

Mellers, B., Schwartz, A., & Ritov, I. (1999). Emotion-based choice. *Journal of Experimental Psychology: General*, 128(3), 332.

Meyer, J.P., Allen, N.J., & Allen, N.J. (1997). *Commitment in the Workplace: Theory, Research, and Application.* Thousand Oaks, CA: Sage Publications.

Meyer, J.P., Allen, N.J., & Smith, C.A. (1993). Commitment to organizations and occupations: Extension and test of a three-component conceptualization. *Journal of Applied Psychology*, 78(4), 538.

Meyer, J.P., Becker, T.E., & Van Dick, R. (2006). Social identities and commitments at work: Toward an integrative model. *Journal of Organizational Behavior: The International Journal of Industrial, Occupational and Organizational Psychology and Behavior*, 27(5), 665–683.

Meyer, J.P., Stanley, D.J., Herscovitch, L., & Topolnytsky, L. (2002). Affective, continuance, and normative commitment to the organization: A meta-analysis of antecedents, correlates, and consequences. *Journal of Vocational Behavior*, 61(1), 20–52.

Naderi Anari, N. (2012). Teachers: emotional intelligence, job satisfaction, and organizational commitment. *Journal of Workplace Learning*, 24(4), 256–269.

O'Connor, B.P. (2000). SPSS and SAS programs for determining the number of components using parallel analysis and Velicer's MAP test. *Behavior Research Methods, Instruments, & Computers*, 32(3), 396–402.

O'Boyle Jr., E.H., Humphrey, R.H., Pollack, J.M., Hawver, T.H., & Story, P.A. (2011). The relation between emotional intelligence and job performance: A meta-analysis. *Journal of Organizational Behavior*, 32(5), 788–818.

Oxman, T.E., Berkman, L.F., Kasl, S., Freeman Jr., D.H., & Barrett, J. (1992). Social support and depressive symptoms in the elderly. *American Journal of Epidemiology*, 135(4), 356–368.

Pilisuk, M. & Parks, S.H. (1986). *The Healing Web: Social Networks and Human Survival.* Hanover, NH: University Press of New England.

Porter, L.W., Crampon, W.J., & Smith, F.J. (1976). Organizational commitment and managerial turnover: A longitudinal study. *Organizational Behavior and Human Performance*, 15(1), 87–98.

Prentice, C. (2008). *Trait Emotional Intelligence, Personality and the Self-perceived Performance Ratings of Casino Key Account Representatives* (Doctoral dissertation, Victoria University).

Prentice, C. (2016). Leveraging employee emotional intelligence in casino profitability. *Journal of Retailing and Consumer Services*, 33, 127–134.

Prentice, C. (2018). Linking internal service quality and casino dealer performance. *Journal of Hospitality Marketing & Management*, 27(6), 733–753.

Prentice, C. & King, B. (2011). The influence of emotional intelligence on the service performance of casino frontline employees. *Tourism and Hospitality Research*, 11(1), 49–66.

Prentice, C., Chen, P.J., & King, B. (2013). Employee performance outcomes and burnout following the presentation-of-self in customer-service contexts. *International Journal of Hospitality Management*, 35, 225–236.

Rafaeli, A. & Sutton, R.I. (1987). Expression of emotion as part of the work role. *Academy of Management Review*, 12(1), 23–37.

Salancik, G.R. (1977). Commitment and the control of organizational behavior and belief. In B.M. Staw and G.R. Salancik (Eds.), *New Directions in Organizational Behavior* (pp. 1–54). Chicago: St. Claire Press.

Schaufeli, W.B., Leiter, M.P., & Maslach, C. (2009). Burnout: 35 years of research and practice. *Career Development International*, 14(3), 204–220.

Schellinck, T. & Schrans, T. (1998). *Nova Scotia Video Lottery Players' Survey*. Report completed by Focal Research Consultants Ltd. for the Nova Scotia Department of Health, Halifax, Nova Scotia.

Schutte, N.S., Malouff, J.M., Hall, L.E., Haggerty, D.J., Cooper, J.T., Golden, C.J., & Dornheim, L. (1998). Development and validation of a measure of emotional intelligence. *Personality and Individual Differences*, 25(2), 167–177.

Schütz, E. (Ed.). (1978). *Zur Aktualität des Kriminalromans* (Vol. 82). Munich: Fink.

Selye, H. (1956). *The Stress of Life*. New York: McGraw-Hill.

Shimazu, A., Shimazu, M., & Odahara, T. (2004). Job control and social support as coping resources in job satisfaction. *Psychological Reports*, 94(2), 449–456.

Slaski, M. & Cartwright, S. (2002). Health, performance and emotional intelligence: An exploratory study of retail managers. *Stress and Health: Journal of the International Society for the Investigation of Stress*, 18(2), 63–68.

Spector, P.E. (1997). *Job Satisfaction: Application, Assessment, Causes, and Consequences* (Vol. 3). Thousand Oaks, CA: Sage publications.

Suh, T., Houston, M.B., Barney, S.M., & Kwon, I.W.G. (2011). The impact of mission fulfillment on the internal audience: Psychological job outcomes in a services setting. *Journal of Service Research,* 14(1), 76–92.

Sutton, J. (1991). *Sunk Costs and Market Structure: Price Competition, Advertising, and the Evolution of Concentration.* MIT Press. Trade Typesetting, Ltd. Hong Kong of America.

Sy, T., Tram, S., & O'Hara, L.A. (2006). Relation of employee and manager emotional intelligence to job satisfaction and performance. *Journal of Vocational Behavior,* 68(3), 461–473.

Tett, R.P., Jackson, D.N., & Rothstein, M. (1991). Personality measures as predictors of job performance: A meta-analytic review. *Personnel Psychology,* 44(4), 703–742.

Varca, P.E. (2004). Service skills for service workers: Emotional intelligence and beyond. *Managing Service Quality: An International Journal,* 14(6), 457–467.

Watson, L. & Kale, S.H. (2003). Know when to hold them: Applying the customer lifetime value concept to casino table gaming. *International Gambling Studies,* 3(1), 89–101.

Wong, C.S. & Law, K.S. (2002). The effects of leader and follower emotional intelligence on performance and attitude: An exploratory study. *The Leadership Quarterly,* 13(3), 243–274.

Wright, T.A. & Bonett, D.G. (2002). The moderating effects of employee tenure on the relation between organizational commitment and job performance: A meta-analysis. *Journal of Applied Psychology,* 87(6), 1183.

CHAPTER 6

EMOTIONAL INTELLIGENCE AND DRAMATURGICAL MARKETING

6.1 Introduction

Chapter 5 discusses how emotional intelligence can be incorporated into internal marketing through providing empirical evidence on how emotional intelligence influences service employees' attitudes and behaviours, which include job satisfaction, employee commitment, job performance and retention. These attitudes and behaviours are linked to, but not directly related to those of customers based on the service profit chain model proposed by Heskett *et al.* (1997). The link is intervened by interactions between employees and customers over the service encounter. Employees' attitudes and behaviours result from internal marketing practice which is often focused on utilising organisational resources such as implementing delivery of superior internal service quality. Emotional intelligence is promoted as a non-organisational resource (employee emotional abilities) to facilitate internal marketing. Whilst acknowledging the influence of internal service quality on employees' job attitudes and behaviours, emotional intelligence is evidently a significant predictor of these employee outcomes.

Moving beyond internal service encounter, the ultimate goal of optimising employee attitudes and behaviours is to ensure that these outcomes can be transferred into positive perceptions over the external service encounter between employees and customers. For example, happy employees (job satisfaction) tend to have positive attitudes towards customers. Employees' service encounter behaviours that form part of employee performance evaluation influence customers' perception of the firm's service quality, which affect their satisfaction with the service provider and subsequent behaviours.

Unlike the internal service encounter that involves co-workers and supervisors who have organisational goals in mind, the encounter between employees and customers is unpredictable and challenging due to diversity of customers with regards to their demands, the purposes of entering the service transaction, cultures and personalities that result in different attitudes and behaviours. Employees' behaviours over the service encounter are largely dependent upon organisational requirements, individual abilities and the context. Service organisations require frontline employees to perform emotional labour, which becomes part of mandatory job descriptions. Therefore prior to discussing how emotional intelligence affects their service encounter behaviours, this chapter looks into the concept of emotional labour and how emotional intelligence is related to emotional labour. Emotional labour is conceptualised as acting strategies in accordance with the requirement of a service organisation and approached from dramaturgical perspective to understand its nature and influence. Therefore, this book refers to the acting strategies as *dramaturgical marketing*. The following presents a review of emotional labour conceptualisation and its relationship with frontline employees. The benefits and negative consequences of emotional labour performance are elaborated, followed by discussion on how emotional intelligence as a marketing tool can facilitate emotional labour strategies.

6.2 Emotional Labour (EL) and Frontline Employees

Service employees, particularly those working in the frontline, are required to perform emotional labour. Emotional labour is defined as managing emotions for a wage, involving enhancing, faking, or suppressing emotions to modify the emotional expression (Hochschild, 1983). This involves two main acting strategies. Firstly, the employee may engage in surface acting to comply with the prevailing rules of display. This type of acting involves simulating emotions that are not felt, and feigning emotions that are not experienced. The second type of performance involves deep acting — making a genuine attempt to experience or feel the emotions that are on display.

Emotional labour has strong applicability to service encounters in the service industry. The function of emotional labour is consistent with the increasing applicability of dramaturgical perspectives to customer interactions and the importance of services to the economy. Available studies on emotional labour in academia focus on frontline service employees who have direct contact with customers. Frontline employees in the service industry perform a necessary communication function between customers and the firm, and play a significant role in influencing organisational effectiveness (Singh, 2000). These employees occupy the interface between an organisation (management and co-workers) and its customers, between employees and customers and form the first point of customer contact. Their jobs involve high social components. Situated in boundary spanning positions, these employees are caught between the demand from customers for attention and quality service provision and the requirement for efficiency and productivity from organisations. Performing emotional labour is an essential part of job requirements for customer-contact employees in service-oriented organisations. Emotional labour designs are means of enhancing task performance and as a strategy for managing service encounters efficiently through appropriate acting to achieve optimal customer-related outcomes such as customer satisfaction and loyalty. Consequently emotional labour can be viewed as a marketing strategy and referred to as ***dramaturgical marketing*** in this book on the basis of frontline employees' dramatic composition over the service encounter with customers.

6.3 Emotional Labour and Performance

Emotional labour has its salient benefits for both organisations and individuals. The display of feelings in the emotional labour process during service interactions strongly impacts the quality of service transactions, the attractiveness of the interpersonal climate, and the experience of emotions. Prescribed sets of responses and patterns of behaviour that EL learned by service employees may facilitate dynamic encounter communications (Mann, 1997), leading to increased product sales, effective handling of customer complaints, and ensuring smooth-running communicative interactions (Hochschild, 1983). In combination, these ultimately lead to better performance. Research has shown that deep acting has a positive relationship with performance (e.g. Brotheridge and Lee, 2002; Grandey, 2003).

Performance enhancement may follow from both task performance (in-role behaviours), and contextual performance, often referred to as organisation citizenship behaviours — OCBs (Borman and Motowidlo, 1997; Carmeli and Josman, 2006; Rousseau, 1990). Task performances refer to employer expectations and requirements of employee behaviours or work performance in return for remuneration (see Borman and Motowidlo, 1997). In the case of frontline employees in the service industry, such performance may concern customer evaluations of service quality leading to satisfaction and loyalty, and ultimately to company profitability (e.g. Zeithaml, Berry and Parasuraman, 1996; Prentice and King, 2012; Singh, 2000). OCBs include "individual behaviours that are discretionary, not directly or explicitly recognised by the formal reward system, and in the aggregate promote the efficient and effective functioning of the organization" (Organ, 1988, p. 4). This approach acknowledges that OCBs are important for improving organisational efficiency and effectiveness and have an indirect effect on customer perceptions of the quality of the firm. Both dimensions of frontline employee performance are important influences on customer perceptions of service quality, whether directly or indirectly.

An empirical study (Prentice and King, 2013) conducted in several hospitality organisations shows that surface acting by hospitality service employees indeed exerts a significant positive influence on both task performance ($\beta = 0.14$, $p < 0.001$) and on OCB ($\beta = 0.09$, $p < 0.05$). A significant association between surface acting and task performance is plausible. Surface acting is the superficial exhibiting of emotions and circumstances where employees act because they are required to conform to organisational display rules. Where employees are able to regulate their emotional expressions on the basis of organisational display rules (surface acting), required duties (task performance) can be accomplished by following the rules of acting. Such behaviour does not need to represent real feelings. In the case of frontline hospitality employees in general, and those working in restaurants and hotels in particular, customer encounters are often short and temporary; acting superficially is more spontaneous and thus facilitates timely task accomplishment. Although OCBs are not required by most organisations, performing such behaviours may be habitual or be undertaken for the sake of making a positive impression. Since surface acting is the "act" required by the organisation, it may in the longer run become habitual, and performing OCB may be part of habitual behaviour.

Interestingly, in the aforementioned study, deep acting is not strongly associated with performance outcomes. Although appearing to contradict the findings of prior research, this outcome may be attributable to the relatively low wages earned by respondents. As stated in the previous section, most of the survey participants earned less than USD $40,000. OCBs are conceptualised as employee behaviours that extend beyond the formal requirements of the role that they play. Since the activities are not remunerated, such behaviours are discretionary and demand a level of conscientiousness. The process of deep acting requires genuine effort in order to experience or feel emotions. Employees may avoid the necessity to "act" deeply when a less onerous approach (surface acting) can accomplish the task, unless an individual is committed to the occupation.

6.4 Emotional Labour and Burnout

Despite the benefits of emotional labour, managing emotions for pay can be detrimental to the employees. Most service employees are typically underpaid, undertrained, overworked, stressed, and susceptible to burnout (Kim and Agrusa, 2011; Lo and Lamm, 2005; Pienaar and Willemse, 2008; Singh, 2000). The incidence of burnout has negative consequences such as low employee self-esteem, health problems, absenteeism, accelerated turnover, job dissatisfaction and poor performance with serious consequences for both individuals and organisations (Dahlin, Joneborg and Runeson, 2007; Houkes *et al.*, 2010; Pienaar and Willemse, 2008).

The pivot on which emotional labour revolves is the fact that there is a discrepancy between emotions expected and those actually experienced. "What is functional for the organization may well be dysfunctional" for the actor (Ashforth and Humphrey (1993, p. 96). Emotional labour is stressful and may result in emotional dissonance and burnout. Portraying emotions that are not felt (surface acting) creates the strain of emotive dissonance that is akin to cognitive dissonance. The dissonance may cause the labourer to feel false and hypocritical. Ultimately, such dissonance leads to personal and work-related maladjustment, such as poor self-esteem, depression, cynicism and alienation from work. On the other hand, deep acting may distort these reactions and impair one's sense of authentic self, and ultimately lead to self-alienation and may impair one's ability to recognise or even experience genuine emotion. When a person is unable to express script emotions, a condition termed burnout is experienced (Jackson and Maslach, 1982).

Consistently, the relevant literature shows that emotional labour-related research focuses on unfavourable consequences. Burnout is the most commonly researched of these various negative connotations. The emotional labour literature extensively attends to burnout. Maslach and Jackson (1986, p. 1) defined burnout as "a syndrome of emotional exhaustion, depersonalization and reduced personal accomplishment that can occur among individuals who do 'people work' of some kind." Emotional exhaustion refers to the affective states characterised by low emotional resources and a shortage of energy (Lee and Ashforth, 1996), which is a central aspect of job burnout (Shirom, 1989). On the other hand, depersonalisation, negative perception of an employee's recipients, can be considered an effort to diminish the emotional resource loss that is a consequence of the continuous need to handle problematic issues with restricted material resources (Wright and Hobfoll, 2004). Similarly, lack of personal accomplishment or feeling ineffective at work involves negative evaluation of one's work. Emotional exhaustion is likely to lead the employee to place an emotional and cognitive distance from work. Depersonalisation provides a means of placing distance between oneself and a recipient of hospitality, and this distancing is an immediate reaction to exhaustion; whereas diminished personal accomplishment appears to be a function of exhaustion and/or depersonalisation.

Researchers generally believe that burnout is positively related to the surface acting element of the emotional labour process but negatively related to deep acting (e.g. Brotheridge and Grandey, 2002; Grandey, 2003; Kim, 2008). In the case of demanding jobs such as frontline positions or so-called job-focused emotional labour where the employee has a low level of control, both types of acting can have negative outcomes (Brotheridge and Grandey, 2002; Pugliesi, 1999). Drawing on Darwin's view that emotional reactions serve a signal function, helping one to make sense of situations, and connecting one to others and to the context, this type of deep acting may distort employee reactions and impair one's sense of the authentic self. The outcome may ultimately lead to self-alienation and reduced capacity to recognise or even to experience genuine emotions. The reworking of authentic emotions (deep acting) has been found to be positively associated with psychological dysfunctions and overall stress (Parkinson, 1991; Rutter and Fielding, 1988). Such stress eventually leads to burnout. Ashforth and Humphrey argue that emotional labour is dysfunctional and that "… the masking or reworking of authentic emotions that one would otherwise prefer to express has been linked to psychological and physical dysfunctions (see Ashforth and Humphrey, 1993, p. 97). Emotional labour can be a double-edged sword, and either surface acting or deep acting is insufficient as means of achieving task effectiveness when managing encounters with highly demanding customers. Both alternatives may have negative psychological consequences: surface acting can cause emotive dissonance and lead to work-related maladjustment; and deep acting can impair individual wellbeing and lead to self-alienation.

Table 6.1 The relationships among emotional labour, performance, and burnout

Variables	EE(β)	ΔR^2	DPA(β)	ΔR^2	DP(β)	ΔR^2	TP(β)	ΔR^2	OCB(β)	ΔR^2
Step 2		0.15***		0.05***		0.15***		0.02**		0.01
SA	0.39***		0.11*		0.37***		0.14**		0.09*	
DA	0.08*		0.12***		0.14**		−0.04		0.03	

Notes: EE = emotional exhaustion, DPA = diminished personal accomplishment, DP = depersonalisation, TP = task performance, OCB = organisation citizenship behaviours, SA = surface acting, DA = deep acting. $*p < 0.05$, $**p < 0.01$, $***p < 0.0005$.

Indeed, Mikolajczak *et al.*'s (2007) study demonstrated a positive relationship between deep acting and three dimensions of burnout. Another study conducted by Prentice, Chen and King (2013) with frontline hospitality employees shows that both surface acting and deep acting had significant effects on three dimensions of burnout: the beta values are 0.39 ($p < 0.0005$) and 0.08 ($p < 0.05$) for surface/deep acting — emotional exhaustion; 0.11 ($p < 0.05$) and 0.12 ($p < 0.0005$) for surface/deep acting — diminished personal accomplishment, and 0.37 ($p < 0.0005$) and 0.14 ($p < 0.005$) for surface/deep acting — depersonalisation (see Table 6.1). These findings may be attributed to the intensifying competition in the service/hospitality industry that has been prevalent in recent years and organisational restructuring. Service employees face the threat of retrenchment as well as excessive job demands. In order to keep their jobs, they may feel obliged to follow organisational rules to "act." Lack of spontaneity and unwillingness in their acting may eventually lead to job dissatisfaction and burnout. If these employees perceive that it is necessary to act genuinely (deep acting) but are unable or unwilling to do so (due to low wages), they may suffer low self-esteem or self-alienation, eventually leading to burnout as well. The new insight into deep acting strategies suggests that researchers should be cautious about promoting deep acting.

6.5 Emotional Intelligence and Emotional Labour

The above discussion presents two contrasting outcomes of performing emotional labour: benefits for the organisation and detrimental effects for individuals (emotional labourer). The majority of emotional labour literature concludes that emotional labour is associated with the negative effects (e.g. burnout) of individual outcomes. Naturally a burnout employee would be unable to perform well at work. For decades researchers and laymen seem to be fixated on the happy-productive worker hypothesis, and deduce the unhappy employees-poor performance relationship (Fisher, 2003). Numerous studies have examined the effect of burnout on performance, and to a certain extent, confirmed a negative relationship between the two albeit inconsistently (e.g. Lazaro, Shinn and Robinson, 1984; Parker and Kulik, 1995; Podsakoff, LePine and LePine, 2007; Randall and Scott, 1988).

Logically, poor performance results in less financial and non-financial rewards and job insecurity, which affects job dissatisfaction. Dissatisfaction with work and pay then leads to burnout. However, the burnout-performance relationship seems to be cyclical rather than a straight linear relationship. Performance can be an antecedent to burnout: good performing employees likely receive financial and non-financial rewards (e.g. promotion, pay rise, a sense of achievement, recognition); with these rewards employees feel motivated and satisfied with their work; with better financial incentives, they can afford more social and entertaining activities for friends, family and themselves (e.g. travelling, sporting); these activities bring them more positive energy and outlook of life and career; they are then more committed to their organisations and career. Consequently, burnout less likely exists in this cycle, or phases out when one is determined to strive for good performance. High performing employees are often positive about challenging situations and may even relish in the opportunity to demonstrate their abilities, test themselves, develop new skills, and learn new subjects. These employees believe inextricability of and in the balance between physical, mental and emotional performance. When overloaded with work commitments and stress, they would opt for some physical activities (e.g. going for a run) to induce endorphins that would boost mental capacity and focus. Hence, they are less likely to burnout.

The performance — burnout relationship can be accounted for by the conservation of resources theory (Hobfoll, 1989). The theory suggests that individuals attempt to attain and preserve resources. The resources can be "objects, personal characteristics, conditions, or energies that are valued by the individual or that serve as a means for the attainment of these objects" (Hobfoll, 1989, p. 516). When an individual's resources are inadequate to meet work demands due to the influence of external environmental/organisational factors and/or individual reasons, burnout often occurs. According to the earlier definition, employee performance can be considered as the result of how an individual utilises his or her resources to accomplish job requirements. In order words, it refers to how employees acquire, preserve and nurture essential resources to not only meet their current work demands but to also prevent further resource loss. As such, poor performance could lead to burnout and vice versa (Wright and Hobfoll, 2004). In fact, Keijsers *et al.* (1995) indicate that subjective perception of performance reflects doubts about one's competence and self-efficacy, and in consequence, guilt and self-blame, all of which are antecedents of burnout.

While burnout is an outcome of task performance, emotional intelligence can be a useful personal resource in dealing with emotional situations and act as a supportive agent in performing duties and deal with work demands to strive for optimal performance (Görgens-Ekermans and Brand, 2012). Highly emotional intelligent individuals are more likely to fathom emotions through cognitive assessment, and to engage coping strategies (King and Gardner, 2006), which can help achieve flexibility and adaptability in stressful environments (Wu, Smith and Rupprecht, 2011). In other words, employees with high emotional intelligence tend to have better interpersonal skills and abilities to gather necessary resources and handle emotional pressure experienced in their work performance, thereby reducing the effect of work performance on propensity for burnout. In contrast, those with low emotional intelligence tend to require more resources such as social support, placing more demands in their task performance, which might result in a stronger effect of performance in inciting burnout. In general, it is expected that highly emotional intelligent employees are more likely than those with a lower level of emotional intelligence to decrease or convert the possible negative effects of task performance towards burnout.

From an organisational perspective, emotional labour is an essential strategy and a job requirement stipulated in job descriptions in most service organisations. Given that emotional labour is particularly relevant to employees who interact with customers, and such encounters involve a high emotional component (e.g. Mattila and Enz, 2002). Employee emotional management skills are necessary to facilitate the emotional labour process in order to reduce burnout risk and achieve enhanced results. Emotional intelligence has particular relevance in the case of service industry personnel and their job-related outcomes because their employment involves substantial interpersonal interactions that require emotional work (Ashforth and Humphrey, 1993; Ashkanasy and Daus, 2005). Emotional intelligence, and its aspects of managing one's own and others' emotions, have the implication of affecting job performance from requiring high emotional labour and in turn, preventing the negative outcomes of such emotional labour. Emotional intelligence can be deployed as a measure to prevent and manage the detrimental effects of performing emotional labour.

6.6 Emotional Intelligence Facilitates Emotional Labour

Emotional intelligence has been primarily discussed as a predictor in the literature. It can in fact, also function as a moderator. For instance, Jordan, Ashkanasy and Hartel (2002) proposed emotional intelligence as a moderator of emotional and behavioural reactions to job insecurity. Emotional intelligence can also facilitate coping with workplace-related stress and moderate the relationship between conscientiousness and performance (Ashkanasy, Ashton-James and Jordan, 2003; Douglas, Frink and Ferris, 2004). In the services context, Gabbott, Tsarenko and Mok (2011) found that emotional intelligence can shape the reaction of customers towards service failure. Although few studies investigate the moderating effect of emotional intelligence in the emotional labour process, Grandy (2008) proposes emotional intelligence as a moderating factor on individual outcomes in the case of the two emotional labour-related acting strategies.

Daus and Ashkanasy (2005) suggest that emotional intelligence might moderate or ameliorate the negative consequences of emotional labour. Studies have been undertaken to demonstrate and confirm the important relationships between emotional intelligence and emotional labour in both laboratory and field studies. With simulated customer service representatives, Daus (2002) found that people who could read emotions in facial expressions felt less of an emotional load from the job, and people who could better manage emotions in themselves felt more of an emotional load. In customer service representatives and sales personnel, Cage *et al.* (2004) found that with respect to the dimension of emotional intelligence, understanding emotions was positively related with the faking positive aspect of emotional labour, whereas expressing negative emotions was negatively associated with actual sales performance. Employing police officers as a sample, Daus, Daus and Saul (2004) and Duas and Ashkanasy (2005) quantitatively demonstrated a definitive link between aspects of emotional labour and emotional intelligence. Based on these studies, Daus and Ashkanasy (2005) concluded that emotional intelligence and its four branches proposed by Mayer and Salovey (1997) were significantly associated with deep acting of emotional labour; while the branch understanding emotions was associated with surface acting, the other three branches were significantly related to suppressing negative emotions; finally, using emotions was related to faking positive emotions.

Salami (2007) reports that emotional intelligence successfully moderates the relationship between surface acting and OCBs. The four hierarchical branches of emotional intelligence may be capable of adjusting the emotional labour process. For example, the first branch may influence surface acting (simulating emotions that are not actually felt). This contention lies in that emotions can only be simulated effectively in circumstances where the perception is accurate, thereby allowing the simulation to fit the context. A nurse may for example simulate sympathy for a patient who has deep concerns about his or her health. In this circumstance the process of simulation is dependent on the nurse possessing the required perception of the patient's concerns. The fourth branch can facilitate deep acting (attempts to experience or feel the emotions that one wishes to display). Mayer *et al.* (2001) indicated that the four branches function hierarchically. The perception of emotions acts as both the most basic branch and as a precursor to the other three. Emotional management may be viewed as the most complex since it occupies the top branch. Once a perception has been acquired, emotions may be deployed in order to facilitate conscious or unconscious thought (Levine, 1997). Emotional knowledge can subsequently be transferred to behaviours (Mayer *et al.*, 2001).

In Prentice, Chen and King's (2013) study on hospitality employees, the results (in Table 6.2) show that emotional intelligence significantly reduced the levels of surface/deep acting on emotional exhaustion ($\beta = -0.36$, $p < 0.0005$; $\beta = -0.18$, $p < 0.05$), on diminished personal achievement ($\beta = -0.16$, $p < 0.0005$; $\beta = -0.09$, $p < 0.05$), and on depersonalisation ($\beta = -0.19$, $p < 0.0005$; $\beta = -0.19$, $p < 0.0005$). The results from the moderation analyses indicate that the incorporation of emotional intelligence as a moderator can be a remedy for enhancing emotional labour-related performance outcomes and reducing emotional labour — caused burnout. Emotional intelligence moderates the relationship between the two emotional labour acting processes and burnout. This finding is consistent with Daus and Ashkanasy's (2005) assertion that emotional intelligence plays a significant role in jobs such as customer service representative which demand high EL. Service encounters between employees and customers often involve a strong emotional component due to unpredictable situational factors and demanding customers (see Ashforth and Humphrey, 1993). Employee emotional intelligence is able to facilitate service transactions by facilitating the management of one's own emotions and those of others. Smooth transactions lead to fewer customer complaints, and consequently, to low employee stress which is a precursor of burnout.

Table 6.2 The moderating effect of emotional intelligence on emotional labour on burnout, task performance and OCB

Variables	EE(β)	ΔR^2	DPA(β)	ΔR^2	DP(β)	ΔR^2	TP(β)	ΔR^2	OCB(β)	ΔR^2
SA*EI	−0.36***	0.11***	−0.16***	0.07***	−0.19***	0.08***	−0.01	0.00	−0.02	0.00
DA*EI	−0.18***	0.06***	−0.09*	0.00	−0.19***	0.08***	0.06	0.00	0.03	0.00
SA*AOC	−0.11*	0.04**	−0.16***	0.07***	−0.06	0.01	0.18***	0.07***	0.16***	0.07***
DA*AOC	−0.03	0.00	−0.14***	0.04***	−0.04	0.00	−0.02	0.00	0.07*	0.01*
SA*COC	0.05	0.01	−0.01	0.01	−0.07	0.01	0.15***	0.05***	0.02	0.00
DA*COC	−0.08	0.01	−0.03	0.00	−0.09	0.13	0.06	0.00	0.03	0.00
SA*NOC	−0.07	0.01	−0.06	0.01	−0.06	0.01	0.05	0.01	0.05	0.01
DA*NOC	−0.03	0.00	−0.04	0.01	−0.04	0.00	0.02	0.00	0.06*	0.01

Notes. EE = emotional exhaustion, DPA = diminished personal accomplishment, DP = depersonalisation, TP = task performance, OCB = organisation citizenship behaviours, SA = surface acting, DA = deep acting, EI = emotional intelligence, AOC = affective occupational commitment, COC = continuance occupational commitment, NOC = normative occupational commitment. *$p < 0.05$, **$p < 0.01$, ***$p < 0.0005$.

6.7 Summary

This chapter presents the concept of emotional labour and its relevance to frontline employees. On the basis of the nature and conceptualisation of emotional labour, this book refers to emotional labour strategies as dramaturgical marketing. The rationale for incorporating emotional intelligence as a marketing tool into emotional labour strategies is presented by elaborating the benefits and negative consequences of performing emotional labour. This elaboration lays foundation for proposing emotional intelligence as a facilitator in regulating emotional labour strategies. Findings from several empirical studies are provided to endorse the influence of emotional intelligence in emotional labour process.

References

Ashforth, B.E. & Humphrey, R.H. (1993). Emotional labor in service roles: The influence of identity. *Academy of Management Review*, 18(1), 88–115.

Ashkanasy, N.M., Ashton-James, C.E., & Jordan, P.J. (2003). Performance impacts of appraisal and coping with stress in workplace settings: The role of affect and emotional intelligence. In P.L. Perrewe and D.C. Ganster (Eds.) *Emotional and Physiological Processes and Positive Intervention Strategies* (pp. 1–43). Bingley, Eng.: Emerald Group Publishing Limited.

Ashkanasy, N.M. & Daus, C.S. (2005). Rumors of the death of emotional intelligence in organizational behaviour are vastly exaggerated. *Journal of Organizational Behaviour*, 26(4), 441–452.

Borman, W.C. & Motowidlo, S.J. (1997). Task performance and contextual performance: The meaning for personnel selection research. *Human Performance*, 10(2), 99–109.

Brotheridge, C. & Grandey, A. (2002). Emotional labour and burnout: Comparing two perspectives of 'people work.' *Journal of Vocational Behavior*, 60(1), 17–39.

Brotheridge, C.M. & Lee, R.T. (2002). Testing a conservation of resources model of the dynamics of emotional labor. *Journal of Occupational Health Psychology*, 7(1), 57.

Cage, T., Daus, C.S., & Saul, K. (2004). An examination of emotional skill, job satisfaction, and retail performance. Paper submitted to the 19th Annual Society for Industrial/Organizational Psychology, as part of the symposium.

Carmeli, A. & Josman, Z.E. (2006). The relationship among emotional intelligence, task performance, and organizational citizenship behaviors. *Human Performance*, 19(4), 403–419.

Dahlin, M., Joneborg, N., & Runeson, B. (2007). Performance-based self-esteem and burnout in a cross-sectional study of medical students. *Medical Teacher*, 29(1), 43–48.

Daus, C.S. & Ashkanasy, N.M. (2005). The case for the ability-based model of emotional intelligence in organizational behaviour. *Journal of Organizational Behaviour*, 26(4), 453–466.

Daus, C.S., Rubin, R.S., Smith, R.K, & Cage, T. (2004). Police performance: Do emotional skills matter? Paper submitted to the 19th Annual Meeting of the Society for Industrial and Organizational Psychologists, as part of the symposium, "Book 'em Danno!: New developments in law enforcement performance prediction."

Daus, C.S. & Jones, R.G. (2002). Emotional intelligence in everyday life. *Personnel Psychology*, Inc. 55.

Douglas, C., Frink, D.D., & Ferris, G.R. (2004). Emotional intelligence as a moderator of the relationship between conscientiousness and performance. *Journal of Leadership & Organizational Studies*, 10(3), 2–13.

Fisher, C.B. (2003). Goodness-of-fit ethic for informed consent to research involving adults with mental retardation and developmental disabilities. *Mental Retardation and Developmental Disabilities Research Reviews*, 9(1), 27–31.

Gabbott, M., Tsarenko, Y., & Mok, W.H. (2011). Emotional intelligence as a moderator of coping strategies and service outcomes in circumstances of service failure. *Journal of Service Research*, 14(2), 234–248.

Görgens-Ekermans, G. & Brand, T. (2012). Emotional intelligence as a moderator in the stress–burnout relationship: A questionnaire study on nurses. *Journal of Clinical Nursing*, 21(15–16), 2275–2285.

Grandey, A.A. (2003). When "the show must go on": Surface acting and deep acting as determinants of emotional exhaustion and peer-rated service delivery. *Academy of Management Journal*, 46(1), 86–96.

Grandy, G. (2008). Managing spoiled identities: dirty workers' struggles for a favourable sense of self. *Qualitative Research in Organizations and Management: An International Journal*, 3(3), 176–198.

Heskett, J.L., Sasser, W.E., & Schlesinger, L.A. (1997, March/April). The service profit chain. *Harvard Business Review*, 164–171.

Hobfoll, S.E. (1989). Conservation of resources: A new attempt at conceptualizing stress. *American Psychologist*, 44(3), 513.

Hochschild, A. (1983). *The Managed Heart: Commercialization of Human Feeling*. Berkeley, CA: University of California Press.

Houkes, I., Janssen, P.P., de Jonge, J., & Nijhuis, F.J. (2001). Specific relationships between work characteristics and intrinsic work motivation, burnout and turnover intention: A multi-sample analysis. *European Journal of Work and Organizational Psychology*, 10(1), 1–23.

Jackson, S.E. & Maslach, C. (1982). After-effects of job-related stress: Families as victims. *Journal of Organizational Behavior*, 3(1), 63–77.

Jordan, P.J., Ashkanasy, N.M., & Hartel, C.E. (2002). Emotional intelligence as a moderator of emotional and behavioral reactions to job insecurity. *Academy of Management Review*, 27(3), 361–372.

Keijsers, G.J., Schaufeli, W.B., Le Blanc, P.M., Zwerts, C., & Miranda, D.R. (1995). Performance and burnout in intensive care units. *Work & Stress*, 9(4), 513–527.

Kim, H.J. (2008). Hotel service providers' emotional labor: The antecedents and effects on burnout. *International Journal of Hospitality Management*, 27(2), 151–161.

Kim, H.J. & Agrusa, J. (2011). Hospitality service employees' coping styles: The role of emotional intelligence, two basic personality traits, and socio-demographic factors. *International Journal of Hospitality Management*, 30(3), 588–598.

King, M. & Gardner, D. (2006). Emotional intelligence and occupational stress among professional staff in New Zealand. *International Journal of Organizational Analysis*, 14(3), 186–203.

Lazaro, C., Shinn, M., & Robinson, P.E. (1984). Burnout, job performance, and job withdrawal behaviors. *Journal of Health and Human Resources Administration*, 213–234.

Lee, R.T. & Ashforth, B.E. (1996). A meta-analytic examination of the correlates of the three dimensions of job burnout. *Journal of Applied Psychology*, 81(2), 123.

Levine, P.A. (1997). *Waking the Tiger: Healing Trauma: The Innate Capacity to Transform Overwhelming Experiences*. Berkeley, CA: North Atlantic Books.

Lo, K. & Lamm, F. (2005). Occupational stress in the hospitality industry: An employment relations perspective. *New Zealand Journal of Employment Relations*, 30(1), 23–47.

Mann, S. (1997). Emotional labour in organizations. *Leadership & Organization Development Journal*, 18(1), 4–12.

Mattila, A.S. & Enz, C.A. (2002). The role of emotions in service encounters. *Journal of Service Research*, 4(4), 268–277.

Mayer, J.D. & Salovey, P. (1997). What is emotional intelligence? In P. Salovey & D.J. Sluyter (Eds.), *Emotional Development and Emotional Intelligence: Educational Implications*, 3, 310

Mayer, J.D., Salovey, P., Caruso, D.R., & Sitarenios, G. (2001). Emotional intelligence as a standard intelligence. *Emotion*, 1, 232–242.

Mikolajczak, M., Menil, C., & Luminet, O. (2007). Explaining the protective effect of trait emotional intelligence regarding occupational stress: Exploration of emotional labour processes. *Journal of Research in Personality*, 41(5), 1107–1117.

Mikolajczak, M. & Luminet, O. (2008). Trait emotional intelligence and the cognitive appraisal of stressful events: An exploratory study. *Personality and Individual Differences*, 44(7), 1445–1453.

Organ, D.W. (1988). A restatement of the satisfaction-performance hypothesis. *Journal of Management*, 14(4), 547–557.

Parker, P.A. & Kulik, J.A. (1995). Burnout, self-and supervisor-rated job performance, and absenteeism among nurses. *Journal of Behavioral Medicine*, 18(6), 581–599.

Parkinson, R.B. (1991). *The Tale of the Eloquent Peasant*. Oxford: Griffith Institute.

Pienaar, J. & Willemse, S.A. (2008). Burnout, engagement, coping and general health of service employees in the hospitality industry. *Tourism Management*, 29(6), 1053–1063.

Podsakoff, N.P., LePine, J.A., & LePine, M.A. (2007). Differential challenge stressor-hindrance stressor relationships with job attitudes, turnover intentions, turnover, and withdrawal behavior: a meta-analysis. *Journal of Applied Psychology*, 92(2), 438.

Prentice, C. & King, B.E. (2012). Emotional intelligence in a hierarchical relationship: Evidence for frontline service personnel. *Services Marketing Quarterly*, 33(1), 34–48.

Prentice, C., Chen, P.J., & King, B. (2013). Employee performance outcomes and burnout following the presentation-of-self in customer-service contexts. *International Journal of Hospitality Management*, 35, 225–236.

Pugliesi, K. (1999). The consequences of emotional labor: Effects on work stress, job satisfaction, and well-being. *Motivation and Emotion*, 23(2), 125–154.

Randall, M. & Scott, W.A. (1988). Burnout, job satisfaction and job performance. *Australian Psychologist*, 23(3), 335–347.

Rousseau, D.M. (1990). Normative beliefs in fund-raising organizations: Linking culture to organizational performance and individual responses. *Group & Organization Studies*, 15(4), 448–460.

Rousseau, D.M. (1995). The 'problem' of the psychological contract considered. *Journal of Organizational Behavior: The International Journal of Industrial, Occupational and Organizational Psychology and Behavior*, 19(S1), 665–671.

Rutter, D.R. & Fielding, P.J. (1988). Sources of occupational stress: An examination of British prison officers. *Work & Stress*, 2(4), 291–299.

Salami, S.O. (2007). Relationships of emotional intelligence and self-efficacy to work attitudes among secondary school teachers in southwestern Nigeria. *Pakistan Journal of Social Sciences*, 4(4), 540–547.

Shirom, A. (1989). Burnout in work organizations. In C.L. Cooper & I.T. Robertson (Eds.), *International Review of Industrial and Organizational Psychology 1989* (pp. 25–48). Oxford, England: John Wiley & Sons.

Singh, J. (2000). Performance productivity and quality of frontline employees in service organizations. *Journal of Marketing*, 64(2), 15–34.

Wright, T.A. & Hobfoll, S.E. (2004). Commitment, psychological well-being and job performance: An examination of conservation of resources (COR) theory and job burnout. *Journal of Business & Management*, 9(4).

Wu, X., Smith, T.G., & Rupprecht, C.E. (2011). From brain passage to cell adaptation: the road of human rabies vaccine development. *Expert Review of Vaccines*, 10(11), 1597–1608.

Zeithaml, V.A., Berry, L.L., & Parasuraman, A. (1996). The behavioral consequences of service quality. *Journal of Marketing*, 60(2), 31–46.

CHAPTER 7

EMOTIONAL INTELLIGENCE AND RELATIONAL ENCOUNTER MARKETING

7.1 Introduction

Last two chapters discuss how emotional intelligence can be integrated into internal marketing practice and how it affects employees' attitudes and behaviours including emotional labour performance. The discussion is focused on employee response over internal service encounter among co-workers. The ultimate goal of internal marketing is to prepare the right employees for the right customers — transferring internal service quality to external value and revenue generalisation. The value and revenue are generated through interactions and transactions over the service encounter in service-oriented businesses or selling encounter in the selling context. Although individuals generally undertake the process of need recognition, information search, evaluation of alternatives, purchase and post-purchase evaluation in their purchase and consumption, most researchers agree that it is the personal encounter between frontline employees and customers that depicts the moment of truth and determine selling success and potential of establishing ongoing relationship with customers.

The personal encounter, depending on the nature of business transactions (intangible services, goods) and types of encounter, can

133

refer to the personal interactions between frontline employees and customers in a face-to-face or remote manner (e.g. call centre). Employees can be service providers in pure service organisations, or sales personnel in companies that primarily produce and sell tangible goods. From relationship marketing perspective, either service providers or sales personnel, despite what they sell or serve, employees should be customer-oriented and relationship-focused. For convenience, both are referred to as frontline employees here. The behaviours and performance by frontline employees facilitate business transactions and buyer-seller relationships.

Employees' encounter behaviours are essentially a relationship marketing practice that is aimed for marketing success and company profitability. Consistent with this view, these overall behaviours from marketing perspective are referred to as *relational encounter marketing*. This marketing practice is a key component of relationship marketing as these encounter behaviours have a direct impact on customers' evaluation of the firm's service quality and their subsequent purchase and loyalty behaviours. Frontline employees are relationship marketers with intention to develop long-term relationships with selected clients (Crosby, Evans and Cowles, 1990). Their behaviours over each personal encounter with customers are hence referred to as *relational encounter behaviours.*

This chapter discusses how emotional intelligence can influence relational encounter marketing through examining the relationships between frontline employees' emotional intelligence and their relational encounter behaviours. The chapter begins with discussing the importance of relational encounter behaviours in the marketing practice, followed by identifying these behaviours from relationship marketing point of view. Subsequently, the relationship between relational encounter behaviours and employee performance is presented. This is an essential step to reinforce the importance of these behaviours in marketing practice since frontline employees' performance is closely related to customers' attitudes and behaviours towards the service providers and the firm. Finally, empirical studies and their findings are provided to reveal the impact of emotional intelligence on employees' relational encounter behaviours.

7.2 Relational Encounter Marketing

Darwin's theory of natural selection — "the fittest survive" resonates well with the marketing evolution. The marketing concept has evolved from hard sale aiming for a single successful transaction without considering customers' future patronage and retention to soft sale aiming for customers' satisfaction and nurturing relationships with them for long-term benefits. The latter approach is referred to as relationship marketing. This marketing approach is focused on the building of mutual trust within the customer/marketer dyad to create long-term relationships with selected customers, and has become a preferred approach that fits well in today's market situations and a firm's competition strategy.

The market situation has changed in the modern economy. The marketplace today in most industries is becoming increasingly competitive domestically and globally, which results in quality products and good services alone being inadequate for a company to gain a competitive advantage. The traditional mass markets involving integrated analysis, planning, and control of the 'marketing mix' variables (the 4Ps or 7Ps), to create exchange and satisfy both individual and organisational objectives, are becoming more and more fragmented. Today, more and more markets are maturing, and the market offerings have become less standardised.

Furthermore, the emergence of digitalisation and advanced technologies in creating computerised databases have enabled most firms to know more about their customers. Based on the information gathered on customers' patterns and preferences from the database, the firm is able to treat different customers accordingly. On the other hand, most customers are becoming increasingly sophisticated. In many situations, customers themselves demand personalised offerings. They no longer want to remain anonymous, and desire individualised treatment and customised service. For many categories of goods and services, customers seek superior ongoing relationships with their suppliers and providers for their own benefits. To align with the market situation and become the "fittest to survive", a firm's marketing approach is naturally evolved into a new paradigm — relationship marketing by focusing on establishing, developing and maintaining long-term relationships with customers. Relationship marketing, as opposed to traditional transaction-oriented marketing is an approach that takes into account customer needs and wants, in order to form relationships with customers across all stages of the buyer-seller relationship (Jolson, 1997).

A firm's relationship marketing strategies are primarily implemented by frontline employees over the personal encounter with customers. Frontline employees are situated in the boundary spanning position. They are the primary source of communication for customers and have traditionally been a vital link between the firm and its customers (Crosby, Evans and Cowles, 1990). These encounter behaviours play a key role in forming customers' perceptions of the firm's quality during their interactions over the encounter, and are important for firms employing them to gain a competitive advantage (Prentice, 2016; Weitz and Bradford, 1999). Their encounter behaviours are aimed for relationship building and viewed as function for developing long-term relationships with customers. The success of a firm's relationship marketing strategy depends to a large extent on the frontline employees' relational encounter behaviours, which become relational encounter marketing.

Researchers (Guenzi, Pardo and Georges, 2004; Wotruba, 1996) proposed and tested a direct link between a firm's relationship marketing approach and its service employees' relational encounter behaviours. Classifying customer orientation, adaptability, team selling, and organisational citizenship behaviours as relational behaviours, Guenzi, Pardo and Georges (2004). found a significant link between a firm's relationship strategy and most categories of its employees' relational behaviours over the personal encounter.

The concept of relational encounter marketing has been supported by several empirical studies (Crosby, Evans and Cowles, 1990; DeCormier and Jobber, 1993; MacIntosh, *et al.*, 1992). Crosby, Evans and Cowles (1990) view the role of frontline employees in the delivering and selling of services as "relationship manager". Using a sample of service frontline employees in the life insurance industry, the authors found that frontline employees' future sales opportunities depend on customer-perceived relationship quality, which comprises two components: trust and satisfaction. Specifically, frontline employees who are engaged in relational behaviours with focus on long-term relationships such as high contact intensity, mutual disclosure, and cooperative intentions had more favourable perceptions of relationship quality by the customers. Their results support the view that relationship-oriented service behaviours can build a strong buyer-provider bond. Another similar study was conducted by Boles, Brashear, Bellenger and Barksdale (2000). Using the three relational-characterised selling behaviours proposed by Crosby, Evans and Cowles (1990), Boles *et al.* investigated the relationships between employee encounter behaviours and job performance respectively and found a positive relationship between two of the three selected behaviours (interaction intensity and mutual disclosure) and sales performance.

Higher performing customer-contact employees tend to be those who focus on relationship building with customers. A study of North American financial service employees by MacIntosh, Anglin, Szymanski and Gentry (1992) found that those focusing on customers' trust achieved better performance. Their second study, using a sample of North American industrial frontline employees working for a distributor of agricultural products, found that those placing importance on relationship building instead of product benefits at early stages of the buyer-seller relationships were greater performers. On the basis of the findings in the two studies, the authors concluded that relationship building and developing trust at early stages of relationship between the buyer-seller or the customer-service provider are important to effective service performance.

DeCormier and Jobber (1993) incorporate personality knowledge and microskills strategies into the use of relationship marketing approach and arrived at similar results. Personality knowledge is referred to understanding the customer's personality style; and microskills are the means through which customer-contact employee can influence the customer. In their study, DeCormier and Jobber employed two groups. One group had training in the aspects of relationship selling method, and the second group had only product knowledge training. They also divided the relationship marketing process into four stages:

1) Introduction that involves rapport, respect and trust building
2) Qualification by means of gathering information to define the problem;
3) Presentation designed to summarise and finalise the finer details of the transaction; and
4) Closing with the focus on asking the prospect to respond to questions about alternatives.

The results indicated that the group who had relationship marketing training demonstrated higher selling effectiveness than the other group. However, the authors pointed out that personality knowledge training alone could not produce significant results without microskills being addressed. They also suggest that relationship marketing approach should incorporate the concepts of adaptability, customer orientation as well as satisfaction.

7.3 Relational Encounter Behaviours

The marketing literature to date has not provided a specific term to define frontline employees' behaviours as relational. Researchers have not reached consensus on what encounter behaviours can be classified as relational. However, since they are relationship-oriented, these behaviour must indicate, "a behavioural tendency exhibited by service representatives to cultivate the buyer-seller relationship and see to its maintenance and growth" (Crosby, Evans and Cowles, 1990, p. 71). According to Guenzi, Pardo and Georges (2004), the characteristics of relational encounter behaviours shall avoid revenue generating behaviours, but aim for buyer-seller relationship building directed toward customer retention. The authors also point out this type of behaviours entails customers' perception of trust in the service employees. Other researchers (Boles *et al.*, 2000) indicate that there is a link between such behaviours and the buyer (customer)–seller (provider) relationship quality, composing of trust and satisfaction. In other words, the relational behaviours should influence employees' performance evaluation by the firm and customers, and should have implications for building trust and customer satisfaction, which are commonly regarded as the antecedents of customer retention (Hennig-Thurau and Klee, 1997).

Consistent with the aforementioned views, the relational behaviours must contain three elements: interaction intensity, mutual disclosure and cooperative intentions. Employees must demonstrate competence and use of low-pressure selling tactics in their interactions with customers to characterise those as relational encounter behaviours. Keillor, Parker and Pettijohn (1999, 2000) originally identified four relational encounter behaviours: customer orientation, adaptability, service orientation and professionalism, and examined their relationships with employee performance satisfaction. At a later stage, they dropped professionalism due to its insignificant effect, and found significant relationships between the remaining three and employees' service performance. Guenzi, Pardo and Georges (2004) characterise customer orientation and adaptability as relational encounter behaviours in their key account management research, but these authors also incorporated team selling and organisational citizenship behaviours into the domain of relationship marketing behaviours.

A review of the relevant literature shows two most cited concepts that can be referred to as relational encounter behaviours: customer orientation and adaptability. Consistent with the above discussion and the characteristics that best describe the relational nature of employee encounter behaviours, customer orientation and adaptability are selected as the relational encounter behaviours for further discussion in the remainder of this chapter. The focus of the discussion is on how the two behaviours are conceptualised and how they influence relationship building with customers, which is reflected in employee performance and customer response.

7.4 Customer Orientation

As early as 1981, Dubinsky and Staples proposed and empirically tested customer orientation as a preferred selling technique which industry frontline employees would use to identify, and cater to the needs of their customers in order to achieve customer satisfaction.

In the following year, Saxe and Weitz (1982) designed a scale called selling orientation and customer orientation (SOCO) to measure customer orientation. They defined it as "the practice of the marketing concept at the level of the individual salesperson and customer" (Saxe and Weitz, 1982, p. 343). It includes the following characteristics: A desire to help customers make satisfactory purchase decisions; helping customers assess their needs; Offering products that will satisfy customers' needs; describing products (and services) adequately; avoiding descriptive or manipulative tactics; and avoiding the use of high pressure selling.

Although the original conceptualisation of customer orientation was based on industrial salesperson, and mainly applied to selling contexts (e.g. Saxe and Weitz, 1982), Kelley (1992) argued that customer orientation played a more important role for service employees in service firms than in other firms because of the intangibility, heterogeneity, perishability and inseparability of services, as the behaviour of service employees affects customers' perception of service quality (Bitner, Booms and Tetreault, 1990). Customer orientation has been frequently used in service settings (e.g. Brady and Cronin Jr., 2001; Brown *et al.*, 2002; Nguyen *et al.*, 2014; Korschun, Bhattacharya and Swain, 2014).

In service contexts, Brown *et al.* (2002) define customer orientation as service employees' tendency or predisposition to meet customer needs in an on-the-job context. They propose two dimensions in a service setting: the needs dimension and the enjoyment dimension. The needs dimension represents employees' beliefs about their ability to satisfy customer needs. This dimension is based on Saxe and Weitz's (1982) conceptualisation of customer orientation. The enjoyment dimension represents the degree to which interacting with and serving customers is motivated for an employee to serve customers by meeting their needs. Based on the requirements that must be met by service employees to satisfy consumers' needs during employee-consumer interaction processes, Hennig-Thurau and Thurau (2003) define customer orientation as the employee's behaviour in person-to-person interactions and suggest a three-dimensional conceptualisation: (1) An employee's customer-oriented skills; (2) His or her motivation to service customers; and (3) His or her self-perceived decision-making authority. The authors argue that only if all dimensions exist, an employee can behave in a fully customer-oriented sense. This was empirically evidenced by Hennig-Thurau (2004), and emphasised the non-compensatory trait of customer orientation dimensions.

The original scale for measuring customer orientation, SOCO, developed by Saxe and Weitz (1982) can be also applied to the service context. However, Daniel and Darby (1996) indicate that the selling-orientation component of the SOCO scale is not applicable in most service contexts. Employing two samples of patients and nurses, Daniel and Darby (1997) modified the original SOCO, and created a new customer orientation scale (COS) with intention to apply to service settings, by dropping the elements related to the selling component of the scale. The authors suggest that COS can be used to measure customer orientation of service providers for those working at non-sales types of service operations. Empirically, the research revealed that customer orientation explains a significant percentage of variance in service employees' service performance (Brown *et al.*, 2002; Prentice and King, 2011).

7.4.1 *Customer orientation and trust*

To classify it as a relational encounter behaviour that implicates relationship marketing practice, customer orientation must manifest its association with customer trust and have implications for establishing a long-term relationship with customers. Studies (Schultz and Good, 2000) show that frontline employees' customer orientation is associated with a long-term buyer-seller relationship. Establishing enduring relationships necessitates developing customer trust. Customer trust is related to customer-oriented behaviours. A study examining industrial frontline employees indicates that customer trust can be earned when the customer-contact employee is perceived as being dependable, honest, competent, likable (Swan, Trawick and Silva, 1985). Contact employees with these characteristics are likely to engage in customer-oriented behaviours.

Additional evidence comes from a meta-analysis of empirical studies of customer trust in the frontline employee. The study finds a positive relationship between benevolence (defined as fair, ethical, and cooperative) and customer trust (Swan, Bowers and Richardson 1999). The customer-oriented employee demonstrates characteristics of benevolence by keeping the customer's interests in mind, which undoubtedly would involve being fair and ethical. Finally, the ability to ask questions (strategic ability) and find creative solutions to customer problems (entrepreneurial ability) was positively related to customer trust in a broad sample of key account frontline employees (Sengupta, Krapfel and Pusateri, 2000). Williams (1998) suggests that customer orientation corresponds with the coordinative style of negotiation behaviour (Dabholkar, Johnston and Cathey, 1994) since it reflects non-opportunistic behaviour that stresses customer-focused solutions and mutual benefits. The coordinative style facilitates mutual trust and commitment, two prerequisites for relationship development (Morgan and Hunt, 1999). Empirically, Schultz and Good (2000) found that an employee's customer orientation was significantly related to long-term relationship orientation through the link with customer trust.

7.4.2 *Customer orientation and customer satisfaction*

According to Saxe and Weitz (1982), customer orientation is a relationship approach to long-term customer satisfaction rather than short-term objectives. They indicate that highly customer-oriented employees engage in behaviours aimed at increasing customer satisfaction, avoiding actions which sacrifice customer interest to increase the probability of making an immediate sale. In examining the determinants of selling effectiveness, Szymanski (1988) noted that customer orientation is a concept which puts emphasis on the customer's product or service acquirement, as indicated in the definition provided by Saxe and Weitz (1982) that customer orientation is referred to as "the degree to which frontline employees practice the marketing concept by trying to help customers make purchase decisions that will satisfy customer needs" (p. 344).

Szymanski argued that a successful deal was not only accounted for by the strategy focusing on a firm's offerings in terms of products or services, but also by the employee's customer-oriented presentations during the interactions with customers.

Goff *et al.* (2001) found that customer orientation explains significant amounts of the variance in customer satisfaction with the customer contact employee, which, in turn positively influences satisfaction with the firm, product and manufacturer. Their findings are an extension of previous studies in demonstrating that a customer contact employee's customer orientation influences consumer satisfaction with a physical product through the mediating constructs of satisfaction with the contact employee and the company. The finding conforms to that of Oliver and Swan's (1989) who found that customer satisfaction with the salesperson led to satisfaction with the company, which, in turn, leads to product satisfaction.

Drawing on a different perspective of four-dimensional customer orientation conceptualisation, Hennig-Thurau (2004), in a sample of nearly 1,000 consumers from book/CD/DVD retailers and travel agencies, find that service employee's customer orientation is strongly related to customer satisfaction, which also significantly impacted customers' emotional commitment to the service employee. Although the results show slight and non-significant relationship between customer orientation and customer retention in the case of travel agencies, the employee's ability in solving customer-related issues has influence on customer retention in the case of media retailers.

7.5 Adaptability

The concept of adaptability was identified four decades ago as a sales approach practiced by customer-contact employees. Adaptive selling is defined as, "altering of sales behaviours during a customer interaction or across customer interactions based on perceived information about the nature of the selling situation" (Weitz, Sujan and Sujan, 1986, p. 175). One of the conditions suitable for adaptive selling, according to Weitz, Sujan and Sujan (1986) is that "frontline employees encounter a wide variety of customers with different needs". Therefore, adaptability becomes one of the key advantages of personal selling as a marketing tool (McIntyre *et al.*, 2000).

Spiro, Perreault and Reynold (1977) noted that buyer and seller strategies are interdependent and may be modified based on actual encounter negotiations. Spiro and Weitz (1990) incorporate the following into the practice of adaptive behaviours over the service encounter: Recognition that different approaches are needed in different service encounter situations; confidence in the ability to use a variety of different marketing approaches; confidence in the ability to alter the marketing approach during the customer interaction; the collection of information to facilitate adaptability; and the actual use of different approaches (p. 61). Thus, adaptive behaviours may present the framework to adopt the appropriate marketing approach for each customer. Jolson (1997) believes that adaptability in service encounter is part of the relationship marketing process, as it entails a service employee's adjustment during service interactions based on his or her perceptions of customers' needs. This view was confirmed by Williams (1998), as adaptability has implication for the employee to delay immediate gratification and aim for long-term relationship.

Adaptability in service contexts is reflected in service employees being flexible and adapting their behaviours to meet the changing needs and requests of customers during service encounter interactions. Hartline and Ferrell (1996) define adaptability in service settings as "the ability of customer-contact service employees to adjust their behaviour to the interpersonal demands of the service encounter" (p.55). It can be described as a continuum ranging from conformity to service personalisation, in which employees must adapt to serve individual customers. The authors indicate that this definition is consistent with that of adaptive selling in the sales management literature proposed by Spiro and Weitz (1990). They are functionally equivalent, because both definitions include two common components: (1) the ability to adjust behaviour and (2) interpersonal situations (Hartline and Ferrell, 1996).

Bitner *et al.* (1990, 1994) indicated that service employees need to be able to recognise customers' various needs, and that inappropriate behaviours in the service encounter can result in dissatisfaction. Being adaptive is the ability of customer contact employees to adjust their behaviour to the interpersonal demands of the service encounter, and it can be described as a service personalisation, in which employees must adapt to serve individual customers (Hartline and Ferrell, 1996). Empirically, Humphrey and Ashforth (1994) provide evidence that employee adaptability is linked with customers' perceptions of the service encounter. Bitner (1990) and Bitner, Booms and Tetreault (1990) show that service employees' adaptability in meeting customers' special needs and requests leads to customer encounter satisfaction. Hartline and Ferrell (1996) attempted to establish a relationship between service employee's adaptability in service encounter and customer's perceived service quality. Their findings indicate that managers must increase employees' self-efficacy in order to increase customers' perceptions of service quality.

7.5.1 *Adaptability and satisfaction*

Adaptive behaviours over the service encounter is classified as relationship marketing approach due to its nature of adapting to the specific needs and beliefs of each customer and implementing a service presentation tailored to each customer. This has implication for customer satisfaction and retention. The customer-employee relationship is affected by the personal characteristics of both the individual customer and employee. These factors lead to the need for adaptability of interpersonal strategies by the employee. While frontline employees have the opportunity to match their behaviour to the specific customer and situation they encounter, the employee is able to evaluate each selling situation and adapt his or her behaviour to the appropriate expectations of the buyer. When customer needs are satisfied, the potential of establishing long-term relationship can be anticipated.

Although few studies have linked adaptability directly with customer satisfaction, the evidenced relationship between adaptability and employee performance has implications for customer satisfaction and customer retention. According to Schultz and Good (2002), when a customer is satisfied with the contact employee, a relationship between the customer and employee can be built and developed; once the relationship is established, the customer tends to purchase more from the employee who thus achieves marketing effectiveness. Empirically, this marketing approach has been evidenced to have direct impact on employee performance (e.g. Franke and Park, 2006; Park and Holloway, 2003; Spiro and Weitz, 1990). A meta-analysis conducted by Franke and Park in late 2006 reports that there is strong positive relationship between adaptability and self-rated performance.

7.5.2 *Adaptability and service performance*

Researchers advocate personal interaction as being the only promotional vehicle which allows its messages to be adapted and adjusted specifically to meet the communication needs of the receiver. Weitz (1978) was the first one to have posited the relationship between adaptability and performance. The author suggests that the employee must recognise and adapt to fit different customer communication styles. Weitz's model of the sales process suggests that the employee's success in influencing the customer is related to his or her ability to perform five activities. The five activities are: developing impressions, formulating strategies, transmitting messages, evaluating reactions, and making appropriate adjustments. The adjustments should be made throughout the whole service/selling process.

The communication styles of service representatives must also be adaptive to suit each individual customers. Some may prefer a direct style of communication whereas others may be more implicit. Self-oriented styles without taking customers' characters into account tend to entice complaints and negatively affect performance evaluations. Task-oriented communicators can be rigid and perceived to be inflexible. This type of communication results in negative evaluations against the employee. Those who adapt their communication style appropriately to interact with the customer are proved to be themost successful employees. An important aspect of practising effective adaptive encounter behaviours is indeed, in having knowledge of the customer's communication style (Weitz, 1978).

Previous findings regarding the relationship between employee adaptability and performance in the selling context are inconsistent. For example, Predmore and Bonnice (1994) found a strong relationship between adaptive selling and sales success. Weilbaker (1990), in two studies involving pharmaceutical frontline employees, found that adaptive selling was positively related to some measures of performance, but unrelated to others. Using a sample of Korean automobile frontline employees, Park and Holloway (2003) found that salesperson adaptability contributed to sales performance and job satisfaction. This study implies the possibility of applying adaptive approach in non-English speaking culture. However, high performers tend to be more adaptive during interactions with customers than low performers. The adaptability–performance relationship has been empirically supported in the service context (Anglin, Stolman and Gentry, 1990; Prentice and King, 2011).

Adaptability style is particularly relevant to the service encounter with customers. Being adaptive means the customer-contact employee tailors encounter behaviours to the customer, and makes rapid strategy adjustments based on the observed customers' reactions to the behaviours (Weitz, Sujan, and Sujan, 1986). In defining the adaptive style in service encounter, Spiro and Weitz (1990) indicate that adaptiveness indicates the concept of the recognition that different approaches are needed in different situations; confidence in the ability to use a variety of different approaches; and confidence in the ability to alter the approach during the customer interaction. Marks, Vorhies and Badovick (2001) interpret this as a customer-contact employee's beliefs of being adaptive in interaction with customers. The authors further indicate that, in some situations, these beliefs do influence behaviour and translate beliefs into performance. Being adaptive may imply less customers being offended; less angry customers may imply less complaints, which implies better job performed by the representative. A few studies have examined and confirmed the direct relationship between adaptability and performance in service context (Cullen *et al.*, 2014; Prentice and King, 2013, 2011; Burke, Pierce and Salas, 2006).

7.6 Emotional Intelligence and Relational Encounter Behaviours

The above discussion depicts customer orientation and adaptability as relational encounter behaviours that constitute relational encounter marketing as part of relationship marketing practice. Viewed as the practice of the marketing concept at the level of the individual marketing person and customer, customer orientation and adaptability are two marketing approaches consistent with the building of long lasting positive relationships between the customer and the company. In the service context, customer orientation and adaptability are referred to as service employees practicing the concept of long-term relationship building with customers through customer satisfaction. The two concepts require the employee to determine customers' needs and adapt him/herself to satisfying those needs better than its competitors. Implementing these behaviours requires employees' abilities to be customer-oriented and adaptive. Individual differences affect these abilities. For instance, a less empathetic employee may have difficulty adapting to diverse needs of different customers. An emotionally incompetent or vulnerable person may not be able to deal with an abusive customer. Given the intense interactions over the service encounter, particularly emotionally charged encounters, employees who demonstrate high levels of emotional intelligence should be better at implementing these relational encounter behaviours.

7.6.1 *Emotional intelligence and customer orientation*

In Goleman, Boyatzis and McKee's (2002) four-cluster emotional competence framework, the fourth cluster is referred to as the relationship management skills. Goleman indicated that this emotional competent ability is crucial for building relationships with others. Saarni (1999) proposed that emotional intelligence can be an essential component of social development and contributes to the quality of interpersonal relationships. Empirically, Schutte and colleagues (2001) investigate the relationships of emotional intelligence to seven aspects of interpersonal relations. The results show that emotional intelligence is significantly and positively related to empathic perspective, taking one dimension of empathy; furthermore, emotional intelligence is found to be significantly and positively associated with social skills.

Being customer-oriented entails the frontline employee's empathy in identifying customer's needs in order to satisfy them. The customer may have different needs in different encounters, and different customers may have different needs in the same encounter. The service representative needs to be empathetic enough to identify and understand the variety of the client's needs in order to deliver appropriate services to them. Sometimes the needs contain emotional elements caused by the customer's personal situations. The employee needs to understand the customer's emotions so to understand his or her demands. In some situations, the client can be over-demanding, which is beyond the empowerment of service representatives, hence the representative has to exhibit negotiation skills.

Williams (1998) suggests that customer orientation corresponds with the coordinative style of negotiation behavior since it reflects non-opportunistic behavior that stresses customer focused solutions and mutual benefits. The coordinative style facilitates mutual trust and commitment, two prerequisites for relationship development (Morgan and Hunt 1994). In a simulated context, Ogilvie and Carsky (2002) linked emotional intelligence with negotiation and stated that negotiators with high levels of emotional intelligence can achieve better outcomes in negotiations. The reasons lie in that negotiators who recognise emotional responses in themselves and others, will be better able to understand the reasons for responses, and thus adopt coordinative style to achieve better outcomes. Understanding how emotions change and transition is also important because the process of negotiation may involve both positive and negative emotions. In other words, emotional intelligence facilitates negotiation.

The empirical evidence on the relationship between emotional intelligence and customer orientation is limited in the relevant literature. However, Rozell, Pettijohn and Parker (2004), using salespeople from a nationwide company that specialises in medical devices as a sample, explored the relationship between emotional intelligence and salesperson's customer orientation. The results show a significantly positive relationship between the two concepts. But the authors recommend further research to be done in this area across a variety of industries as their sample only represents an educated group in a very specialised industry. Later in 2010, Pettijohn, Rozell and Newman examines the relationships between salespeople's emotional intelligence and customer-orientation levels in pharmaceutical marketing using 71 pharmaceutical salespeople working in the UK. The findings indicate that the salespeople's emotional intelligence levels are positively correlated with their customer-orientation scores.

Prentice and King (2011) conducted a study in a casino settling to understand the influence of emotional intelligence on frontline service employees' customer orientation. Emotional intelligence is operationalised into mood regulation, experiencing of emotions, utilisation of emotions, and appraisal of emotions. Their findings (Table 7.1) show that emotional intelligence in total explained 26 percent variance in customer orientation, $F(4, 147) = 25.60$, $p < 0.0005$. Among the four emotional intelligence dimensions, mood

Table 7.1 Relationship between emotional intelligence and customer orientation

	Coefficients		
Predictor	Beta	T	Sig.
Mood Regulation	0.55	5.86	0.00
Experiencing Emotions	−0.22	−2.66	0.01
Utilisation of Emotions	0.15	1.89	0.06
Appraisal of Emotions	0.16	1.89	0.06
df (4, 147)	$F = 25.60$	Sig. $F = 0.00$	R-squared $= 0.41$

regulation and social skills made statistically significant and unique contributions to customer orientation, with β = 0.55, t = 5.86, $p <$ 0.0005 for mood regulation, and β = –0.22, t = –2.66, $p <$ 0.01 for social skills.

7.6.2 *Emotional intelligence and adaptability*

No two customers are alike, and different customers are spurred to patronise a business out of different consumption/purchasing motives, each bringing with them another set of infinitely variable expectations and valuation criteria. Different customers have different expectations in their needs and wants. The same customer may have different experiential expectations and valuations criteria from one occasion to another (Macomber, 1999).

Creating a memorable and lasting impression in the customer's mind has positive impact on customers' satisfaction and intention to return. However, Weitz, Sujan and Sujan (1986) note that the effectiveness of using the adaptive approach is affected by the frontline employee's ability and skills to practice the technique. The ability and skills are gained from knowledge of the structure of encounter situations; encounter behaviours, and contingencies that link specific behaviours to situations. Therefore, gaining of knowledge is also an information collection process. During the process, Boorom, Goolsby and Ramsey (1998) found that the relational communication skills of attentiveness (willingness to listen and observe non-verbal cues), perceptiveness (ability to interpret observations of the customer), and responsiveness (knowing what message to present and when to present it) all were correlated with the ability to apply adaptive approaches towards the customer.

Emotional intelligence in the literature has constantly been linked with a person's communication skills. More emotionally intelligent people are said to succeed at communicating their ideas, goals and intentions in more convincing ways (Goleman, 1998). Perception is another dimension of emotional intelligence. In a high contact service context, as the interactions between employees and customers contain high emotional contents, being able to

Table 7.2   Relationship between emotional intelligence and employee adaptability

	Coefficients		
Predictor	Beta	*T*	Sig.
Mood Regulation	0.51	5.83	0.00
Social Skills	−0.03	−0.44	0.66
Utilisation of Emotions	−0.00	−0.03	0.97
Appraisal of Emotions	0.27	3.28	0.001
df (4, 147)	*F* = 25.60	Sig. *F* = 0.00	*R*-squared = 0.41

perceive the customer's emotions can facilitate the communication process, which leads to adaptive responsiveness.

In Prentice and King's (2011) study, which examined how casino employees' emotional intelligence affects their adaptability in dealing with gaming customers, the results (Table 7.2) indicate that emotional intelligence explained 48 percent variance in employee adaptability, $F(4, 147) = 33.47$, $p < 0.0005$. Examination of the coefficients results reveals that only mood regulation ($\beta = 0.51$, $t = 5.83$, $p < 0.0005$) and appraisal of emotions ($\beta = 0.27$, $t = 3.28$, $p < 0.001$) made statistically significant contributions to the adaptability measure. In addition to having been proposed and tested as a predictor, Chen and Jaramillo (2014) found that emotional intelligence with respect to regulation of emotions plays a moderator role in enhancing employees' adaptability in the selling context.

7.7 A Hierarchical Effect of Emotional Intelligence on Relational Encounter Marketing

Results of a meta-analysis conducted by Churchill *et al.* (1985) indicate that personal factors play an important role in determining job performance. Another meta-analysis (Frei and McDaniel, 1998) also found that personality traits are predictive of job performance. Although significant, only a small portion of variance in job performance was explained by personal factors (e.g. Boles *et al.*, 2000; Hurley, 1998). The weak relationship between personality traits and performance rating thus suggests the incorporation of surface trait, as proposed by Brown *et al.* (2002).

The term "surface traits" was first used by Allport (1961) to describe a collection of surface behaviours as opposed to specific focal behaviours such as specific service behaviours, for example, number of calls taken, number of smiles, response time (cf. Brown *et al.*, 2002). The surface behaviours are classified as traits, according to Mowen and Spears (1999). The reason is that they represent an enduring tendency to behave within particular situational contexts. Therefore, surface traits are contextual, representing "dispositions, inclinations or tendencies to behave in certain ways in certain situations and are more abstract than concrete behaviours" (Brown *et al.*, 2002, p. 112). Compared to surface traits, basic personality traits are enduring dispositions to behave across diverse situational contexts. The difference between surface traits and basic traits is that the former is context specific and results from the interaction of basic traits and the situational context.

According to Brown *et al.* (2002), the induction of surface traits lies in that personality traits may be too far from actual focal behaviours to be able to predict employee performance well, which is reflected in the observation that basic personality traits do not appear to account for a large proportion of variance in ratings of employee performance in a direct model. While surface traits, compared to basic personality traits, are regarded as being closer to the specific behaviours that form performance rating, and also believed to be able to increase the ultimate performance. Therefore, the surface traits surface between the time that the basic personality traits operate to influence the performance result and their direct impact on the performance, and the effect of personality trait exerted on performance is indirect and through surface traits. In other words, the surface traits mediate between personality factors and performance evaluation.

On the basis of the above argument about basic traits and surface traits, Brown *et al.* (2002) applied the concepts in a service setting, and proposed a hierarchical model of a surface trait that mediated between basic traits and service employees' service performance.

The model included personality factors as basic traits and customer orientation as a surface trait. The authors further proposed that the incorporation of the surface trait as a mediator would increase the variance of performance ratings over the model without mediation. The results of their study confirmed the hierarchical model and supported their propositions.

Based on the conceptualisation of service encounter, the concept of a surface trait can be considered as being equivalent to that of service encounter behaviours. Service encounter behaviours are referred to those activities a service employee conducts during a specific interaction with the client, which often form customers' perception of service quality and customer satisfaction (Farrell, Souchon and Durden, 2001; Winsted, 2000). Service quality and customer satisfaction have implications for the frontline employee's performance, because a satisfied customer tends to come back to purchase more products or services that will ultimately affect the employee's performance evaluation (Schultz and Good, 2000). The specific interaction is a situational context, and therefore, every service encounter is a context, and the behaviours over the encounter are contextual.

The foregoing discussion informs plausibility of a hierarchical relationship between the basic personality traits, service encounter behaviours and the service performance. Emotional intelligence can be such a basic personality trait. As indicated in previous literature, trait emotional intelligence is regarded as a personality trait and embedded in the personality framework, (Petrides and Furnham, 2001). The relational encounter behaviour are referred to as surface traits. Emotional intelligence influence relational encounter behaviours which have direct impacts on employee service performance. These relationships can be functioned hierarchically.

Customer orientation is referred to as "the ability of the service provider to adjust to his or her service to take account of the circumstances of the customer" (Daniel and Darby, 1997 p. 133), and adaptability as "the ability of contact employees to adjust their behaviour to the interpersonal demands of the service encounter" (Hartline and Ferrell, 1996, p. 55). These two relational service encounter behaviours can be referred to as surface traits. The relevant literature also confirm this assertion and shows that customer orientation and adaptability have been tested as surface traits mediating between basic traits and the actual performance outcome (McIntyre *et al.*, 2000). McIntyre *et al.* found that a person's cognitive style, such as information intake by intuiting and information processing by thinking predicted his or her adaptability and customer orientation, which exerted influence on the self-perceived selling performance.

Prentice and King (2012) tested a hierarchical relationship between emotional intelligence, customer orientation and adaptability as two separate surface traits and the performance of service employees. The hierarchical relationship can be referred to as a mediation or a mediational model. It takes place when a variable surfaces between the time the independent variables operate to influence the dependent variable and their impact on the dependent variable (Sekaran, 1984). The variable is named *mediator* or *intervening variable.* According to Sekaran, it acts as a function of the independent variable, helping to conceptualise and explain the influence of the independent variable(s) on the dependent variable. In Brown *et al.*'s (2002) hierarchical model, the surface trait surfaces as a function of the basic personality traits influencing the performance outcome. Therefore, the surface traits can be referred to as mediators, and the basic personality traits as independent variables. Based on this conceptualisation, customer orientation and adaptability can be posited to be the mediators in the mediational model of the current study where emotional intelligence is the independent variable, and the service performance is the dependent variable.

The four step approach was deployed to examine this hierarchical relationship. The first step tests the relationship between emotional intelligence and service performance without including the mediator. The results showed that emotional intelligence explained 35 percent variance in the performance outcome, $p < 0.0005$. The second step tests the relationship between emotional intelligence and customer orientation. The former explains 41.10 percent of variance, ($p < 0.0005$). The third step investigates if customer orientation scale as the presumed mediator explained variance in service performance (the dependent variable). This condition was tested by a simple regression analysis, with the total score of customer orientation scale used in the regression equation. The results indicated that customer orientation made a statistically significant contribution to the dependent variable. The beta value for customer orientation was 0.43 ($p < 0.0005$). The fourth step assesses if the effect of emotional intelligence on the service performance became zero or is reduced after controlling for customer orientation. Review of the results shows that the variance explained by the whole model reduced from 36.3 percent to 18 percent. The results indicate that customer orientation did mediate between emotional intelligence and employee service performance; however, the mediation effects was not reduced to zero. Therefore, it appears that the indirect effects were partially mediated by customer orientation indicating a partial mediation (Table 7.3).

When testing adaptability as the mediator between emotional intelligence and the service performance, the results indicated that emotional intelligence explained 48 percent variance in the adaptability scale, $p < 0.0005$. Adaptability as the presumed mediator explains variance (0.58, $t = 8.73$, $p < 0.0005$) in the service performance (the dependent variable). This finding indicates that adaptability did make a statistically significant contribution to the service performance. In determining if the effect of trait EI on the service performance became zero or was reduced after controlling

Table 7.3 Hierarchical regression analysis for customer orientation scale as mediator between emotional intelligence and service performance

IV	Beta	Mediator	Beta	DV	DE	IE
Mood regulation	0.55				0.34***	0.26*
Appraisal of emotions	−0.22	COS	0.17	SP	−0.10	−0.04
Social skills	0.14				−0.09	−0.07
Utilisation of emotions	0.16				0.41***	0.38***

Notes: IV = independent variables, DV = dependent variable, DE = direct effect of independent variables on the dependent variable, IE = indirect effect after the inclusion of COS as a control, COS = customer orientation scale, SP = service performance. *$p < 0.05$, **$p < 0.01$, ***$p < 0.001$.

Table 7.4 Hierarchical regression analysis for adaptability scale as mediator between Trait EI and the service performance

IV	Beta	Mediator	Beta	DV	DE	IE
Mood regulation	0.51				0.34***	0.16
Appraisal of emotions	–0.03				–0.10	–0.06
Social skills	0.00	ADAPT	0.58	SP	–0.09	–0.09
Utilisation of emotions	0.27				0.41***	0.31**

Notes: IV = independent variables, DV = dependent variable, DE = direct effect of independent variables on the dependent variable, IE = indirect effect after the inclusion of COS as a control, ADAPT = adaptability scale, SP = service performance. $*p < 0.05$, $**p < 0.01$, $***p < 0.001$.

for the effect of adaptability, a hierarchical regression analysis was conducted, with adaptability entered at Step 1, emotional intelligence measure entered at Step 2, and with the service performance serving as the dependent variable. The results indicate that the change of R-squared value was 0.08, $p < 0.005$. Again, the indirect effects did not become zero, indicating that adaptability partially mediated between trait EI and the service performance (Table 7.4).

These findings indicate that emotional intelligence indeed has both significant direct and indirect effects on employee service performance. Possessing a high level of emotional intelligence is necessary, but not sufficient to predict performance. Employees must be able to utilise emotional skills to manage service encounter behaviours (customer orientation and adaptability), which in turn leads to greater performance. Including these relational encounter behaviours enhances performance evaluation. Therefore, emotional intelligence plays a significant role in service encounter marketing by exerting hierarchical effects on encounter behaviours and service employee performance. Service performance influences customers' evaluation of the company's service quality, future patronage and loyalty.

7.8 Summary

This chapter moves beyond internal service encounter and focuses on interactions between employees and customers and the relationship behaviours performed by customer-contact employees. These behaviours are referred to as relational encounter marketing as they have implications for optimal marketing outcomes. Customer orientation and adaptability are the most cited relationship behaviours and selected as relational encounter behaviours in this chapter. This chapter explains how emotional intelligence can be incorporated into the relational encounter marketing practice through influencing employees' encounter behaviours. A direct relationship between emotional intelligence and the encounter behaviour is demonstrated to understand the link between emotional intelligence and relationship marketing. The chapter also embarks on presenting a relatively new concept surface traits to reveal the hierarchical effect of emotional intelligence on relational encounter marketing outcome manifested in employees' customer-oriented behaviours and performance.

References

Allport, G.W. (1961). *Pattern and Growth in Personality.* New York: Halt, Rinehart, and Winston.

Anglin K.A., Stolman, J.J., & Gentry, J.W. (1990). The congruence of manager perception of salesperson performance and knowledge-based measures of adaptive selling. *Journal of Personal Selling and Sales Management,* 10(4), 81–90.

Bitner, M.J. (1990). Evaluating service encounters: The effects of physical surroundings and employee responses. *Journal of Marketing,* 54(2), 69–82.

Bitner, M.J., Booms, B.H., & Tetreault, M.S. (1990). The service encounter: Diagnosing favorable and unfavorable incidents. *Journal of Marketing,* 54(1), 71–84.

Bitner, M.J., Booms, B.H., & Mohr, L.A. (1994). Critical service encounters: The employee's viewpoint. *Journal of Marketing,* 58(4), 95–106.

Boles, J.S., Brashear, T., Bellenger, D., & Barksdale Jr., H. (2000). Relationship selling behaviours: Antecedents and relationship with performance. *Journal of Business and Industrial Marketing,* 15(2/3), 141–153.

Boorom, M.L., Goolsby, J.R., & Ramsey, R.P. (1998). Relational communication traits and their effect on adaptiveness and sales performance. *Journal of the Academy of Marketing Science,* 26, 16–30.

Brady, M.K. & Cronin Jr., J.J. (2001). Customer orientation: Effects on customer service perceptions and outcome behaviors. *Journal of Service Research*, 3(3), 241–251.

Brady, M.K. & Cronin Jr., J.J. (2001b). Some new thoughts on conceptualizing perceived service quality: A hierarchical approach. *Journal of Marketing*, 65(3), 34–49.

Brown, T.J., Mowen, J.C., Donavan, D.T., & Licata, J.W. (2002). The customer orientation of service workers: Personality trait effects on self-and supervisor performance ratings. *Journal of Marketing Research*, 39(1), 110–119.

Burke, C.S., Pierce, L.G., & Salas, E. (Eds.). (2006). Understanding adaptability: A prerequisite for effective performance within complex environments. In *Advances in Human Performance and Cognitive Engineering Research*, Vol. 6. Emerald Group Publishing Limited.

Chen, C.C. & Jaramillo, F. (2014). The double-edged effects of emotional intelligence on the adaptive selling–salesperson-owned loyalty relationship. *Journal of Personal Selling & Sales Management*, 34(1), 33–50.

Churchill Jr., G.A., Ford, N.M., Hartley, S.W., & Walker Jr., O.C. (1985). The determinants of salesperson performance: A meta-analysis. *Journal of Marketing Research* (JMR), 22(2), 103–118.

Crosby, L.A., Evans, K.A., & Cowles, D. (1990). Relationship quality in services selling: An interpersonal influence perspective. *Journal of Marketing*, 54(3), 68–81.

Cullen, K.L., Edwards, B.D., Casper, W.C., & Gue, K.R. (2014). Employees' adaptability and perceptions of change-related uncertainty: Implications for perceived organizational support, job satisfaction, and performance. *Journal of Business and Psychology*, 29(2), 269–280.

Dabholkar, P.A., Johnston, W.J., & Cathey, A.S. (1994). The dynamics of long-term business-to-business exchange relationships. *Journal of the Academy of Marketing Science*, 22(2), 130–145.

Daniel, K. & Darby, D.N. (1997). A dual perspective of customer orientation: A modification, extension and application of the SOCO scale. *International Journal of Service Industry Management*, 8(2), 131–147

DeCormier, R.A. & Jobber, D. (1993). The counselor selling method: Concepts and constructs. *Journal of Personal Selling and Sales Management*, 13(4), 39–60.

Dubinsky, A.J. & Staples, W.A. (1981). Are industrial salespeople buyer oriented? *Journal of Purchasing and Materials Management*, 17(3), 12–19.

Farrell, A.M., Souchon, A.L., & Durden, G.R. (2001). Service encounter conceptualisation: Employees 'service behaviours and customers' service quality perceptions. *Journal of Marketing Management*, 17(5–6), 577–593.

Franke, G.R. & Park J-E. (2006). Salesperson adaptive selling behaviour and customer orientation: A meta-analysis. *Journal of Marketing Research*, 43(4), 693–702.

Frei, R.L. & McDaniel, M.A. (1998). Validity of customer service measures in personnel selection: A review of criterion and construct evidence. *Human Performance*, 11(1), 26–42.

Goff, B.G., Boles, J.S., Bellenger, D.N., & Stojack, C. (2001). The influence of salesperson selling behaviours on customer satisfaction with products. *Journal of Retailing*, 73(2), 171–184.

Goleman, D. (1998). *Working with Emotional Intelligence.* New York: Bantam Books.

Goleman, D., Boyatzis, R., & McKee, A. (2002). *Primal Leadership: Realizing the Power of Emotional Intelligence.* Boston, MA: Harvard Business School Publishing.

Guenzi, P., Pardo, C., & Georges, L. (2007). Relational selling strategy and key account managers' relational behaviors: An explanatory study. *Industrial Marketing Management*, 36(1), 121–133.

Hartline, M.D. & Ferrell, O.C. (1996). The management of customer-contact service employees: An empirical investigation. *Journal of Marketing*, 60 (October), 52–70

Hennig-Thurau, T. (2004). Customer orientation of service employees: Its impact on customer satisfaction, commitment, and retention. *International Journal of Service Industry Management*, 15(5), 460–478.

Hennig-Thurau, T. & Klee, A. (1997). The impact of customer satisfaction & relationship quality on customer retention: A critical reassessment and model development. *Psychology and Marketing*, 14(8), 737.

Hennig-Thurau, T. & Thurau, C. (2003). Customer orientation of service employees — toward a conceptual framework of a key relationship marketing construct. *Journal of Relationship Marketing*, 2(1), 1–32.

Humphrey, R.H. & Ashforth, B.E. (1994). Cognitive scripts and prototypes in service encounters. *Advances in Services Marketing and Management*, 3(C), 175–199.

Hurley, R.F. (1998). A customer service behaviour in retail settings: A study of the effect of service provider personality. *Journal of the Academy of Marketing Sciences*, 26(2), 115–227.

Jolson, M.A. (1997). Broadening the scope of relationship selling. *Journal of Personal Selling and Sales Management*, 17(4), 75–88.

Keillor, B.D., Parker, R.S., & Pettijohn, C.E. (1999). Sales force performance satisfaction and aspect of relational selling: Implications for sales managers. *Journal of Marketing,* 7(1), Winter, 101–115.

Keillor, B.D., Parker, R.S., & Pettijohn, C.E. (2000). Relationship-oriented characteristics and individual salesperson performance. *Journal of Business and Industrial Marketing,* 15(1), 7–22.

Kelly, S.W. (1992). Developing customer orientation among service employees. *Journal of the Academy of Marketing Services,* 20(1), 27–36.

Korschun, D., Bhattacharya, C.B., & Swain, S.D. (2014). Corporate social responsibility, customer orientation, and the job performance of frontline employees. *Journal of Marketing,* 78(3), 20–37.

MacIntosh, G., Anglin, K.A., Szymanski, D.M., & Gentry, J.W. (1992), Relationship development in selling: A cognitive analysis. *Journal of Personal Selling & Sales Management,* 12(4), 23–34.

Macomber, D.M. (1999). *Target guest entertainment experience delivery system.* Retrieved May 30, 1999, from www.urbino.net.

Marks, R., Vorhies, D.W., & Badovick, G.J. (2001). A psychometric evaluation of the ADAPTS scale: A critique and recommendations. *Journal of Personal Selling and Sales Management,* 16(4), 53–65.

McIntyre, R.P., Claxton, R.P., Anselmi, K., & Wheatley, E.W. (2000). Cognitive style as an antecedent to adaptiveness, customer orientation, and self-perceived selling performance. *Journal of Business and Psychology,* 15(2), 179–196.

Morgan, R.M. & Hunt, S. (1999). Relationship-based competitive advantage: The role of relationship marketing in marketing strategy. *Journal of Business Research,* 46(3), 281–290.

Moven, J.C. & Spears, N. (1999). A hierarchical model approach to understanding compulsive buying among college students. *Journal of Consumer Psychology,* 8(4), 407–430.

Nguyen, H., Groth, M., Walsh, G., & Hennig-Thurau, T. (2014). The impact of service scripts on customer citizenship behavior and the moderating role of employee customer orientation. *Psychology & Marketing,* 31(12), 1096–1109.

Ogilvie, J.R. & Carsky, M.L. (2002). Building emotional intelligence in negotiation. *International Journal of Conflict Management,* 13(4), 381–400.

Oliver, R.L. & Swan, J.E. (1989). Consumer perceptions of interpersonal equity and satisfaction in transactions: A field survey approach. *Journal of Marketing,* 53(2), 21–35.

Park, J.E. & Holloway, B.B. (2003). Adaptive selling behaviour revisited: An empirical examination of learning orientation, sales performance and job satisfaction. *Journal of Personal Selling and Sales Management*, 23(3), 239–251.

Petrides, K.V. & Furnham, A. (2001). Trait emotional intelligence: Psychometric investigation with reference to established trait taxonomies. *European Journal of Personality*, 15(6), 425–448.

Pettijohn, C.E., Rozell, E.J., & Newman, A. (2010). The relationship between emotional intelligence and customer orientation for pharmaceutical salespeople: A UK perspective. *International Journal of Pharmaceutical and Healthcare Marketing*, 4(1), 21–39.

Predmore, C.E. & Bonnice, J.G. (1994). Sales success as predicted by a process measure of adaptability. *Journal of Personal Selling and Sales Management*, 14(4), 55–66.

Prentice, C. (2016). Leveraging employee emotional intelligence in casino profitability. *Journal of Retailing and Consumer Services*, 33(c), 127–134.

Prentice, C. & King, B. (2011). The influence of emotional intelligence on the service performance of casino frontline employees. *Tourism and Hospitality Research*, 11(1), 49–66.

Prentice, C. & King, B.E. (2012). Emotional intelligence in a hierarchical relationship: Evidence for frontline service personnel. *Services Marketing Quarterly*, 33(1), 34–48.

Prentice, C. & King, B.E. (2013). Impacts of personality, emotional intelligence and adaptiveness on service performance of casino hosts: A hierarchical approach. *Journal of Business Research*, 66(9), 1637–1643.

Rozell, E.J., Pettijohn, C.E., & Parker, R.S. (2004). Customer-oriented selling: Exploring the roles of emotional intelligence and organizational commitment. *Psychology and Marketing*, 21(6), 405–424.

Saarni, C. (1999). *The Development of Emotional Competence*. New York: Guilford Press.

Saxe, R. & Weitz, B.A. (1982). The SOCO scale: A measure of the customer orientation of sales people. *Journal of Marketing Research*, 19(14), 343–351.

Schultz, D.E. & Bailey, S. (2000). Customer/brand loyalty in an interactive marketplace. *Journal of Advertising Research*, 40(3), 41–52.

Schultz, R.J. & Good, D.J. (2000). Impact of the consideration of future sales consequences and cusomer-oriented selling on long-term buyer-seller relationships. *Journal of Business & Industrial Marketing*, 15(4), 200–215.

Schutte, N.S., Malouff, J.M., Bobik, C., Coston, T.D., Greeson, C., Jedlicka, C., & Wendorf, G. (2001). Emotional intelligence and interpersonal relations. *The Journal of Social Psychology*, 141(4), 523–36.

Sekaran, U. (1984). *Research Methods for Business.* (2nd edition). New York: John Wiley & Sons, Inc.

Sengupta, S., Krapfel, R.E., & Pusateri, M.A. (2000). An empirical investigation of key account salesperson effectiveness. *Journal of Personal Selling and Sales Management,* 20(4), 253–262.

Spiro, R., Perreault, W., & Reynolds, F. (1977). The personal selling process: A critical review and model. *Industrial Marketing Management,* 5(6), 351–364.

Spiro, R.L. & Weitz, B.A. (1990). Adaptive selling: Conceptualization, measurement, and nomological validity. *Journal of Marketing Research,* 27(1), 61–69.

Swan, J.E., Bowers, M.R., & Richardson, L.D. (1999). Customer trust in the salesperson: An integrative review and meta-analysis of the empirical literature. *Journal of Business Research,* 44(22), 93–107.

Swan, J.E., Trawick, I.F., & Silva, D.W. (1985). How industrial salespeople gain customer trust. *Industrial Marketing Management,* 14(3), 203–211.

Szymanski, D.M. (1988). Determinants of selling effectiveness: The importance of declarative knowledge to the personal selling concept. *Journal of Marketing,* 52(1), 64–77.

Weitz, B.A. (1978). The relationship between salesperson performance and understanding of customer decision making. *Journal of Marketing Research,* 15(4), 501–516.

Weitz, B.A. & Bradford, K.D. (1999). Personal selling and sales management: A relationship marketing perspective. *Journal of the Academy of Marketing Science,* 27(2), 241–254.

Weitz, B.A., Sujan, H., & Sujan, M. (1986). Knowledge, motivation, and adaptive behaviour: A framework for improving selling effectiveness. *Journal of Marketing,* 50(4), 174–191.

Weilbaker, D.C. (1990). The identification of selling abilities needed for missionary type sales. *Journal of Personal Selling & Sales Management,* 10(3), 43–58.

Williams, M.R. (1998). The influence of salesperson's customer orientation on buyer-seller relationship development. *Journal of Business and Industrial Marketing,* 13(3), 271–287.

Winsted, K.F. (2000). Service behaviours that lead to satisfied customers. *European Journal of Marketing,* 34(3/4), 399–417.

Wortuba, R.R. (1996). The transformation of industrial selling: Causes and consequences. *Industrial Marketing Management,* 25(12), 327–338.

CHAPTER 8

EMOTIONAL INTELLIGENCE AND EXTERNAL MARKETING

8.1 Introduction

The preceding chapter 7 discusses how employees' emotional intelligence can affect their job attitudes and behaviours. The discussion includes how emotional intelligence can be positioned as an internal marketing tool to manage co-worker relationships, employee job satisfaction, commitment, retention and performance. On the basis of the service profit chain model proposed by Heskett and Sasser (2010), these employees' job attitudes and behaviours are related to those of customers, which leads to business profitability. The internal marketing is focused on internal service encounter among co-workers, supervisors and management. Employees are viewed as internal customers. The encounter, like any other interpersonal encounters, is emotionally loaded. The goal of internal marketing is to ensure an optimal level of internal service quality with the organisation to manage co-worker relationships and employee productivity.

Emotional intelligence is proposed as an extra internal marketing tool from personal competence perspective to achieve internal marketing objectives. Employee commitment and loyalty can also be influenced by their emotional skills as emotional intelligent employees are able to manage job-related stress resulted from conundrums associated with the boundary spinning position. Employees with a high level of emotional intelligence may view the stress as a challenge and a source of gratification. This logic is confirmed with empirical evidence as presented in previous chapters.

Admittedly, employees with a higher level of emotional intelligence tend to provide better service (Bardzil and Slaski, 2003), and perform better over the service encounter (Prentice and King, 2011; Prentice, Chen and King, 2013). Service performance by frontline employees often forms customer perception of service quality which influences customer satisfaction and loyalty (Liao and Chuang, 2004; Shi, Prentice and He, 2014). On this basis, emotional intelligence is positioned as a relational encounter marketing tool to influence employees' relational encounter behaviours.

Employees' attitudes and behaviours resulting from internal and relational encounter marketing practices are not directly related to customers' response, but through the medium of the moment of truth or service encounter between employees and customers. Their job attitudes and behaviours from internal marketing can be reflected in their attitudes and behaviours towards customers, which form part of customers' perception of the firm's quality and affect customer responses towards these employees and the firm. For example, employee job satisfaction and commitment serve as impetus to manage the dyadic relationships with customers or satisfy their needs and wants. Employee loyalty indicates that the firm likely implements appropriate internal marketing and instils pleasant service culture. High employee turnover indicates problematic internal management and employee dissatisfaction.

Given the emotional contents loaded in the interpersonal service encounter as previously discussed, it is imperative for frontline employees to possess emotional competence and intelligence to understand and manage their own emotions and emotions of customers so they can achieve positive outcomes on both counts. Employees' emotional intelligence affects customers' responses through its influence on employees' attitudes and behaviours. On this basis, this chapter contends that employee emotional intelligence can have a direct impact on customers' attitudes and behaviours.

8.2 Emotional Intelligence and Customer Response

Besides recognising and managing one's own emotions, emotionally intelligent individuals are able to understand, manage, and regulate others' emotions, which likely influences their mood, attitudes, and behaviours (Prentice, 2016). Intuitively one would prefer to deal with emotionally intelligent individuals as they are more empathetic and understanding. Understanding one's own emotions implicates understanding others' emotions, including positive and negative ones. This understanding prompts appropriate behaviours in interactions. Similarly in business transactions over a service encounter, customers would expect employees they are in contact with to be more empathetic and person-oriented rather than business-focused. Wong (2004) reported that customers' emotional satisfaction was positively associated with service quality assessment, relationship quality, and customer loyalty.

In some service encounters such as holiday resorts or psychological counselling, customers enter the transaction for a pleasant service experience. These services involve interactions between customers and employees that are characterised by intimacy, the exchange of content-rich information, extensive interaction times, and, in some cases, high emotional load (Prentice, 2013). The interactions with employees form an essential part of their experience. Through interpersonal interactions, customers seek cues and emotional expression in employees to assess quality of the service. Employees' emotional intelligent expressions affect customers' reactions in an unconscious manner according to emotional contagion phenomenon. Emotional contagion refers to individuals' proneness to duplicate or synchronise "facial expressions, vocalizations, postures, and movements with those of another person and, consequently, to converge emotionally" (Hatfield, Cacioppo and Rapson, 1994, p. 4). When one person in an interaction expresses positive (or negative) feelings, the other person tends to experience a corresponding positive (or negative) affective state (Hatfield *et al.*, 1994).

Giardini and Frese (2008) draw upon emotional contagion theory and argue for existence of a reciprocal relationship between employee and customer positive affect over the service encounter.

Other researchers (Pugh, 2001; Tsai and Huang, 2002) have found a link between the employee's display of positive emotions (e.g. smiling or a friendly greeting) and the customer's positive affective state. The flow of affective information can channel either from employees to the customers or from customers to employees. Employees' emotional expressions trigger similar response from customers. Positive emotions trigger positive affective state of the customer. Customers' emotional feedback leads to the synchronisation of the display of feelings and to the convergence of affective states of employee and customer. For example, empathy manifested in employees can be interpreted as being kind and caring by customers. Naturally customers would respond with similar reactions based on the norm of reciprocity (Gouldner, 1960).

Some customers intentionally and spontaneously enter the service encounter to interact with employees and other customers for social purposes. Working professionals may seek to get away from their hectic work or business life; whereas single seniors may seek ways to escape loneliness and boredom. Customer emotions in these service encounters on the one hand form expectations from the service provider, and on the other hand provide employees with useful information about their needs and wants (Mattila and Enz, 2002). This requires contact employees' emotional abilities in order to understand and manage those emotions. Each individual's abilities may vary substantially in assessing and understanding customers' emotional needs and to strive for relationship building with them. Employees with a high level of emotional intelligence are able to minimise emotional issues derived from interpersonal interactions to create and maintain an appropriate service climate suitable to the context. To a certain degree, employee emotional intelligence constitutes customers' service experience. The four branches of emotional intelligence conceptualised by Mayer *et al.* (2003) explain its impact on customers' attitudes and behaviours.

8.2.1 *Perceive emotions and customer response*

Despite the culture difference and geographic diversity, human emotions are expressed in similar ways and function as a form of social communication. These emotions are recognisable either through facial expressions, voice or body movements. Most emotions are manifested in human facial expressions. The ability to accurately perceive emotions in others' face, voice or body language is an essential starting point for communication and exchanges both within social and commercial contexts. A customer would prefer to converse with an employee who understands his or her needs and emotions, and is social and enthusiastic about communicating with the customer. Since the interaction involves two parties, an employee would similarly prefer to deal with emotionally intelligent customers. Here is a personal experience:

> *One Friday afternoon before business closing hours, I rang up a call centre to enquire about a bank statement. The call centre representative picked up the call and conversed with me unenthusiastically. I could tell from his voice that he was tired and probably fed up with answering phone calls especially at the end of a Friday. Instead of blaming his attitude, I initiated an apology that I called so late and I understand he must be tired and eager to go home to enjoy regular happy Friday hours. There was suddenly a change in the representative's voice and he expressed appreciation of my understanding. In the end, we had a very pleasant conversation and had the business transaction done efficiently. We probably could become friends if we wanted to.*

8.2.2 *Using emotions and customer response*

Emotions can be used to facilitate thoughts and behaviours. This branch depicts emotional intelligent individuals as able to use emotions to guide the cognitive system in promoting or prioritising thinking. In the case of service encounter, negative emotions exhibited by customers could be derived from employees' inappropriate attitudes, behaviours or services; or from customers' own behaviours or situations. These negative emotions guide the customer contact employee to modulate their attitudes and behaviours to help soothe agitated customers and look for a solution to resolve the unhappy encounter. Employees' effort to convert customers' negative emotions could result in surprising outcomes as customers would appreciate employees' endeavour and reciprocate with positive attitudes and purchase. A customer's positive moods or emotions may indicate that he or she has had pleasant interactions with the employee and is happy with the business transaction. Employees could utilise the customer's emotions and nurture relationship with the customer for future purchases and loyalty behaviours, including being the business's advocate and initiating influential referrals.

8.2.3 *Understanding emotions and customer response*

Emotions convey messages. Each emotion conveys a pattern of possible messages, and actions associated with those messages. When someone is upset or angry, it indicates that this person is unhappy with the situation or has unsatisfied demand. Anger indicates a potential or possibility to attack or harm others. This anger may be triggered by unfair treatment, which may lead to attacking, retribution and revenge-seeking, or withdrawal to seek peace, depending on the specific situation. Fear indicates a tendency to avoid or escape. Happiness usually indicates a desire to join or reunite with other people. Understanding emotional implications and the possible actions associated with emotions is a very important skill in the service encounter. When identifying a customer's emotional messages and potential actions, an emotionally intelligent employee is able to comprehend the meaning of emotions, has the capacity to reason with those emotional messages and play for appropriate actions.

8.2.4 *Managing emotions and customer response*

Emotions can be managed. A person can perceive, understand and utilise emotions but not necessarily manage them. To manage emotions, the person must understand the information or messages conveyed in the emotions, and most importantly wants to work on the emotions. Some individuals can manage their own emotions but not others', or vice versa. Managing one's own negative emotions can limit negative consequences triggered by negativity and impulsiveness, for instance, through utilising positive emotions to achieve greater outcomes or performance. Managing emotions of others can smooth interactions. In the case of service encounter between employees and customers, the latter can be unreasonably demanding and emotional. Employees are inevitably in contact with and affected by these emotions according to the emotional contagion phenomenon. How employees internalise these emotions would affect their communication with customers. If they are susceptible to negative emotions, the employees may lash out or suffer burnout. If they neglect customers' positive emotions and fail to express appreciation, the employees may have missed a great opportunity to establish an ongoing profitable relationship with the customer. Managing one's own emotions in the service encounter is not adequate to ensure a successful transaction. Employees must be able to manage customers' emotions. Negative emotions which are left unmanaged would likely result in complaints and customers' switching to competitors. Positive emotions are reflective of appreciating employees' customer-oriented performance over the encounter. Employees must be able to manage both to nurture a positive encounter and long-term relationship with the customers.

In Prentice's (2008) PhD thesis on emotional intelligence and employee performance in the casino setting, she describes how gaming customers can be abusive, extremely demanding and emotional during their casino visit and stay. Emotional intelligence was identified as the best tool to manage customers' emotional responses. In her own professional experience as a casino marketing manager dealing with high rollers, she recalls:

> *Gamblers are emotional, and these emotions permeate every stage of their travel. Most VIP clients (high rollers) were busy business people. Typically, they had made no advance plans to visit a casino. They often decided at the last minute shortly before the visa office was due to close, and air tickets were on waiting list or fully booked. They did not normally listen to or accept the circumstances but assumed everything would be ready for them whenever they wanted. When this was not the case, they tended to be accusing and abusive. It was essential to show understanding and empathy, to calm them down and let them accept the alternatives.*
>
> *Travelling with these high rollers was a major challenge. They were often unreasonably abusive if the plane was delayed; if there was long queue*

at immigration after disembarkation; if they were accidentally assigned a limousine without the number 8 on the number plate (the number designated for high rollers), or a driver with a pointy face (a characteristic believed to bring them back luck). However, it was not within the power of the casino staff to make the plane take off on time; tell immigration officers to offer them privileges; or even order another limo with a round-faced driver before their patience runs out. Instead, I managed to mitigate their emotions and convince them to calmly accept the unexpected, which I now realise has a lot to do with emotional intelligence.

Upon their arrival at the casino hotel reception, my job of escorting these players to the destination was technically complete. From this point casino hosts were required to look after them. However, they often expressed discomfort with the prospect of encountering new faces and forcefully demanded my presence during their playing time. This was not appreciated by the researcher's superiors and was considered a violation of company rules. This led to another emotional confrontation, indicative of a discrepancy between clients and employer expectations.

The most challenging part of the job as a gambler-contact employee was to regulate players' winning or losing-related emotions. Those could be the source of conflict, anger, never-return intentions, and spreading of negative word-of-mouth. For example, some winning gamblers would demand entertainment such as a "gentleman's club" or prostitutes. Those are commonly available in places like Macau and Las Vegas, but not available in the casino I was working for. Under such circumstance, these players tended to be harsh and critical towards casino hosts. This response was exacerbated when these gamblers had just experienced a big loss. At such times they could be wildly emotional and abusive. Some complained that the croupier had a killing face, or a pretty female casino host had approached them to bring bad luck. They might also demand something that the casino could not, or was unable to deliver. Then the casino host or shift manager dealing with them might be severely accused or abused, even if they had done nothing wrong. However, they still had to behave in a friendly manner and present a smiling face towards the abusive customers and try their best to serve them. In other words, they were performing emotional labour. I was often called up to deal with clients' spontaneous anger or emotional outburst.

When these players completed their first trip to the casino, irrespective of their gambling results, they often expressed the wish to visit again and became loyal clients. I was informed that the decision by these gamblers to visit a casino was not based on the casino location, gaming or non-gaming related facilities, or a big win on the previous trip, but on the casino representatives they had dealt with. In this case, I as one of the casino marketing representatives who has the foremost interactions with the clients was often the reason that these gamblers frequently patronise the casino, despite the setbacks encountered during previous trips. The researcher was informed that most clients (in fact all of them) after having heard that the researcher was leaving stopped visiting the casino. Some of them have established ongoing relationship and extended into other businesses with her.

The story of her work experience has the following implications. First, although casino services include both tangible elements such as limousine services and free accommodation, and the intangible elements of the services performed by casino frontline employees, it is the intangible component that attracts gambler patronage. Second, the service encounters between casino frontline employees and clients are characterised by emotional events, so the emotional intelligent performance of the employee is critical in shaping gambler perceptions of casino service quality. Finally, this story suggests that the employees are a key factor in gaming customer retention. Specifically, it is the employee's emotional competence that influences customer retention and loyalty. This relationship is possible through the establishment of rapport.

8.3 Emotional Intelligence Instils Rapport

Employee emotional intelligence influences customer attitudes and behaviours through rapport. The connection between two interactants on a personal, professional or spiritual level is referred to as rapport. Despite cultural and personal differences, people in dyadic relationships experience rapport when they feel there is some kind of chemistry that connects them on a single or different levels (Tickle-Degnen and Rosenthal, 1990). In the service context, particularly in businesses characterised as people-concentrated or as providing high-contact services where employee-customer interactions form the majority of the services, rapport is especially important for a smooth transaction over the service encounter through one or more personal interactions. Rapport is reflective of pleasant interactions and bond building between the customer and service provider (Gremler and Gwinner, 2000, 2008; Hennig-Thurau *et al.*, 2006). The level of rapport is indicative of relationship quality between the two parties in the dyad and has been proved to affect customer satisfaction and loyalty in the employee-customer dyad (Gremler and Gwinner, 2000; Hennig-Thurau *et al.*, 2006); these outcomes in turn are related to company profitability.

The interactions that instil rapport between customers and contact employees are often loaded with positive emotions, sympathy and empathy, and stimulated with cognitive evaluations of the exchange with the service provider. Rapport bridges employee emotional intelligence and customer outcomes. Employees with high levels of emotional intelligence perceive and understand customer emotions that help them customise the service offering to address customer needs and build rapport. Perceived rapport translates into higher levels of customer satisfaction and loyalty. The affect-as-information theory proposed by cognitive psychologists presents a useful framework for understanding how emotionally intelligent employees establish rapport with customers. According to this theory, individuals often make judgments by questioning themselves on how they feel (Schwarz and Clore, 1983). Their feelings or emotions are used as information to influence their judgments.

In the dyadic encounter between customers and employees, emotions play an especially important role in the dyadic interactions (Grandey *et al.*, 2005). Employees often draw upon their own emotions to understand those of customers. When customers display emotions, employees with higher levels of emotional intelligence are able to perceive and understand customers' emotions implicitly or explicitly. Based on the information derived from these emotions, they take the necessary measures to create a positive service environment and interact with customers via the most appropriate methods (Mattila and Enz, 2002). On this basis, emotionally intelligent employees are naturally better in establishing rapport with customers.

There are a plethora of studies in the literature that examine how emotional intelligence affects one's own attitudes and behaviours. Research on its influence on that of others is however, limited. In spite of this, a few studies have shown that employee emotional intelligence directly impact customers' attitudes and behaviours in high-contact services.

8.4 Emotional Intelligence and Customer Satisfaction

Customer satisfaction is a central construct in marketing research and reflective of customer attitudinal response towards the service provider. The level of satisfaction determines customers' subsequent purchase and loyalty behaviours. Customer satisfaction refers to as an overall feeling of pleasure or disappointment that emerges from comparing perceived performance of a service or product, with pre-service expectations (Oliver, 1980). It is indicative customers' emotions towards the service employees and the company. These emotions can be resulted from discrete elements or events over a single transaction or a holistic assessment of all experience encounters forming overall evaluation of customer experience.

Dissatisfaction is manifested in negative emotions that convey information indicating unpleasant experience with the service. This information requires customer contact employees' emotional intelligence to recognise and assess customer emotions so that they can customise appropriate service offering to cater for customers' specific needs (Mattila and Enz, 2002). Emotional intelligent performance moderates interpersonal behaviors (e.g. familiarity, care, commercial friendship, listening behavior, customer orientation), which affect customer satisfaction (Dagger, Sweeney and Johnson, 2007; de Ruyter and Wetzels, 2000; Gremler and Brown, 1998; Price and Arnould, 1999). On the basis of Forgas's (1995) theory of affect infusion, a person's affective state influences his or her judgment, and supports this expectation — in a positive affective state induced by an emotionally intelligent employee, customers are less critical and thus, more satisfied with the service encounter.

In their empirical study, Kernback and Schutte (2005) examine whether higher emotional intelligence displayed by service providers leads to customer satisfaction. The study used a community sample of 150 participants (86 of them were male) from Queensland,

Australia. Participants were recruited through snowball sampling from rotary club meetings and various business organisations, a technical training institute in different regions of Queensland. The participants viewed video clips depicting a service provider displaying three different levels of emotional intelligence in high or low service difficulty transactions. The results show that higher emotional intelligence displayed by the service provider led to greater reported satisfaction with the service transaction. They also found a link between emotional intelligence of the service provider and transaction difficulty. In the low transaction difficulty condition, there was progressively more satisfaction at each higher level of emotional intelligence of the service provider. In the high transaction difficulty condition, there was low satisfaction in the low service provider emotional intelligence condition. Finally, no significant difference was found in satisfaction between the high and medium levels of service provider emotional intelligence.

Giardini and Frese (2008) tested a relationship between employee emotional intelligence and customer positive effect in a dyadic setting (banking customers and employees) in banks. The study recruited 53 bank consultants from five banks in different cities in Germany and 394 customers of the bank. The study finds that employee emotional intelligence is positively related to customer evaluation of the encounter which is positively related to customer satisfaction.

8.5 Emotional Intelligence and Customer Loyalty

Delcourt and colleagues (2013) were the first to propose a direct link of emotional intelligence exhibited in employees, and customer satisfaction and loyalty. The rationale for this is built upon Gouldner's (1960) norm of reciprocity. The reciprocity theory indicates that business exchanges reflect the use of a subjective cost-benefit analysis and comparisons of alternatives. One party reciprocally obligates another upon receiving expected and unexpected benefits to balance giving and receiving relationships (Blau, 1964; Robinson, Nye and Thomas, 1994).

According to the authors, emotionally intelligent employees are better at regulating interpersonal behaviours; building strong interpersonal bonds; displaying respect and efforts to address customers' issues and problems; and are more focused on understanding customer needs and keeping the customer satisfied (or more customer-oriented). In return, a customer likely recognises a benefit and thus feels indebted to the employee. To feel less indebted, the customer may engage in behaviours that restore balance. In other words, customers reciprocate employees with positive attitudes and loyalty behaviours.

In their empirical testing, Delcourt *et al.* chose a high-contact service business (hairstyling) as the study context. The reason for this option was due to the fact that a hairstylist is in close proximity to customers — the service encounter with customers is emotionally charged according to Price, Arnould and Tierney's (1995) service encounter categorisation and highly interactive, requiring inputs from the hairstylist and the customer to co-produce value (Lusch, Vargo and O'Brien, 2007; Vargo and Lusch, 2004). The researchers classified three types of interactions between the customer and hairstylist: service encounters (when customers interact with an employee from a different hair salon each time), pseudo-relationships (when customers interact with different employees each time, but within a single hair salon), and service relationships (when customers have repeated contact with the same employee within a single hair salon) (Gutek, 1995; Gutek *et al.*, 1999). The interactions between a hairstylist and customer are key to successful ongoing relationships. Since the encounter is emotionally loaded, the hairstylist's emotional intelligence can be influential in determining customer evaluations and behaviour.

In the test, 247 observations were collected with 61 percent being male respondents. 89 percent of respondents indicated they had regularly visited the same hairstylist, and 47 percent indicating use of the service at least five times per year, which suggests that most respondents have sufficient knowledge of their hairstylist. The results show a significant and positive relationship between the service employee's emotional intelligence with satisfaction ($\beta = 0.34$; $t = 6.19$), and with customer loyalty (β = 0.23; t = 4.27). The study also tested whether rapport between the hairstylist and the customer is related to emotional intelligence and customer outcomes. The testing through a non-parametric bootstrapping procedure shows that rapport is partially mediated by the relationship between the hairstylist's emotional intelligence and customer satisfaction as well as loyalty. The finding indicates that the employee's emotional intelligence instils rapport in customers, which is transferred into positive attitudes and behaviours.

Prentice (2018) recently tested the relationship between employee emotional intelligence and customers' response in the casino context with a focus on casino dealers and gaming customers. Following Price, Arnould and Tierney's (1995) service encounter categorisations on the basis of the levels of affective contents, Prentice contends that the encounter between casino dealers and gaming customers over gaming tables has high affect content and can be categorised as a highly emotionally charged service encounter. The high-affect context refers to services that offer affective benefits in both functional (the process) and technical (the outcome) aspects. Gaming, as a risk-taking activity and the primary service offered by casinos, has high affective content in both the gambling process (the functional aspect) and outcome (the technical component). The emotions displayed during gambling are attributed to uncertainty of the outcome (winning or losing). Indeed, prior studies (Mellers, Schwartz and Ritov, 1999; O'Connor, 2000; Schellinck and Schrans, 2004) show that regular gamblers experience the range and strength of emotions during gambling on the basis of their cortical responses to the expectation of winning. They often appear to be anxious and hysterical, as reflected in their impatience towards the dealer's performance and yelling while expecting the outcome of turning the cards.

Gambling outcomes also trigger gamblers' emotional responses. Win seeking is one of the primary motives of people who come to a casino to play. and the feeling of fulfilment from winning is very emotional (Lee *et al.*, 2010). Admittedly, the odds are generally not in their favour (Watson and Kale, 2003). Whilst some gamblers treat gambling as a recreational activity and accept the outcome (regardless of win or loss) without making a fuss; others who have experienced a big loss can be wildly emotional and abusive, complaining about the dealer for their own mistakes and bad play (Prentice, 2008).

Gamblers' emotions during gambling or after each play are often transferred to the interactions with casino dealers who are in direct contact with the gambler. The dealers not only bear a noisy working environment and physical exhaustion from conducting croupier duties (Chan, Wan and Kuok, 2015), but are also the victims of gamblers' emotional outbursts (Prentice, 2016). Following organisational job descriptions, the dealers are compelled to deal with these outbursts to ensure a smooth operation, acting in a friendly manner with smiling faces towards emotional customers. Like any other customer-contact employee, the dealers engage in emotional labour which is performed through acting strategies (deep or surface acting; Hochschild, 1983). Either acting strategy in the long run has detrimental effects (i.e. self-alienation, burnout) on employees, particularly those working in the hospitality industry (Federici and Skaalvik, 2012; Prentice, Chen and King, 2013).

In the case of casino dealers, salaries in some jurisdictions such as Macau consist of base payment by the casino and tips from gamblers. Tips are sourced from gamblers' voluntary "giving", depending on their winning and moods at the time. The same gambler may experience a few losses and wins within each play session, hence, his or her moods vary. The dealer must be able to understand the gambler's volatile moods and emotional reactions and act accordingly in order to generate more positive reactions including generous tipping. Since emotional intelligence indicates the individuals' capacity to perceive and understand their own and others' emotions, and to use this understanding to guide their thinking and behaviours (Goleman, 1998), it is possible to connect a casino dealer's emotional intelligence level with tipping income.

Theoretically, the dealer with higher emotional intelligence is more likely to understand gamblers' moods and emotions, and to display a higher level of interpersonal skills to sooth them. For instance, the dealer can be congratulatory when gamblers win, be empathetic and initiate jokes to entertain them when they lose, or direct these gamblers to other recreational activities within the casino premises to ensure their positive experience with the casino. As customer response refers to evaluation of service offerings and experience (Bolton and Drew, 1991), these types of dealer interpersonal skills form the basis of positive customer response towards the dealer. Consequently, the gambler may prefer to return to the same dealer or the casino on his or her future trips. This discussion informs a connection between dealer emotional intelligence and gaming customer's loyalty.

On the basis of the rationale provided, Prentice (2018) conducted her study from 22 casinos in Macau with both casino dealers and supervisors who rated customer response towards the dealer. 738 usable match-up responses were received. Of the total usable dealer sample, about half respondents (52%) were male, and half (48%) were female. The results show that dealer emotional intelligence has a significant impact on gaming customer loyalty ($\beta = 0.607$, $p < 0.0005$).

8.6 Summary

This chapter extends relational encounter marketing from elaborating the influence of emotional intelligence on relational encounter behaviours in understanding the direct relationship between emotional intelligence and customers' response. Whilst acknowledging that employees' encounter behaviours affect customer response, emotional intelligence with its four branch abilities demonstrated by employees can directly affect customers' attitudes and behaviours. This relationship is built through the rapport between the dyadic parties. Anecdotes and empirical studies are provided to illustrate the direct impact of employee emotional intelligence on customer responses. This illustration reinforces the role of emotional intelligence in relationship marketing with regard to relational encounter marketing practice. Emotional intelligence is related to marketing outcomes through its influence on the attitudes and behaviours of both employees and customers in the dyadic service encounter.

References

Bardzil, P. & Slaski, M. (2003). Emotional intelligence: Fundamental competencies for enhanced service provision. *Managing Service Quality*, 13(2), 97–104.

Blau, H. (1964). *The Impossible Theater: A Manifesto*. New York: Macmillan.

Bolton, R.N. & Drew, J.H. (1991). A multistage model of customers' assessments of service quality and value. *Journal of Consumer Research*, 17(4), 375–384.

Chan, S.H., Wan, Y.K.P., & Kuok, O.M. (2015). Relationships among burnout, job satisfaction, and turnover of casino employees in Macau. *Journal of Hospitality Marketing & Management*, 24(4), 345–374.

Dagger, T.S., Sweeney, J.C., & Johnson, L.W. (2007). A hierarchical model of health service quality: Scale development and investigation of an integrated model. *Journal of Service Research*, 10(2), 123–142.

de Ruyter, K. & Wetzels, M. (2000). Customer equity considerations in service recovery: A cross-industry perspective. *International Journal of Service Industry Management*, 11(1), 91–108.

Delcourt, C., Gremler, D.D., Van Riel, A.C., & Van Birgelen, M. (2013). Effects of perceived employee emotional competence on customer satisfaction and loyalty: The mediating role of rapport. *Journal of Service Management*, 24(1), 5–24.

Federici, R.A. & Skaalvik, E.M. (2012). Principal self-efficacy: Relations with burnout, job satisfaction and motivation to quit. *Social Psychology of Education*, 15(3), 295–320.

Forgas, J.P. (1995). Mood and judgment: The affect infusion model (AIM). *Psychological Bulletin*, 117(1), 39.

Giardini, A. & Frese, M. (2008). Linking service employees' emotional competence to customer satisfaction: A multilevel approach. *Journal of Organizational Behaviour*, 29(2), 155–170.

Goleman, D. (1998). *Working with Emotional Intelligence*. New York, NY: Bantam Books.

Gouldner, A.W. (1960). The norm of reciprocity: A preliminary statement. *American Sociological Review*, 25(2), 161–178.

Grandey, A.A., Fisk, G.M., Mattila, A.S., Jansen, K.J., & Sideman, L.A. (2005). Is "service with a smile" enough? Authenticity of positive displays during service encounters. *Organizational Behavior and Human Decision Processes*, 96(1), 38–55.

Gremler, D.D. & Brown, S.W. (1998, January). Service loyalty: Antecedents, components, and outcomes. In *American Marketing Association. Conference Proceedings* (Vol. 9, p. 165). American Marketing Association.

Gremler, D.D. & Gwinner, K.P. (2000). Customer-employee rapport in service relationships. *Journal of Service Research*, 3(1), 82–104.

Gremler, D.D. & Gwinner, K.P. (2008). Rapport-building behaviors used by retail employees. *Journal of Retailing*, 84(3), 308–324.

Gutek, B.A. (1995). *The Dynamics of Service: Reflections on the Changing Nature of Customer/Provider Interactions*. San Francisco, CA: Jossey-Bass.

Gutek, B.A., Bhappu, A.D., Liao-Troth, M.A., & Cherry, B. (1999). Distinguishing between service relationships and encounters. *Journal of Applied Psychology*, 84(2), 218–233.

Hatfield, E., Cacioppo, J. T., & Rapson, R. L. (1994). Emotional contagion: *Cambridge Studies in Emotion and Social Interaction*. Cambridge, UK: Cambridge University Press.

Hatfield, E., Rapson, R.L., & Le, Y.C.L. (2011). Emotional contagion and empathy. In J. Decety & W. Ickes (Eds.), *The Social Neuroscience of Empathy*, (pp. 19–30). Cambridge, MA: MIT Press.

Hennig-Thurau, T., Groth, M., Paul, M., & Gremler, D.D. (2006). Are all smiles created equal? How emotional contagion and emotional labor affect service relationships. *Journal of Marketing*, 70(3), 58–73.

Heskett, J.L. & Sasser, W.E. (2010). The service profit chain. In C.A. Paul & P. Maglio (Eds.), *Handbook of Service Science* (pp. 19–29). Boston, MA: Springer.

Hochschild, A.R. (1983). *The Managed Heart*. Berkeley, CA: University of California Press.

Kernbach, S. & Schutte, N.S. (2005). The impact of service provider emotional intelligence on customer satisfaction. *Journal of Services Marketing*, 19(7), 438–444.

Lee, C.K., Kang, S.K., Long, P., & Reisinger, Y. (2010). Residents' perceptions of casino impacts: A comparative study. *Tourism Management*, 31(2), 189–201.

Liao, H. & Chuang, A. (2004). A multilevel investigation of factors influencing employee service performance and customer outcomes. *Academy of Management Journal*, 47(1), 41–58.

Lusch, R.F., Vargo, S.L., & O'Brien, M. (2007). Competing through service: Insights from service-dominant logic. *Journal of Retailing*, 83(1), 5–18.

Mattila, A.S. & Enz, C.A. (2002). The role of emotions in service encounters. *Journal of Service Research*, 4(4), 268–277.

Mayer, J.D., Salovey, P., Caruso, D.R., & Sitarenios, G. (2003). Measuring emotional intelligence with the MSCEIT V2.0. *Emotion*, 3(1), 97.

Mellers, B., Schwartz, A., & Ritov, I. (1999). Emotion-based choice. *Journal of Experimental Psychology: General*, 128(3), 332.

O'Connor, B.P. (2000). SPSS and SAS programs for determining the number of components using parallel analysis and Velicer's MAP test. *Behavior Research Methods, Instruments, & Computers*, 32(3), 396–402.

Oliver, R.L. (1980). A cognitive model of the antecedents and consequences of satisfaction decisions. *Journal of Marketing Research*, 17(4), 460–469.

Prentice, C. (2016). Leveraging employee emotional intelligence in casino profitability. *Journal of Retailing and Consumer Services*, 33, 127–134.

Prentice, C. (2018). Linking internal service quality and casino dealer performance. *Journal of Hospitality Marketing & Management*, 27(6), 733–753.

Prentice, C. & King, B. (2011). The influence of emotional intelligence on the service performance of casino frontline employees. *Tourism and Hospitality Research*, 11(1), 49–66.

Prentice, C., Chen, P.-J., & King, B. (2013). Employee performance outcomes and burnout following the presentation-of-self in customer-service contexts. *International Journal of Hospitality Management*, 35, 225–236.

Prentice, C. (2008). *Trait Emotional Intelligence, Personality and the Self-perceived Performance Ratings of Casino Key Account Representatives*. (Doctoral dissertation, Victoria University).

Price, L.L. & Arnould, E.J. (1999). Commercial friendships: service provider-client relationships in context. *Journal of Marketing*, 63(4), 38–56.

Price, L.L., Arnould, E.J., & Tierney, P. (1995). Going to extremes: Managing service encounters and assessing provider performance. *Journal of Marketing*, 59(2), 83–97.

Pugh, S.D. (2001). Service with a smile: Emotional contagion in the service encounter. *Academy of Management Journal*, 44(5), 1018–1027.

Robinson, E.J., Nye, R., & Thomas, G.V. (1994). Children's conceptions of the relationship between pictures and their referents. *Cognitive Development*, 9(2), 165–191.

Schellinck, T. & Schrans, T. (2004). Identifying problem gamblers at the gambling venue: Finding combinations of high confidence indicators. *Gambling Research: Journal of the National Association for Gambling Studies (Australia)*, 16(1), 8–24.

Schwarz, N. & Clore, G.L. (1983). Mood, misattribution, and judgments of well-being: Informative and directive functions of affective states. *Journal of Personality and Social Psychology*, 45(3), 513–523.

Shi, Y., Prentice, C., & He, W. (2014). Linking service quality, customer satisfaction and loyalty in casinos, does membership matter? *International Journal of Hospitality Management,* 40 (July), 81–91.

Tickle-Degnen, L. & Rosenthal, R. (1990). The nature of rapport and its nonverbal correlates. *Psychological Inquiry,* 1(4), 285–293.

Tsai, W.C. & Huang, Y.M. (2002). Mechanisms linking employee affective delivery and customer behavioral intentions. *Journal of Applied Psychology,* 87(5), 1001–1008.

Vargo, S.L. & Lusch, R.F. (2004). Evolving to a new dominant logic for marketing. *Journal of Marketing,* 68(1), 1–17.

Watson, L. & Kale, S.H. (2003). Know when to hold them: Applying the customer lifetime value concept to casino table gaming. *International Gambling Studies,* 3(1), 89–101.

Wong, A. (2004). The role of emotional satisfaction in service encounters. *Managing Service Quality: An International Journal,* 14(5), 365–376.

CHAPTER 9

EMOTIONAL INTELLIGENCE AND IMPERSONAL ENCOUNTER MARKETING

9.1 Introduction

Service organisations today are increasingly putting emphasis on physical environment that is reflective of the firm's service environment. Service environment is a commercial place that is designed to provide the customer with a unique service experience, and to differentiate a service provider from others. The service environment consists of all aspects of the organisation's physical environment as well as other tangible facilities that facilitate service transactions. The physical environment is referred to as *servicescape* (Bitner, 1992). Servicescape constitutes the core component of service environment where service production and delivery takes place, and influence the attitudes and behaviours of both employees and customers (Bitner, 1992). Servicescape is often purposefully designed to exert affective and cognitive effects on customers in order to entice their favourable behavioural responses such as purchase and consumption of the service (Harris and Goode, 2010; Zeithaml, Parasuraman and Malhotra, 2002).

Chapter 2 introduces the concept of service encounter and its two general categories: personal and impersonal encounters. The foregoing chapters focus on personal encounters and how emotional

185

intelligence demonstrated by service employees impact their attitudes and behaviours as well as those of customers. Customers' attitudes and behaviours towards the employees and the firm are manifested in their purchasing/repurchasing, consuming and recommending of the firm's products/services. Emotional intelligence as an individual trait or ability (depending on the model of choice) has been conceptualised as a marketing tool to be incorporated into internal, dramaturgical, and relational encounter marketing practices. Internal marketing emphasises the role of employees as internal customers in influencing external customers. Dramaturgical marketing describes the influence of employees' acting strategies on employees' customer-oriented performance. The relational encounter marketing is focused on the relational interactions between employees and customers.

This chapter contends that the concept of emotional intelligence can be injected into service design with respect to the servicescape. The context of the discussion is focused on the impersonal encounter between customers and the servicescape. The servicescape is personified here and viewed as an organic physical environment that can be armed with emotional intelligent skills to attract positive attitudes and purchase behaviours from customers. This practice is referred to as *Impersonal Encounter Marketing* in this book.

Specifically, this chapter discusses how the concept of emotional intelligence can be used by the firm to design appropriate non-human elements of the service environment (referred to as servicescape) to manage and influence the impersonal encounter between the servicescape and customers. The discussion will be centred on how an emotionally intelligent servicescape would affect customer attitudes and behaviours. The research on servicescape and employees to date is fairly scant but is nevertheless worth exploring. This chapter is focused on the relationship between external customers and the service organisation's servicescape. Bitner's (1992) framework for understanding environment-user relationships will be drawn up to explain necessity of incorporating emotional intelligence into servicescape design to influence customer-related outcomes.

9.2 Typology of Servicescapes

In the pre-digital era, Bitner (1992) developed a typology of service-scapes based on three classifications of service businesses: self-service, remote services and interpersonal services. Each of the service categories can be classified as lean or elaborate servicescapes. *Lean* servicescapes refer to services that require relatively few elements and few interpersonal interactions between customers and employees such as kiosks, vending machines, self-service retail outlets and fast food outlets. Lean servicescapes are simple and straightforward. *Elaborate* servicescapes comprise multiple spaces, are rich in physical elements and symbolism, and involve high contact services with many interactions between customers and employees. The elaborate servicescape includes the provider's exterior (style of décor, land-scape, exterior design, signage, parking and surrounding environment) and interior (furnishings, interior design, equipment and layout), and ambient conditions (noise, music, odour, air quality, temperature and lighting), for instance, an internationally branded hotel with guest accommodation, concierge, bars, restaurants, swimming pools, gymnasiums and other supplementary services where guests interact with multiple personnel during their stay. According to Bitner, the servicescapes for self-service settings could be designed to convey positioning and segmentation strategies. For remote services, the aim of servicescape design is to focus on employee satisfaction and productivity because of the minimal or no presence of customers in those settings. For interpersonal services, the servicescapes can be utilised to build relationships.

In the digital era, with the disproportionately increasing popularity of e-commerce facilitated by advanced information and communication technologies, research on e-servicescapes has emerged rapidly, and its importance in influencing customers' attitudes and behaviours for e-merchandising has been recognised (Hopkins *et al.*, 2009; Lee and Jeong, 2012; Lai *et al.*, 2014). E-merchandise often comprises information search assistance (search engines, site maps, and categorisation); product presentation such as product view and display method, colour and methods of presentation, detailed views, swatches, and mix and match; and environment atmospherics, also referred to as e-servicescapes. Regardless of tangible physical environment or e-servicescapes, the ultimate goal of service design is to entice positive responses from the users.

9.3 Servicescape Components

Servicescape generally consists of tangible components. Tangible servicescapes refer to the physical elements within the service environment and consist of three broad categories: ambient conditions; space/function; signs, symbols, and artefacts. Ambient conditions refer to the controllable, observable stimuli such as air temperature, lighting and noise. For example, music used in service environment, which has been found to influence consumer behaviours. Joyful music stimulates more thoughts and feelings than negatively valanced music. Playing pleasant music reduces the negative effects of waiting since it serves as a distraction. Changing the background music to a quicker tempo in a retail store may influence the consumer to move through the space at a quicker pace, thereby improving traffic flow. On the other hand, the ambient conditions can also be adjusted to encourage avoidance behaviour before closing the store, service employees can turn the air conditioning up, turn up the lights, turn off the background music and start stacking chairs on top of tables. These actions send a signal to patrons that it is closing time.

Internal elements such as space and function primarily serve a functional role. The comfort of furniture and spatial layout enhances customers' in-store experience and encourage customers to stay longer since longer stays result in more opportunities to sell services. Furnishings may serve a functional role in that they provide seating where customers can wait for friends and family, or simply enjoy a quiet rest. Quality of materials may serve a symbolic role in which they may signify an elegant, up-market store or an inexpensive, family-friendly venue.

The environmental elements of signs, symbols and artefacts not only serve a functional or utilitarian role, but also communicate symbolic meanings. For example, signage provides information and direction that may assist customers in navigating their way through a complex service environment. Luxurious settings represent prestige of this service provider. The use of colour communicates at a symbolic level in ways that impact behaviour. Artefacts imply some type of cultural, historical or social interest for customers. They are the tangible reminders of the service experienced by consumers. Artefacts may be purpose-designed objects that serve as souvenirs or mementoes of a pleasant experience. Many services, such as museums, galleries, theatres and tourist attractions, manufacture artefacts that form the basis of a merchandise collection.

E-servicescapes refer to the firm's website design that includes visual and auditory cues including music, colours, borders, fonts, animation, videos, display, background colours, page layout, navigation bar, decorative graphics as well as ambient conditions, function, and signs (Éthier, *et al.*, 2006; Kim, Kim, and Lennon, 2006; Mummalaneni, 2005). These can be categorised into high and low task-relevant environmental cues, the former is products-related such as in providing information about price, terms of sale, delivery, return policies etc. whereas the latter is non-product related to focusing on ambient factors, design factors and social factors (Ezeh and Harris, 2007).

The other area of e-servicescapes is focused on social factors. The social factors of the online environment are growing in the form of social network sites and virtual community research (Flavián and Guinalíu, 2005; Ku, 2011). The social dimensions of online shopping focus on new features implemented on various websites that include links to share information on social media sites as well as Facebook groups and pages where customers can chat and share thoughts of the particular brand or products of interest. Some websites also implement chat with advisory facility that offers the opportunity to speak to an advisor as in offline stores. Use of a personalised avatar — a pictorial representation of a human in a chat environment is also popular, which may enhance the effectiveness of web-based sales channels (Holzwarth, Janiszewski, and Neumann, 2006). Although unable to enable sensory experience of tasting, touching, and smelling in the manner of physical settings, e-servicescape can evoke customers' emotional response (Rosenbaum, 2009) and affect customer loyalty (Kwon and Lennon, 2009) and purchase behaviours (Fagerstrøm, 2010).

9.4 The Roles of Servicescapes

Depending on the service type (self-service, remote, interpersonal or digital services), servicescape serves as a holistic service environment that is used to interact with customers and satisfy their needs. It holds strategic importance to the organisation and has been viewed as a primary organisational value proposition (Bitner, 1992; Hightower, 2003; Rosenbaum, 2009). In general, the servicescape performs four strategic and functional roles: packaging, facilitator, socialiser, and differentiator. The role of packaging indicates the outward appearance to the public through environmental cues and surrounding physical evidence, acts like a "product's package" — by communicating a total image to customers and providing information about how to use the service; for instance, a facilitator would guide for an efficient flow of activities; a socialiser would convey expected roles to both employees and customers; and a differentiator serves as a point of difference by signalling the segments of the market to which various services can be rendered thus conveying competitive difference and positioning the organisation towards these service functions and goals.

These roles ultimately contribute to explain customers' attitudes and behaviours. There are two original prototypes of servicescapes in the literature to depict its impact on individuals' attitudes and behaviours. The earliest one is the stimulus–organism–response model (the SOR model) proposed by Mehrabian and Russel in 1974. The SOR model describes the way that organisms, including customers and employees, respond to environmental stimuli (e.g. lighting, music, interior design). In essence, the model proposes that individuals exhibit three broad types of responses to stimuli in the external environment: physiological, emotional (affective) and behavioural responses. A simple stimulus–organism–response model is depicted as Stimulus (physical environment) → Organism (customers and employees) → Response (comfort, pleasure, approach, avoidance).

Although Mehrabian and Russel included three broad types of responses (physiological, emotional (affective) and behavioural responses) to the external environment as stimuli in their model, the focus is on the impact of the environmental cues on emotional responses which arguably mediate between the servicescape factors and behaviours as shown in Figure 9.1 below. The emotional responses are operationalised into three dimensions: pleasure, arousal and dominance. Each emotional response functions in a continuum rather than being discrete. For instance, pleasure–displeasure refers to the emotional state reflecting the degree to which an individual is satisfied with the service experience. Arousal–nonarousal refers to the emotional state that reflects the degree to which an individual feels excited and stimulated. Dominance–submissiveness refers to the emotional state that reflects the degree to which one feels in control and able to act freely within the service environment.

According to Mehrabian and Russell, environmental stimuli can be categorised into high or low load based on the degree of information processing and stimulation. High load environments refer to those that are unfamiliar, novel, complex, unpredictable or crowded. Such environments tend to make people feel alert and stimulated. Low load environments refer to familiar, simple, unsurprising and well-organised environments. These environmental elements tend to make people feel relaxed, calm and even sleepy. For mundane and routine tasks, a stimulating environment would be beneficial. Complex or difficult tasks may require a low load environment. The emotional arousal in either situation is dependent upon the context.

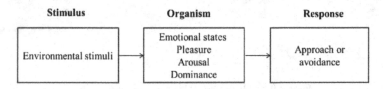

Figure 9.1 The SOR model proposed by Mehrabian and Russel (1974)

For example, intense emotions may be more necessary for physical training; whereas relaxing environment should be more appropriate for a leisure setting. It is imperative for service organisations to design the service environment (servicescapes) that specifically caters for customers' emotional needs in order to attract their positive affective state and approach behaviours. Inappropriate emotional arousal can be counter-effective. For example, an intense business negotiation cannot be conducted in a noisy pub. The noise may trigger a blunt objection to the deal.

Building on environmental psychology research, Bitner (1992) developed a comprehensive servicescape model (Figure 9.2), which links the service environment to various consumer behavioural outcomes (e.g. attraction, to stay/explore and spend more, and satisfaction) through the role of consumer and employee responses. Bitner in his seminar articulates the dimensions and attributes of the service environment and provides theoretical background to understand the details involved in crafting the physical setting. In particular, the three core dimensions of perceived service environment — ambient conditions (i.e. temperature, air quality, noise and music), space and function (i.e. layout, equipment, facilities and

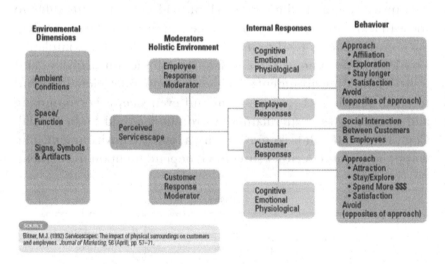

Figure 9.2 Bitner's (1992) servicescape model
Source: Bitner, 1992.

furnishings), and signs, symbols and artifacts (i.e. signage, style of decor, and personal artefacts) — provide customers a holistic view of the physical surrounding in the service encounter (Bitner, 1992; Lovelock and Wirtz, 2007).

Although the two pioneer models seemingly differ in the degree of complexity and elaboration in terms of the dimensionality of servicescapes and the influence of extraneous factors, they propose similar outcomes: emotional and behavioural responses. Both models depict stimuli from the service environment to influence consumers' sensory experience and lead to arousal and positive affective responses including strong impulses to approach specific services (Rosenbaum, 2009). Some researchers propose concurrence of emotional and behavioural outcomes, empirical evidence shows that emotional responses mostly play a mediation role in the relationship between servicescapes and behavioural responses such as favourable consumer behaviours and loyalty outcomes (Hightower Jr., Brady and Baker, 2002). Mattila and Wirtz's study (2001) show that congruence between physical atmosphere and the customer leads to favourable customer evaluation of perceived service quality as well as a higher level of approach and impulse buying behaviours in retail stores. In conclusion, in the service context, servicescape can be crafted to exert direct impact on customers' emotional responses, which in turn, can lead to behavioural outcomes.

9.5 Emotional Intelligence and Servicescapes

Given that servicescape can be crafted to exert emotional and behavioural consequences for both employees and customers in a commercial service setting, it is plausible to incorporate the concept of emotional intelligence in designing the servicescapes. Although emotional intelligence is an individual trait or cognitive ability, servicescapes are non-human elements but designed and created by human beings who can utilise their emotional capacity in the process of designing servicescapes to inject emotional intelligence into the design. The four branches of emotional intelligence depict the abilities of perceiving, utilising, understanding and managing emotion.

The first branch, perceiving emotions, entails the service provider having a better idea of what their prospective customers seek from the service. Customers enter a service environment to experience the service — to relax (e.g. a spa), to be entertained (e.g. live performance), to be excited (e.g. theme parks). The service provider must understand customers' expectations that stem from their emotions and their intention to seek the emotional benefits from the service environment. The servicescape should be designed to deliver such emotional benefits. A spa or massage parlour needs to be fragranced with the appropriate aroma (e.g. lavender scent), and the use of dim lighting will enable customers to feel relaxed. Night clubs should be accompanied with lively music and flash lighting for busy professionals who seek to unwind from work-related stress after a hectic day. The service provider needs to understand their market segments and perceive their emotional needs to ensure customers' positive service experience and attract their patronage.

The second branch of emotional intelligence — using emotions to facilitate thought refers to emotions being utilised to guide the cognitive system and to promote thinking. Emotions can be used to trigger cognitive activity such as through purchase and active recommendation of products and services. The servicescape can be designed to attract shoppers' attention and instigate their impulse to purchase or consume. Impulse is an emotionally loaded urge. For example, the fragrance in a cosmetic store can attract consumers to purchase a bottle of perfume; aroma permeating a pastry shop induces hunger; the spinning and winning hubbub in a casino simulates patrons' urge to punt. While these shoppers may have no prior intention to engage in any consumption, the emotions derived from the servicescape may drive them to engage.

The third branch of emotional intelligence — understanding emotions refer to abilities of diagnosing the meaning behind the emotions (happiness, upset, anger etc.). Servicescapes play various strategic and functional roles of packaging, facilitating, socialising and differentiating as aforementioned. The design must be in accordance with understanding customers' underlying motives of engaging with the service environment and the service provider. An elegant French restaurant must carefully select exquisite and delicate servicescapes to attract customers who seek a romantic atmosphere and elegant delicacies, thus exemplifying how servicescape elements are personified with emotional intelligence to cater to customers' emotional needs (indulgency in luxury). The designer of the servicescapes must understand such needs of potential customers. A VIP club has to be designed with luxurious décor and classy atmospherics to make VIP clients feel differentiated and valued.

The fourth brand of emotional intelligence — managing emotions refers to abilities of regulating and responding to the emotions of others appropriately to achieve optimal outcomes. In a service setting, this skill is often implemented by customer contact employees to manage emotional customers with idiosyncratic demands. The servicescapes of a hospital or clinic should be designed with the intention to manage anxiety and convey a sense of urgency for patients in need. The queue design in airport security and immigration areas must take into account passengers' anxiety to reach departure gates in time. These designs often affect customers' perception of the airport service quality (Prentice and Kadan, 2019).

By the same token, the design of servicescapes should also attend to employees' emotional response. As discussed previously, employees are internal customers. They must be happy with their jobs to be able to perform well and stay loyal to the organisation. Their performance influences customers' perceptions of the firm's service quality. Their commitment and loyalty to the organisation have implications on customer loyalty (Prentice, 2018). For employees working at the backstage, appropriate servicescapes could facilitate their productivity and collaboration with co-workers. For frontline employees, pleasant servicescapes are conducive to their performance over the service encounter with customers. Although the servicescapes are designed for enhancing customer satisfaction and consumption or purchase, in a context where employees must be present to deliver the products/services, the design of servicescapes is equally important in influencing employee attitudes and behaviours. For example, Prentice (2018) shows that the servicescapes in the casino gaming floor have a significant impact on casino dealers' job satisfaction and performance. Dealers are situated in a very uncomfortable working environment due to noise from gaming customers and intense atmosphere on the gaming floor. A staff room with pleasant atmospherics and relaxing ambient conditions could help dealers recuperate from their mundane duties during their break time, and to relieve them of the noisy and intense environment. The service design must cater to employees' emotional needs in this case in order to ensure productivity and successful service transactions, and to a certain extent, to prevent customer complaints.

Emotional intelligence has been widely acknowledged to affect employees' attitudes and behaviours, as well as those of customers in service settings. Although most research has focused on its impact on employees, studies that link employee emotional intelligence and customers' attitudes and behaviours are emerging. This chapter contends that servicescapes are created by the service provider who could instil the concept of emotional intelligence into service design and personalise servicescapes, in their aim to manage customers' attitudes and behaviours with emotionally intelligent servicescapes. The following section provides empirical evidence on how servicescapes can be designed to generate emotional benefits for the service providers. The benefits discussed here are customer's experiences and impulsion, which are emotionally loaded concepts that describe customers' feelings and emotions. The following section discusses how these emotional outcomes drive subsequent behaviours.

9.6 Servicescape in Impersonal Encounter Marketing

9.6.1 *Servicescape and customer experience*

With intensified competitions and much improved services among service providers around the globe, customers are looking for better services and a constellation of service experience. Economic transactions today have progressed into experience-oriented encounters dominated by staged service experiences that differentiate providers primarily based on emotional and gratifying offerings, and are backed by customers' need for sensations. Service experience is defined as the customer's emotions and feelings over the service encounter with the service provider (Hui and Bateson, 1991). Such emotional feelings can be converted into experiential values consisting of aesthetics, entertainment, enjoyment, escape, efficiency, economic, excellence, and social interaction (Pine and Gilmore, 1998). Wang and Prentice (2015) propose that service experience equity can supersede value equity. The former refers to a constellation of lavished services including the service environment, or broadly, value, novelty, brand experience, and perceived luck (Wong, 2013). In turn, each of these attributes contribute to propel a total service experience that customers seek.

Pine and Gilmore (1998) propose that service experience, in particular the memorable experience, has a cascading effect on customers long-term loyalty. This proposition has been widely confirmed in the literature in that customers, who enjoy their experience at the provider's premises, often expressed greater loyalty propensity and actual behaviours through brand preference, patronage, word of mouth, and willingness to spend more (Lucas, 2003; Prentice and Wong, 2015; Zhang, Cheng and Boutaba, 2010). Building a strong brand with memorable service experience has significant implications to service providers as properties with a favourable position in the mind of customers often enjoy greater competitive advantage with loyal customers (Wong and Wu, 2013).

This experience-driven value prompts organisations to deliver experience-centric services with the customer experience becoming the core of the service offering (Zomerdijk and Voss, 2010). The core aim of delivering experience-centric services is to connect customers with the service provider in a personal, memorable way, and engage customers emotionally, physically and intellectually (Pine and Gilmore, 1998; Pullman and Gross 2004). Such engagement builds the emotional connections that promote repeat purchase and positive word of mouth.

Servicescapes can be used to intensify engagement and emotional connections and is the primary concern of experience design (Pullman and Gross, 2004). The servicescapes send customers the cues that create and influence their experience. The physical environment with carefully crafted servicescapes can be designed to evoke particular emotions and responses, and the effective management of atmospheric variables can create compelling service experiences and produce specific emotional effects in the buyer that enhance purchase propensity (Hoffman and Turley, 2002; Kotler, 1973; Turley and Milliman, 2000). The five senses (sight, sound, smell, taste and touch) are crucial when designing tangible elements in experience-centric services. Customers gain information about their physical environment through their senses which can be a direct route to customers' emotions (Roberts, 2004). The more effectively an experience engages the senses, the more memorable it will be (Haeckel, Carbone, and Berry 2003; Pine and Gilmore 1998).

Lin and Mattila (2010) conducted a field study in a Japanese restaurant to understand the relative impact of the servicescape (e.g. lighting, temperature, colour of the wall, colour of the floor, music, theme, comfort level, and the uniqueness of the interior layout and design) and service encounters (i.e. the interaction between customers and service staff) on customers' emotions and satisfaction in a restaurant setting. The interior walls of the restaurant are bright green and yellow with red columns; it has a brown ceiling. The exterior looks shabby, and is poorly lit without signs. Their study explored the congruency effects between two sets of factors (the store atmosphere and the type of food served, and the exterior look and the interior décor) and their potential impact on consumer emotions (e.g. pleasure and arousal), and also examined the interactive effects of perceived congruency and emotions on satisfaction. The study involved 183 males and 295 females who were approached in both peak (lunch and dinner) and nonpeak hours. The results show a significant impact of servicescape and service encounter on emotional responses (i.e. pleasure and arousal) (standardised β = 0.35, $t = 7.36$, $p < 0.001$) and service encounter (standardised $\beta = 0.35$, $t = 7.32$, $p < 0.001$) both enhance individual's pleasure level. They account for 38% of customers' pleasure level. Furthermore, the use of servicescape was found to be positively linked to arousal (standardised $\beta = 0.12$, $t = 1.93$, $p < 0.05$).

Given the impact of servicescapes on customers' emotional response and behaviours, selection of the elements and design should be undertaken with emotional intelligence, aiming for customers' optimal service experience, and derived from identified attitudes and behaviours. Customers' service experience is enhanced by the emotionally intelligent design of servicescapes.

9.6.2 *Servicescape, impulse buying, and brand related outcomes*

Dating back to the rise and fall of Adam and Eve, it is not uncommon for humans to experience impulse to act and behave without deliberation in their daily lives. Impulse involves a tendency to act on a whim and to behave with little consideration of the consequences (Evenden, 1999). Impulse is a sudden, irresistible and powerful urge to engage in an unplanned activity, and often stimulated biochemically and psychologically. The onset of a psychological impulse is instantaneous and spontaneous. According to Wolman (1973), the biological stimulation function neurophysiologically as waves of active change that continue along a nerve fibre and trigger a particular somatic or mental reaction. The psychological urge function as mentally stimulating and motivating agents that are derived from both conscious and unconscious activity. In a commercial setting, consumers can be driven to purchase and consume out of impulse. Consequently impulse buying is defined as an immediate and unplanned purchase or consumption driven by a persistent urge (Rook, 1987).

The impulse in the process of buying is emotionally and hedonically loaded. It is irresistible as impulsive buyers often result in anticipated or unanticipated pleasurable experiences. To a certain degree, impulsive buying tends to generate positive emotional outcomes. Gardner and Rook (1988) reported that 75% of respondents felt better after their impulse purchase, and over 90% felt within the "somewhat" to "extremely" happy range, although nearly 40% did feel guilty after their impulsive purchase. These figures suggest that consumers experience triggering of immediate gratification after an impulsive purchase. Impulsive buying, compared to compulsive buying, is less likely to lead to severe outcomes, depending on the nature of purchasing and the product. Admittedly, some impulsive buyers can end up experiencing a series of problems including financial trouble, disappointment with the product, and disapproval from family and friends (Di Nicola *et al.*, 2010; Evenden, 1999; Sohn and Choi, 2014). However, research shows that impulsive buying accounts for about 80% of sales in some product categories (see Dawson and Kim, 2009).

Although consciously unplanned, an impulse often arises immediately upon confrontation with a certain stimulus (Wolman, 1973). A plethora of research provides understanding to the causes of triggers of impulsive buying. The identifiable antecedents in the literature fall into two main categories: internal and external characteristics. Internal factors are primarily focused on individual motives, wants, needs and personality (Rook and Fisher, 1995). These factors play an insignificant role in the case of impulsive/accidental buying. External factors such as service environment with well-designed servicescapes mostly induce a buying impulse.

Service environment generally includes marketing stimuli and buying environment (Piron, 1991; Schiffman and Kanuk, 2010; Youn and Faber, 2000). Rook and Fisher (1995) indicate that impulse buying behaviour is almost exclusively stimulus-driven. Various marketing promotions and cues can stimulate an instantaneous buying tendency (Youn and Faber, 2000). The tangible environment and atmosphere, including physical appearance of the shopping place, ambience, design, background music, lighting, floor coverings, colours, sounds, odours, and even dress and behaviour of sales and service personnel induce the buying impulse. Mattila and Wirtz (2008) found that a stimulating shopping environment had a positive effect on impulsive buying behaviour. These stimuli tend to lessen self- regulation/control and rationalisation of one's action, which likely increases chance of impulsive buying (Baumeister, 2002; Verplanken and Herabadi, 2001). Admittedly situational factors such as time availability and spending power may also influence buying impulse (Jeffrey and Hodge, 2007). The more time a shopper spends in the shopping outlets, the better chance he or she will engage in impulse purchases. Such impulse can lead to subsequent loyalty behaviours.

The hypothesis of the impulse — loyalty relationship can be accounted for by the positive feeling generated from impulse engagement, which may be attributed to the novelty and surprise from the product purchased that has unexpectedly desirable benefits. Such novelty and surprise likely result in a higher degree of enjoyment and satisfaction than that from a planned purchase, where consumers are already aware of the outcome. These benefits, through one impulsive purchase, likely prompt consumers to repurchase the product. The repurchasing experiences eventually develop into attachment to the product or brand (Keller, 2003, Park *et al.*, 2010). Ultimately the initial impulsive purchasers likely stay loyal to the brand. Impulsive purchase can lead to brand attachment and customer loyalty.

Researchers generally agree that brand attachment precedes and differs from loyalty to a brand (e.g. Amine, 1998; Park *et al.*, 2010; Thomson, MacInnis and Park, 2005). Brand attachment is referred to as consumers' emotional commitment to the brands; whereas brand loyalty is indicative of behavioural elements including repetitive purchase, spreading positive word of mouth, and brand referral (Oliver, 1999). When a customer is attached to a brand, he or she tends to be the brand advocate. Highly attached consumers are often motivated to defend their chosen brands and devote themselves to the brand through brand communities and social media promotion. Customers' brand attachment has a positive significant influence on their loyalty behaviours.

Taking a service management and marketing perspective, many researchers concur on a view that service environment (including the servicescapes, ambience, and physical surroundings) has a significant influence on customer satisfaction, desire to stay, and intention to revisit. For example, Wong and Fong (2010) show that service environment is the most important predictor to customer satisfaction and revisit intention. Prentice and Woodside (2013) find that customer perception of ambience and facilities associated with a service organisation influences both their first choice of visit to the business and on their propensity to switch venues. Although these factors may not determine customer intention and behaviours, Lio and Rody's (2009) study indicates that service environment can enhance customer mood and service experience in the business premises, which prompts their purchase behaviours.

Prentice and Wong (2015) empirically tested a chain relationship from servicescapes to brand-related outcomes in casino setting (see Figure 9.3). Their study reveals that service environment ($b = 0.55$, $p < 0.001$), has a significant relationship with impulse buying. The

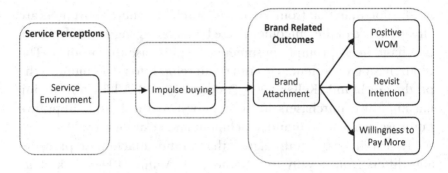

Figure 9.3   Proposed research framework: the chain effects of service quality perceptions on impulsive buying and brand related outcomes

Table 9.1   Results of hierarchical linear modelling estimates of impulse buying and brand attachment

	Model 1	Model 2	Model 3	Model 4
	Impulse buying	Impulse buying	Brand Attachment	Brand Attachment
Main Effects				
Brand equity		1.70***		1.13***
Service environment	0.55***	0.52***		
Buying impulse			0.23***	0.23***
R^2	0.10	0.13	0.14	0.19

Notes: ***$p < 0.0005$.

Parameter estimates are unstandardised.

results for the effect of impulse buying on brand attachment show that the two variables are significant and positively related ($b = 0.23$, $p < 0.001$). The results for the proposed model are show in Table 9.1.

Further from that study, Wong and Prentice (2015) added that servicescapes should be construed as a firm's service environment comprising both individual and organisational levels. The authors argue that service environment and its impact on customers should be considered at both individual and organisational levels, as Figure 9.4 depicts. In fact, this framework heeds the call from Russell and

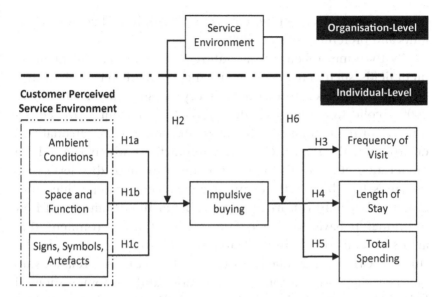

Figure 9.4 Organisational-level service environment × signs, symbols, and artefacts interaction on buying impulsion

Mehrabian (1976). The authors contend that there are two classes of variables that explain consumer behaviours: "Those variables describing differences in environments... and those variables describing differences in the persons" (p. 62). This premise addresses the divide between the consumer-psychology view, which focuses on the linkage between environmental stimuli and individual perceptions, and the organisational-resource view, which focuses on utilising the environment as a strategic asset and competitive advantage. More specifically, Wong and Prentice (2015) contend that organisational-level service environment should not only influence impulse buying and other consumer behaviours, but also moderate the relationship between customer-perceived service environment and impulse buying. This view is reinforced by the institutional theory. The theory posits that the organisation can shape the actors' perceptions and behaviours. The environment "[creates] lenses through which actors view the world and the very categories of structure, action, and thought" (DiMaggio and Powell, 1991, p. 13). Such an institutional system and its environment exert strong effects on the individual actor's behaviours and preferences (Scott, 2001).

By the same token, the literature in psychology and management fields, such as the contingency theory (Battilana and Casciaro, 2012) and person-environment fit theory (Greguras and Diefendorff, 2009), collectively suggests that individual outcomes are consequences of the combined influences emanating from personal and environmental variables. Cross-level interactions, which assessed the moderating effect of the research context on individual-level relationships, have been at the centre stage in recent academic literature because they help researchers gain a better understanding of how individual behaviours are contingent on the environment that actors are embedded within (Mathieu *et al.*, 2012). For example, the study by Grizzle and colleagues (2009) shows that the relationship between employee-customer orientation and customer-oriented behaviours (individual-level) is moderated by the organisational environment (e.g. customer orientation climate), in that the individual-level relationship is strengthened in organisations with a high level of customer orientation climate. Accordingly, the relationship between customer-perceived service environment and impulse buying should be strengthened in organisations that offer good service environment.

To understand how the different levels of service environment affect customer response, Wong and Prentice (2015) conducted an empirical study that tested the moderation of firm-level service environment on the relationship between service environment and impulse buying in the casino setting. The study also tested the relationship between the three dimensions of servicescape adapted from Bitner's (1992) study and impulsive gambling at the individual level. The results in Table 9.2 show that customer-perceived ambient conditions ($b = 0.16$, $p < 0.10$); space and function ($b = 0.21$, $p < 0.01$); and signs, symbols, and artefacts (SSA) ($b = 0.19$, $p < 0.05$) are positively related to impulse buying. Servicescape also has a cross-level moderating effect at the casino level on the relationship between the three servicescape dimensions and impulse gambling at the individual level. The cross-level direct main effect leads from the

Table 9.2   Results of hierarchical linear modelling estimates of gambling impulsion

	Model 1	Model 2
Main effects		
Organisation-level service environment (OSE)	1.04**	1.04**
Ambient conditions	0.16†	0.17*
Space and function	0.21**	0.20**
Signs, symbols, and artefacts (SSA)	0.19*	0.15†
Cross-level Moderating effects		
OSE × ambient conditions	—	−0.12
OSE × space and function	—	0.05
OSE × SSA	—	0.39*
R^2	0.42	0.44

Notes: †$p < 0.10$, *$p < 0.05$, **$p < 0.01$.

Parameter estimates are unstandardised.

casino-level service environment to the customer impulsive gambling behaviours. Results show a significant relationship of the two variables ($\gamma = 1.04$, $p < 0.01$). The results for testing the cross-level interaction in **Model 2** indicate only the organisational-level service environment × SSA interaction is significant ($\gamma = 0.39$, $p < 0.05$). Following Aiken and West's (1991) approach, the study defines the moderator as high and low service environment and graphically illustrates the interaction effects by plus and minus one standard deviation from the mean (see Figure 9.5). The results suggest that the effect of customer-perceived SSA on impulse buying is positive only when a casino offers a good overall service environment.

When testing a direct relationship leading from impulse buying to three behavioural variables — FOV, LOS, and total spending — in Model 3, the results in Table 2 indicate that the effect of impulse buying is significant for FOV ($b = 0.11$, $p < 0.05$) and spending ($b = 77.81$, $p < 0.05$), but not for LOS ($b = 0.04$, n.s.). When testing a cross-level moderating effect of the service environment at the organisational level, on the relationship between impulsive gambling and the three endogenous behavioural variables, the cross-level direct main effect

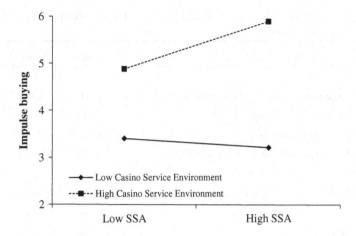

Figure 9.5 Casino-level service environment × impulse buying with regards to customers' length of stay

Table 9.3 Results of hierarchical linear modelling estimates of frequency of visit (FOV), length of stay (LOS), and total spending

	Model 3			Model 4		
	FOV	LOS	Spending	FOV	LOS	Spending
Main effects						
Organisation-level service environment (OSE)	0.45**	0.47**	285.34*	0.45**	0.47**	284.52*
Impulse	0.11*	0.04	77.81*	0.11*	0.02	75.07*
Cross-level moderating effects						
OSE × impulse	—	—	—	0.01	0.20*	46.66
R^2	0.08	0.13	0.09	0.08	0.14	0.09

Notes: $*p < 0.05$, $**p < 0.01$.
Parameter estimates are unstandardised.

leads from the organizational-level service environment to the three endogenous variables. Results show a significant cross-level effect emanating from organisational-level service environment to FOV ($\gamma = 0.45$, $p < 0.01$), LOS ($\gamma = 0.47$, $p < 0.01$), and spending ($\gamma = 285.34$, $p < 0.05$). The cross-level interaction was tested in **Model 4**. The results in Table 9.3 indicate that only the organisational-level service environment × LOS is significant ($\gamma = 0.20$, $p < 0.05$). The results suggest that the effect of impulse buying on LOS is positive if a firm offers a good overall service environment, while the effect is negative if a firm provides low-quality service environment. In short, impulse buying has a divergent effect on customers' length of stay with the service provider, in that the effect is contingent on the firm's overall service environment. A comfortable and well-designed environment keeps people in the service environment to spend more ($r_{LOS, Spending} = 0.11$, $p < 0.05$).

Furthermore, Wong and Prentice tested the mediating effect of buying impulse with respect to the effect emanating from customer-perceived service environment to the three endogenous variables using the Sobel test (Preacher and Leonardelli, 2001) reveal that buying impulse fully mediates the relationships leading from ambient conditions and SSA on FOV, LOS, and spending as well as the relationship leading from space and function on LOS. In addition, buying impulse partially mediates the relationships leading from space and function to FOV ($Z = 1.98$, $p < 0.10$) and spending ($Z = 1.71$, $p < 0.10$). Finally, the cross-level mediating effect led from organisational-level service environment to the three behavioural variables through buying impulse. The results support a partial mediating effect of impulsive buying on the relationship between organisational-level service environment and FOV ($Z = 1.98$, $p < 0.05$) and spending ($Z = 1.87$, $p < 0.10$), and a full mediating effect of impulsive buying on relationship between organisational-level service environment and LOS ($Z = 0.59$, n.s.).

9.7 Summary

This chapter takes a fresh perspective and proposes a new concept impersonal encounter marketing by delving into the service design and the characteristics of servicescapes to understand customers' attitudes and behaviours. In particular this chapter personifies servicescapes and discusses how the concept of emotional intelligence can be injected in the design of servicescapes to exert the influence on customers' attitudes and behaviours towards the service providers and the firm. This chapter extensively presents the evidence for incorporating the concept into design of the servicescape by demonstrating the customers — related outcomes derived from the design through several empirical studies. Although no empirical evidence can be provided to link emotional intelligence and the servicescape, the chapter is intended to provide the rationale for integrating the concept of emotional intelligence into design of the servicescapes. Hence, emotional intelligence can be positioned as a marketing tool to generate business profitability through the association with the impersonal encounter marketing.

References

Aiken, L.S., West, S.G., & Reno, R.R. (1991). *Multiple Regression: Testing and Interpreting Interactions.* New Bury Park, USA: Sage.

Amine, A. (1998). Consumers' true brand loyalty: The central role of commitment. *Journal of Strategic Marketing*, 6(4), 305–319.

Battilana, J. & Casciaro, T. (2012). Change agents, networks, and institutions: A contingency theory of organizational change. *Academy of Management Journal*, 55(2), 381–398.

Baumeister, R.F. (2002). Yielding to temptation: Self-control failure, impulsive purchasing, and consumer behavior. *Journal of Consumer Research*, 28(4), 670–676.

Bitner, M.J. (1992). Servicescapes: The impact of physical surroundings on customers and employees. *Journal of Marketing*, 56(2), 57–71.

Dawson, S. & Kim, M. (2009). External and internal trigger cues of impulse buying online. *Direct Marketing: An International Journal*, 3(1), 20–34.

DiMaggio, P.J. & Powell, W.W. (Eds.) (1991). *The New Institutionalism in Organizational Analysis* (Vol. 17, pp. 1–38). Chicago, IL: University of Chicago Press.

Di Nicola, M., Tedeschi, D., Mazza, M., Martinotti, G., Harnic, D., Catalano, V., Pozzi, G., Bria, P., & Janiri, L. (2010). Behavioural addictions in bipolar disorder patients: Role of impulsivity and personality dimensions. *Journal of Affective Disorders*, 125(1–3), 82–88.

Éthier, J., Hadaya, P., Talbot, J., & Cadieux, J. (2006). B2C web site quality and emotions during online shopping episodes: An empirical study. *Information & Management*, 43(5), 627–639.

Evenden, J.L. (1999). Varieties of impulsivity. *Psychopharmacology*, 146(4), 348–361.

Ezeh, C. & Harris, L.C. (2007). Servicescape research: A review and a research agenda. *The Marketing Review*, 7(1), 59–78.

Fagerstrøm, A. (2010). The motivating effect of antecedent stimuli on the web shop: A conjoint analysis of the impact of antecedent stimuli at the point of online purchase. *Journal of Organizational Behavior Management,* 30(2), 199–220.

Flavián, C. & Guinalíu, M. (2005). The influence of virtual communities on distribution strategies in the internet. *International Journal of Retail & Distribution Management,* 33(6), 405–425.

Gardner, M.P. & Rook, D.W. (1988). Effects of impulse purchases on consumers' affective states. *Advances in Consumer Research,* Association for Consumer Research (U.S.), 15, 127–130.

Greguras, G.J. & Diefendorff, J.M. (2009). Different fits satisfy different needs: Linking person-environment fit to employee commitment and performance using self-determination theory. *Journal of Applied Psychology,* 94(2), 465–477.

Grizzle, J.W., Zablah, A.R., Brown, T.J., Mowen, J.C., & Lee, J.M. (2009). Employee customer orientation in context: How the environment moderates the influence of customer orientation on performance outcomes. *Journal of Applied Psychology,* 94(5), 1227–1242.

Haeckel, S.H., Carbone, L.P., & Berry, L.L. (2003). How to lead the customer experience. *Marketing Management,* 12(1), 18–23.

Harris, L.C. & Goode, M.M. (2010). Online servicescapes, trust, and purchase intentions. *Journal of Services Marketing,* 24(3), 230–243.

Hightower, J. (2003, October). From position to place. In *Proceedings of The 2003 Workshop on Location-Aware Computing* (pp. 10–12), part of the 2003 Ubiquitous Computing Conference.

Hightower Jr., R., Brady, M.K., & Baker, T.L. (2002). Investigating the role of the physical environment in hedonic service consumption: An exploratory study of sporting events. *Journal of Business Research,* 55(9), 697–707.

Hoffman, K.D. & Turley, L.W. (2002). Atmospherics, service encounters and consumer decision making: An integrative perspective. *Journal of Marketing Theory and Practice,* 10(3), 33–47.

Holzwarth, M., Janiszewski, C., & Neumann, M.M. (2006). The influence of avators on online consumer shopping behavior. *Journal of Marketing,* 70(4), 19–36.

Hopkins, C.D., Grove, S.J., Raymond, MA., & LaForge, M.C. (2009). Designing the e-servicescape: Implications for online retailers. *Journal of Internet Commerce,* 8(1–2), 23–43.

Hui, M.K. & Bateson, J.E. (1991). Perceived control and the effects of crowding and consumer choice on the service experience. *Journal of Consumer Research,* 18(2), 174–184.

Jeffrey, S.A. & Hodge, R. (2007). Factors influencing impulse buying during an online purchase. *Electronic Commerce Research,* 7(3–4), 367–379.

Keller, K.L. (2003). Brand synthesis: The multidimensionality of brand knowledge. *Journal of Consumer Research*, 29(4), 595–600.

Kim, M., Kim, J.H., & Lennon, S.J. (2006). Online service attributes available on apparel retail web sites: An ES-QUAL approach. *Managing Service Quality: An International Journal*, 16(1), 51–77.

Kotler, P. (1973). Atmospherics as a marketing tool. *Journal of Retailing*, 49(4), 48–64.

Ku, E.C. (2011). Recommendations from a virtual community as a catalytic agent of travel decisions. *Internet Research*, 21(3), 282–303.

Kwon, W.S. & Lennon, S.J. (2009). What induces online loyalty? Online versus offline brand images. *Journal of Business Research*, 62(5), 557–564.

Lai, K.P., Chong, S.C., Ismail, H.B., & Tong, D.Y.K. (2014). An explorative study of shopper-based salient e-servicescape attributes: A Means-End Chain approach. *International Journal of Information Management*, 34(4), 517–532.

Lee, S. & Jeong, M. (2012). Effects of e-servicescape on consumers' flow experiences. *Journal of Hospitality and Tourism Technology*, 3(1), 47–59.

Lin, I.Y. & Mattila, A.S. (2010). Restaurant servicescape, service encounter, and perceived congruency on customers' emotions and satisfaction. *Journal of Hospitality Marketing and Management*, 19(8), 819–841.

Lio, H.L.M. & Rody, R. (2009). The emotional impact of casino servicescape. *UNLV Gaming Research & Review Journal*, 13(2), 17–25.

Lovelock, C. & Wirtz, J. (2007). *Services Marketing: People, Technology, Strategy*. Upper Sadle River, NJ: Pearson/Prentice Hall.

Lucas, A.F. (2003). The determinants and effects of slot servicescape satisfaction in a Las Vegas hotel casino. *UNLV Gaming Research & Review Journal*, 7(1).

Mathein, T. (2012). GER Lloyd, Disciplines in the Making: Cross Cultural Perspectives on Elites, Learning and Innovation. Reviewed by *Philosophy in Review*, 32(4), 304–306.

Mattila, A.S. & Wirtz, J. (2001). Congruency of scent and music as a driver of in-store evaluations and behavior. *Journal of Retailing*, 77(2), 273–289.

Mattila, A.S. & Wirtz, J. (2008). The role of store environmental stimulation and social factors on impulse purchasing. *Journal of Services Marketing*, 22(7), 562–567.

Mehrabian, A. & Russel, J.A. (1974). *An Approach to Environment Psychology*. Cambridge, MA, USA: MIT Press.

Mummalaneni, V. (2005). An empirical investigation of web site characteristics, consumer emotional states and on-line shopping behaviors. *Journal of Business Research*, 58(4), 526–532.

Oliver, R.L. (1999). Whence consumer loyalty? *Journal of Marketing*, 63(4), 33–44.

Park, C.W., MacInnis, D.J., Priester, J., Eisingerich, A.B., & Iacobucci, D. (2010). Brand attachment and brand attitude strength: Conceptual and empirical differentiation of two critical brand equity drivers. *Journal of Marketing*, 74(6), 1–17.

Pine, B.J. & Gilmore, J.H. (1998). Welcome to the experience economy. *Harvard Business Review*, 76, 97–105.

Piron, F. (1991). Defining impulse purchasing. *Advances in Consumer Research*, Association for Consumer Research (U.S.), 18, 509–514.

Prentice, C. (2018). Linking internal service quality and casino dealer performance. *Journal of Hospitality Marketing & Management*, 27(6), 733–753.

Prentice, C. & Kadan, M. (2019). The role of airport service quality in airport and destination choice. *Journal of Retailing and Consumer Services*, 47, 40–48.

Prentice, C. & Wong, I.A. (2015). Casino marketing, problem gamblers or loyal customers? *Journal of Business Research*, 68(10), 2084–2092.

Prentice, C. & Woodside, A.G. (2013). Problem gamblers' harsh gaze on casino services. *Psychology & Marketing*, 30(12), 1108–1123.

Preacher, K.J. & Leonardelli, G.J. (2001). Calculation for the Sobel Test. Retrieved January 20, 2009.

Pullman, M.E. & Gross, M.A. (2004). Ability of experience design elements to elicit emotions and loyalty behaviors. *Decision Sciences*, 35(3), 551–578.

Roberts, K. (2004). *Lovemarks: The Future Beyond Brands*. New York, NY: Powerhouse Books.

Rook, D.W. (1987). The buying impulse. *Journal of Consumer Research*, 14(2), 189–199.

Rook, D.W. & Fisher, R.J. (1995). Normative influences on impulsive buying behavior. *Journal of Consumer Research*, 22(3), 305–313.

Rosenbaum, M.S. (2009). Restorative servicescapes: Restoring directed attention in third places. *Journal of Service Management*, 20(2), 173–191.

Russell, J.A. & Mehrabian, A. (1976). Environmental variables in consumer research. *Journal of Consumer Research*, 3(1), 62–63.

Schiffman, L.G. & Kanuk, L. (2010). *Consumer Behavior, Global Edition, 10th International Edition*. Harlow: Pearson Education Limited.

Scott, G. (2000). Accountability for service excellence. *Journal of Healthcare Management*, 46(3), 152–50.

Sohn, S.H. & Choi, Y.J. (2014). Phases of shopping addiction evidenced by experiences of complusive buyers. *International Journal of Mental Health and Addiction*, 12(3), 243–254.

Thomson, M., MacInnis, D.J., & Park, C.W. (2005). The ties that bind: Measuring the strength of consumers' emotional attachments to brands. *Journal of Consumer Psychology*, 15(1), 77–91.

Turley, L.W. & Milliman, R.E. (2000). Atmospheric effects on shopping behavior: A review of the experimental evidence. *Journal of Business Research*, 49(2), 193–211.

Verplanken, B. & Herabadi, A. (2001). Individual differences in impulse buying tendency: Feeling and no thinking. *European Journal of Personality*, 15(S1), S71–S83.

Wolman, B.B. (1973). *Concerning Psychology and the Philosophy of Science*. Oxford, Eng.: Prentice Hall.

Wong, I.A. (2013). Exploring customer equity and the role of service experience in the casino service encounter. *International Journal of Hospitality Management*, 32, 91–101.

Wong, I.A. & Fong, V.H. (2010). Examining casino service quality in the Asian Las Vegas: An alternative approach. *Journal of Hospitality Marketing & Management*, 19(8), 842–865.

Wong, I.A. & Prentice, C. (2015). Multilevel environment induced impulsive gambling. *Journal of Business Research*, 68(10), 2102–2108.

Wong, I.A. & Wu, J.S. (2013). Understanding casino experiential attributes: An application to market positioning. *International Journal of Hospitality Management*, 35, 214–224.

Youn, S. & Faber, R.J. (2000). Impulse buying: Its relation to personality traits and cues. *Advances in Consumer Research*, Association for Consumer Research (U.S.), 27, 179–185.

Zeithaml, V.A., Parasuraman, A., & Malhotra, A. (2002). Service quality delivery through web sites: A critical review of extant knowledge. *Journal of the Academy of Marketing Science*, 30(4), 362–375.

Zhang, Q., Cheng, L., & Boutaba, R. (2010). Cloud computing: State-of-the-art and research challenges. *Journal of Internet Services and Applications*, 1(1), 7–18.

Zomerdijk, L.G. & Voss, C.A. (2010). Service design for experience-centric services. *Journal of Service Research*, 13(1), 67–82.

INDEX

Printed in the United States
By Bookmasters